GARDENS
OF KARMA

GARDENS
OF KARMA

Harvesting Myself
Among the Weeds

– A MEMOIR –

SUSAN WEST KURZ

White River Press
Amherst, Massachusetts

First published 2021 by White River Press, Amherst, Massachusetts 01004
whiteriverpress.com

ISBN: 978-1-887043-83-0 paperback
        978-1-887043-85-4 ebook

Book and cover design by Lufkin Graphic Designs, Norwich, Vermont 05055
www.LufkinGraphics.com

Library of Congress Cataloging-in-Publication Data

Names: Kurz, Susan West, author.
Title: Gardens of karma : harvesting myself among the weeds / Susan W.
   Kurz.
Description: Amherst, Massachusetts : White River Press, [2021] | Summary:
   "This memoir is a journey of self-discovery through the mazes of
   addiction and anthroposophy as illustrated by the gardens in the
   author's life"-- Provided by publisher.
Identifiers: LCCN 2020046907 (print) | LCCN 2020046908 (ebook) | ISBN
   9781887043830 (paperback) | ISBN 9781887043854 (ebook)
Subjects: LCSH: Kurz, Susan West, | Women--United States--Biography. |
   Self-consciousness (Awareness) | Gardens--Social aspects. |
   Gardens--Symbolic aspects.
Classification: LCC HQ1120.U5 K87 2021 (print) | LCC HQ1120.U5 (ebook) |
   DDC 126--dc23
LC record available at https://lccn.loc.gov/2020046907
LC ebook record available at https://lccn.loc.gov/2020046908

Contents

Prologue

"TELL US YOUR NAME, where you live, and where you would like to live," Natalie Goldberg instructed during the first morning of the Great Summer Writer's Retreat at Omega Institute in August 2016. She stood, barefoot in yellow capris, on the polished wooden floor in the Zen-like Lake Theater where sixty of us had gathered. Her unexpected question hung in humidity so thick it could make rain sweat.

"My name is Susan Kurz," I said when it was my turn to reply. "I live in Jamestown, Rhode Island, and love it, but I would also love to live in Sicily, the home of Demeter, the goddess of agriculture." I returned to my comfortable BackJack floor chair in the first row.

I was familiar with Demeter's magnificent home. When I had turned sixty-five, I told my husband, Clifford, that I wanted to take a real vacation, one that did not include camping on his man cave, which is how I referred to his old sailboat, *Voyager*. After doing some research, he found the *Anna Tasca Lanza Cooking Experience* held at Tasca d'Almerita's nineteenth-century wine estate, located in the village of Vallelunga Pratameno in the remote Sicilian countryside. I was pleased and impressed with his choice; I've always loved cooking, and though I don't always follow the recipe, I do try to follow my heart when it comes to food and nourishing those I love.

When we arrived, an English-speaking apprentice named Lauren escorted us to a distressed cobalt blue wooden door that led to our rooms. She said the surrounding area was referred to as "the womb of Demeter." Then she explained that Demeter, the goddess of fertility, the earth, and agriculture, had once stood up to Zeus. Mythology claims that, when lonely Hades kidnapped Demeter's daughter, Persephone, in order to marry her in the Underworld, Demeter became so grief-stricken she wandered many days and nights in search of her daughter and refused to nourish the Earth. All of life on Earth faced extinction, but, thankfully, all was resolved.

For me, ours was a holiday made in heaven. We prepared fresh pasta daily from local wheat, grown and ground near the estate. Fabrizia Lanza, the marchioness, was a stunning woman with short, curly white hair, cerulean blue eyes, and a wide smile enhanced by clear red lipstick. She taught us simple traditional recipes for making lemon sorbet, *Scaccia Ragusana* (a kind of pizza), *Flan di Giri* with broccoli, and *Sfince di San Giuseppe* (fried puffs with honey).

Between cooking classes I sat in the garden among the vegetables and herbs in a small area that was shaded by a canvas awning near a lemon tree. The garden overlooked the valley below and across to a neighboring hilly slope. I realized that being close to plants felt like a soul spa for me. Although I was alone, I felt a presence, almost as if the garden were an alive being. I could smell lavender and rosemary; I heard honeybees careening around, seeking nectar. The garden and the view beckoned an early childhood reminiscence of being in my aunt's garden. It was a bittersweet memory. I recalled how I loved visiting my aunt and uncle: They had a pretty house at the top of an incline in the middle of fourteen acres of land. A large garden was on one side of the house; on the other side, blueberry bushes were bountiful, and there were lots of trees to climb. My aunt and uncle didn't have children of their own and loved to have me stay at their house and buy me presents. I especially remembered the life-size cotton Pinocchio doll that they gave me. I loved that doll. After my uncle left for his business each day, Pinocchio and I followed my aunt out to the garden where I helped her weed and harvest green beans, tomatoes, and corn during the long summer weeks I spent there.

When I was around six, my uncle died. It wasn't fun to be there anymore. My aunt hardly spoke when she was home. Then, every morning, she had to leave me alone for several hours while she went to work. I would sit on the back steps for a while with her dog, Cinder; with Midgi, the black cat; and with my much-loved Pinocchio doll. Lonely and sad, I often retreated to her garden, where I made crowns out of bittersweet vines and pretended to be a princess. Then I crept among the vegetable plants, looking under leaves for red ladybugs and smelling each tomato and green bean that I picked. Decades later, as I sat in the garden in Sicily, the memories of that time were vivid, but I no longer felt alone. I knew then how deeply my karma was intimately connected to gardens, how sweetness could lead to bitterness and bitterness back to sweetness.

On that wonderful vacation, Clifford always sensed when it was time to come and find me in my meditative thoughts. I heard his Teva-clad footsteps before his six-foot-two-inch frame appeared before me—salt now more apparent in his hair than pepper. We took lovely walks through the surrounding vineyards and olive groves where the word *culture* still thrives in the word *agriculture.* All ingredients used in our "cooking experience" came from the garden estate or local farms.

Another favorite moment was when a friend of Fabrizia's drove us to a hilltop museum near Mount Etna. Once a monastery, the museum has a statue of Demeter that had recently been returned after a twenty-two-year visit at the Getty Museum in Los Angeles—a visit that had been embroiled by her controversial purchase. I loved her noble presence and took her photo: it greets me each morning when I open my laptop. The Sicilians who talked about the returned treasure laughed at the Americans who had not known she was Demeter but, instead, had mistaken her for Aphrodite.

"Of *course*, it's Demeter," a group of several old men exclaimed as they sat in front of small cafes, sipping strong coffee and smoking hand-rolled cigarettes. "She's from Sicily, the breadbasket of Rome! She makes all our grains—the best in the world!"

Pasta made from Demeter's wheat left no guilt on my palate. *If only my gluten-free friends could see me now*, I thought with a laugh. Pasta in any form has always been my comfort food of choice, including German späetzle and Eastern European pierogies (ravioli-like dumplings filled with sauerkraut, potatoes, ground meat, or prunes).

The pasta of my childhood wasn't called pasta—it was simply *noodles* and *spaghetti.* After all, I had come a long way from Providence, Rhode Island, on a journey filled sometimes with joy and sometimes sorrow, but always laced with sweet riches found woven through its garden paths.

Fast-forward to years later, when I was at the five-day writer's retreat at the Omega Institute. We gradually learned that our wonderful writing instructor, Natalie Goldberg, had a rare and serious form of cancer. She said, "I'm here to teach you writing as a practice. If you've got cancer, get your treatment, then come home and write; if your mother, dies bury her, then come home and write. Writing is where you live, where you inhabit wherever you are."

It was then that I knew that, whether I lived in Jamestown, Rhode Island, or in the village of Vallelunga Pratameno in Sicily, if I were writing, I would feel at home. Eventually, writing led me to follow the thread of my life back to the gardens, the place where I really *was* home. The place where I found myself.

Following the Thread

WHEN I RAN HOME from Broad Street Elementary School for my short lunch break each day, my father heated up a can of Campbell's Beef Consommé and served it over Pennsylvania Dutch Noodles. It was my favorite meal because of the noodles, and because my father was my favorite person back then. He was the oldest member of my family, more a grandfather than a father; I was the youngest, and we spent many quiet days together—him smoking cigars, reading detective stories, copying landscapes from art books using oil paints, or playing on the piano the theme song of *The Quiet Man*—a classic, award-winning 1950s film starring John Wayne and Maureen O'Hara; me, waiting for him to read me *Jack and the Beanstalk* or take me somewhere. My father wasn't an active parent, but I was happy to be with him and thrilled when he took me for an occasional pony ride in Roger Williams Park or skating at the Duck Pond.

I left Broad Street Elementary and my father's lunches after the sixth grade, when I transferred to Elmhurst Academy, a private Catholic girls' school. Academically, Elmhurst was more challenging, so the nuns and my mother decided that I had some catching up to do, especially since the other students had been studying French since the fourth grade. So I repeated grade six. But there was more catching up for me than with French. Elmhurst Academy was a well-groomed environment, with well-groomed rose gardens in front of the Italian villa-like building of the motherhouse—a well-groomed, large red brick building with shiny wooden floors and a wide staircase, where the aroma of freshly ground coffee escaped from the refectory and followed us through the halls to classes. The gardens and grass playing fields were beautifully maintained by a groundskeeper who lived over a utility building. The other five girls in the sixth grade were also well-groomed and had been since birth.

And though the uniforms of gray cotton A-line skirts, gray cotton cardigan sweaters, gray cotton knee socks, and white blouses with Peter Pan collars (the cotton was replaced with wool in late autumn until early spring) combined to provide me with a suitable-enough, well-groomed look, I felt ungroomed and lonely on the inside, a feeling that accompanied me for a long time. The small class left me nowhere to hide and no time to gaze out the large-framed windows as I had done at Broad Street.

Hungry to fit in, I found my comfort zone by playing field hockey. I was chosen to play center forward on the seventh grade team—an honor hard-won and admired. My tomboy days of playing touch football in a neighborhood populated with boys gave me an edge with the upper-class girls. (In touch football, I'd learned that I could catch almost any ball thrown to me and run like the wind over the goal line.) By springtime, I finally had begun to feel like part of the Elmhurst community. Academically, I was doing well, and, as I brought fame to the field hockey team, I forgot about my ungroomed background. For a while.

Then, suddenly, a whiplash from a small car accident while my mother was driving and I was holding my ten-month-old nephew, her firstborn grandchild, ended my field hockey career.

I watched the end of the season from the sidelines wearing a neck brace and a broken heart. That September, as I was about to enter the seventh grade, Elmhurst Academy moved from Providence to Portsmouth. The added distance was too far for my father to drive me each day, and the school was too expensive for me to be a boarder. My mother enrolled me in another private Catholic girls' school closer to home that provided bus service and a less-groomed environment.

In September 1961, the first day of school, I walked past my father, who sat rocking in his chair on the porch, smoking his cigar. I was on my way to the corner of Alabama Avenue and Narragansett Boulevard, where I would catch the school bus that would take me to Bay View Academy. My new uniform—a navy blue rayon jumper and white blouse—wasn't as stylish as the Elmhurst one. Once down the stairs, I walked past the curb where I had sat as a younger child with my arms wrapped around my skinny legs, waiting to be chosen to play softball, dodge ball, or my favorite, football, with the boys. I continued on, past the Arrigos' house, where Mrs. Arrigo (the woman whom I wished was my mother) used to pinch my cheeks and say, "You're so sweet, I want to eat you up." Next, I walked by the widow Reed's house, the home of the old retired librarian who once said to my mother: "It isn't right for a young girl to be playing football in the streets with boys." Then I moved past the empty lot, where I had caught grasshoppers in jars by myself. At the time, I didn't realize I was walking past my childhood and into puberty.

Finally, I reached my destination. The bus pulled up and stopped; the driver pushed a lever to open the door. "Susan West?" he asked, looking straight ahead. Mumbling, "Yes that's me," I climbed three black rubber-matted steps and, as the number forty-three yellow bus began to move, I wobbled from side to side in the aisle. Suddenly, the bus accelerated into its

"45 mph" zone: the sounds of shrieking girls erupted. I shrank behind the noise and looked for an empty seat. The front of the bus was filled with girls dressed like me, but, as I went farther back, I noticed that the older girls—upperclassmen, I figured—wore blazers and pleated skirts, the black shoes and knee socks of junior high apparently having been replaced with nylons. My gaze darted around, but I kept my head straight. I wanted to sit where I could become invisible instead of standing in plain view. But the only seats left were way in the back.

Finally, I reached an empty aisle seat; a girl dressed like me was sitting near the window. She said, "Sit here." I quickly fell in beside her. "I'm so pretty no one likes to sit with me," she added as I turned to take a quick look at her.

"My name is Sally Ann Pause, the pause that refreshes, actually the pause that's fresh." She giggled. Recognizing the Coca-Cola slogan, I giggled a little, too. Then I looked at Sally: she wasn't pretty; she was beautiful, like a Greek goddess I had read about in sixth-grade history when we learned about ancient civilizations. She looked familiar—almost like the actress in the movie *Picnic* that my sister had taken me to see one day when my mother wasn't home. As Sally continued to talk, I studied her thick, chin-length, wavy dark blonde hair; her large, green, leaf-shaped eyes that appeared to be made up but weren't; her clear, very white skin; and her lips that were full of color, a bluish-red. I knew right away that I wanted to be just like her.

On that school bus ride, the first day of school, Sally and I talked all the way to East Providence, and when we pulled into the parking lot filled with yellow buses she said, "Follow me. Let's be best friends. School is boring, but this year on Friday nights we can start going to the dances at Hendricken High, and lots of boys will be there."

I followed Sally into the seventh-grade classroom and stood behind her as she walked up to the nun at the head of the class. "Sister," she said. "Susan is going to sit beside me because she's new here. Okay?" The nun looked at her with a big smile and nodded. For the next two years, I lived in Sally's world, a world where her beauty got its way. And to my twelve-year-old eyes, she wasn't only beautiful—everything about her life was beautiful. Her house in Warwick, a suburb of Providence, was a white Cape Cod cottage with a breezeway decorated with wicker furniture and blue and white pillows. There was also a large, fenced-in yard with bountiful flower beds forming the border— unlike my backyard, where a small forsythia struggled to bloom in a dark corner. I had known in an instant that Sally's home was where I wanted to be. I didn't want to be at my own house where two of my siblings no longer lived and one was never home, and where, when not working, my mother was angry, suffering from a migraine, depressed, or too busy for me, and where my father was too quiet.

Sally lived with her parents, Harry and Viola, and her grandfather. Her father worked as a meteorologist at TFG airport and her mother, Viola (the same name as my mother's), worked at Warwick Shoppers World. Except for their names, our mothers were very different. Sally's mother was blonde and cheerful. She worked while Sally was at school; she bought her pretty clothes, movie magazines, makeup, and the latest records. Whatever Sally asked for, Sally received. My mother seemed old, was burdened, and had to work to pay for four children's educations, mortgage payments, and only the bare essentials of life. There was no frivolous spending for her.

5

I spent much of my non-school time at Sally's house, and she shared all her treasures with me. We played her music: Bobby Darin, B.B. King, and The Marvels, and we memorized the lyrics to "Spanish Harlem," "Run Around Sue," and "Moon River"—songs we heard on the radio. We jumped on her couch and sang with the music that we played at top volume when her parents weren't home. (Her grandfather was deaf and never complained.) She gave me her leftover *'Teen* magazines and I collected sixty photos of my favorite TV star, George Maharis, who played Buz Murdock on *Route 66*. Sally's favorite was Tod Stiles, the character on the same show played by the actor Martin Milner.

Then we went to work on my looks. Slowly, Sally transformed my ash brown hair, which had the remnants of a bad home permanent still visible. My mother had given it to me when she'd cut off my ponytail, when she'd hoped I would become less of a tomboy. Sally carefully combed Clairol blonde dye though my hair, which resulted in blonde streaks. (I told my mother the streaks were from lemon juice that we put on our hair when tanning in the sun.) By the end of the eighth grade I had very long and very blonde hair. At the Friday night dances, I watched Sally—blonde, beautiful, and sexy—pretend that she didn't see all the boys looking at her. One night, however, a tall, broad-shouldered guy with ruddy skin stared boldly at her. As we walked by him, Sally smiled, holding his eyes with her beautiful ones. We stopped while she pretended to talk to me until the stranger asked her to dance. It turned out that his name was Jerry, and he was a football player from a high school across town; he quickly became her steady. She didn't want anything else in life except to graduate from high school and marry Jerry. She subsequently became less interested in me, and she mostly used our friendship as an excuse to go out with him. One night the three of us went to a dance at a beach hotel in Newport. Jerry and Sally left me there. "For just a little while," they said, but they didn't return until the next morning. I spent the night in the lobby fighting off advances from Rich, the owner, who wanted me to go upstairs to his room. There was no Demeter in my life, wandering the earth, trying to figure out how to rescue me from the Underworld.

I didn't find a boyfriend at the dances. Sally told me not to worry, that I would find someone like Jerry someday. "You're not beautiful like I am, but there's something about you, and you're tall, with blonde hair and brown eyes. You're . . ."

I can't remember what Sally said next, but what actually happened was that, at the end of the eighth grade, I left Sally with the nuns at Bay View Academy and entered Classical High School as a blonde and a wild freshman. It both amazes and saddens me to realize what little effort I put into my studies in high school and college, and how much effort I put into boys and men. Gone was any interest in field hockey or sports. At Classical, I survived on emotional intelligence and was able to cross boundaries between cliques: the rich Jewish girls; the cool, Weejun loafer-wearing girls who wanted to learn French and travel to Europe; the geeks who wore thick glasses and were good in science and math; and the *mondos*, as we called the ones who teased, greased, and sprayed their hair and wore tight black skirts.

One night, I convinced two of my rich Jewish friends to drive to Boston for a lobster dinner because shellfish was forbidden in their homes. We not only ate lobster at a fancy hotel on the Boston Common, but I signed the check to a room number I made up, and we ran out on the bill and drove back to Providence in my friend's white sports car—laughing and shrieking all the way. I felt wild and free. With other cliques I went downtown after school, and we dared each other to steal silly things like orange gloves or a man's tie from the Outlet Company department store. I would risk anything for attention and friendship by being as wild and reckless as possible.

Lots of boys were interested in me, but I wouldn't consider any of the freshmen or sophomores: I set my aim on the most popular juniors and seniors. As soon as one asked me on a date, I lost interest and moved on to the next. It was like an addiction to see if I could get anyone I wanted to ask me out. I felt wild but in control until the summer of 1965.

Driving around the east side of Providence near Brown University and Rhode Island School of Design, and then parking on River Road near the Swan Point Cemetery was a popular thing to do. Many students from local high schools and community colleges hung out there, talking, smoking cigarettes, and hoping to meet someone. That's where I met Walter one Friday night. My friend Pam had been driving. (My parents hadn't let me have the family car that night—my mother was very random about when she would let me use it.) Pam parked the car, but we left the radio on. Soon, a guy wearing black jeans and a crisp white shirt with rolled up sleeves stopped next to the car. Under his left arm, he was holding a black helmet. When he stuck his head in the passenger side of the car, I was no longer angry with my parents for not letting me drive. When he smiled, I pushed back the seat and placed my feet up on the dashboard. His hair looked kind of brown (hard to tell in the dark), but his pale blue eyes dominated, especially when he smiled. I quickly learned a lot about him. While an undergraduate at Princeton, he had held up a train on horseback. In addition to the motorcycle that went with his helmet, he also owned a Husqvarna—an off-road bike—and a vintage gray Porsche. He worked in Woonsocket in his college roommate's family business, a company that manufactured artificial Christmas trees.

8

He didn't learn much about me because I lied and said I was a junior in college. I thought he must have been about twenty-two, and I didn't want him to know I was only sixteen. But he seemed to like me, even though I said little. He especially seemed to like my blonde hair that he kept touching and combing back behind my ears with his fingers.

I got out of Pam's parents' black Ford, and Walter took me for a ride on his motorcycle. We roared past the cemetery and made a U-turn; I screamed and laughed loudly, because we were making so much noise on Blackstone Boulevard, where all the rich people lived. My body was crushed up against his back, my arms held tightly around his thin frame. We slid smoothly around a curve onto the highway and crossed the bridge toward East Providence. The upper end of Narragansett Bay was filled with lights from the electric company plant and the shipping docks where the large containers were unloaded. He drove fast. I felt free and excited as my hair whipped around my face and neck.

We returned to River Road and found Pam leaning against the driver's side of her parents' car, talking to a football player from Mount Pleasant High School. Walter opened the car door; I slid into the front seat, adjusted my denim cutoffs, and smoothed my hair. I stretched out my long, tanned legs and put my feet back up on the dashboard. Walter leaned in and kissed my right knee then pulled a pen out of his shirt pocket. He handed it to me and asked for my telephone number. He held out his arm, and I wrote *Hopkins 1-3812* just above his wrist. That was the most exciting and romantic moment of my sixteen-year-old life. I was in love.

At the end of that summer when I didn't "go back to college," I had to tell Walter that I was really a junior in high school. He stopped asking me out as often. But still we went to new restaurants for dinner sometimes (where I ordered Harvey's

Bristol Cream Sherry), to foreign films at the Cable Car Cinema, and to Thompson Speedway in Thompson, Connecticut, where I watched Walter race his Husqvarna dirt bike on weekends.

During my last two years of high school, I lived between my family's house and my sister's. She was newly divorced and had two young children. I made big pots of chicken soup seasoned with parsley and dill that I grew among her flower beds. Herbs are hardy and don't need much care. I did hours of babysitting while my sister worked on her master's degree, and I sat for her neighbor's children, too. My sister and her friends took diet pills to lose weight and gave them to me so I could work harder. I helped with yard work, then went home and cleaned my family's house, ironed clothes, and spent my babysitting money buying dresses for my mother, hoping to make her happy, all the time waiting for Walter to say, "I love you." I continued to stare out the window in school. I wrote Walter's name all over my notebooks and yearned to be tangled up in his life.

Somehow, I made it through the rest of high school relatively unscathed and was accepted at the University of Rhode Island. At the time I had no idea that my real journey had only begun.

– 2 –

Reckless Hunger

AT THE END of my sophomore year in college, my roommates Linda—a beautiful and intelligent blonde—Margie—a blue-eyed brunette in the honors program—and I decided to move "down the line." If not the first young women to live off campus in 1969, we certainly were among the first, and soon became some of the most famous. Along the way, we stopped at a women's health clinic in a nearby town and got prescriptions for birth control pills, which were relatively new on the market and still controversial.

To avoid any resistance from my parents about my decision to move off campus, I got a job at Iggy's, a local Italian restaurant and, except for my tuition, I started to support myself. The restaurant was the favorite hangout for college students. The waitresses were locals, married or divorced with children, who expected to live in the neighborhood forever. I wore a miniskirt when I applied for the opening, and I was hired immediately. Iggy, the owner, was thrilled when several of my attractive college friends soon followed me in joining his staff.

My roommates and I rented a house in Bonnet Shores, a seasonal beach community seven miles from campus. It was up the hill from a house on the bay where guys who were studying business were also running a successful venture selling marijuana, hashish, and an occasional sheet of orange sunshine, a psychedelic drug that was just beginning to appear in the community.

I heard about a guy named Jim Walsh before I saw or met him. He had recently moved into the house down the hill. One night, Margie came home from the restaurant and told me that a friend introduced her to him.

"He's really smart, went to Tübingen, the Harvard of Germany, till his father died. Then his family moved to Rhode Island because his mother's family lives here. He finished his last two years here at URI."

"What's he like? What does he look like?" I asked.

"He's not really handsome, more like attractive, but there's something about him. He's interesting. After graduation, he moved to New York and got a job as a social worker, and then he went to Boston to work on an underground newspaper called *Avatar*. He came back here 'cuz he knows someone in the theater department."

Linda and Margie were dating the star basketball and football players respectively. I was dating three guys. One was a noncommissioned officer in the Air Force, named Manzie, whom I'd met the previous summer in Plattsburg, New York, where I'd been staying with my brother, George, and his new wife. George was an officer who navigated planes over Vietnam; Manzie played the trumpet in a jazz bar and had an apartment over the bar where he lived when he wasn't on duty. He was a peaceful and funny young guy who reminded me of Dustin Hoffman. In addition to his trumpet he owned a glockenspiel, where he hid grass and hash that I often borrowed and took back to my college friends. My black 1960 Chevy Nova hand-me-down family car finally died when I was visiting Manzie during a long holiday weekend. He gave me his old, though newly painted, gold 1957 Mercedes Benz to take home. It was a standard shift with red leather seats and very fun to drive. Since he thought we were kind of engaged, he was happy for me to keep it.

"My dad picks up old cars all the time," he said. "We fix 'em up when I'm home in Louisville," which Manzie pronounced *loooooville*. "It's a great car even though it's old." He waved as I drove away.

I was also dating a guy named Bill who had a loud motorcycle. He was a fraternity brother of Linda's boyfriend; Linda and I were inseparable, and we liked to double date, which was much of the reason I was even dating him. And there was Walter, who never did say, "I love you," but who took my heart and virginity the month before I started college; he took them to Japan where he went to organize a factory that was manufacturing artificial Christmas trees to keep up with U.S. demand. Before leaving he wrote me a *Dear Susan* letter saying he hated good-byes but that he would see me again. He left no return address. At the time I was crushed. Two years passed before he contacted me; by then he was living in New Haven. He came to our house bearing gifts: an Yves Saint Laurent scarf, a bottle of "L'Air du Temps" perfume, and enough rolls of uncut silver tinsel to wallpaper my room. I wasn't as lovesick over Walter as I had been in high school, but I did enjoy the intrigue of visiting him at his very interesting apartment near Yale. At our home down the line, Walter was another story to share with Linda and Margie interspersed with the gossip I heard at the restaurant.

Iggy's was a fun and lucrative place to work. Jim Walsh came there with different sets of friends: the guys from down the road who were always high on the best grass available; a group of theater students and their director, who were doing very edgy productions on campus; and graduate students from the psychology department. Jim was always the last one to leave the restaurant. One night when I was waiting on his table I really looked at him. He was wearing an oversized overcoat, the lining of which hung below ripped sleeves that he'd rolled up, no doubt to fit him better; frayed jeans; ankle-high leather boots that looked old but polished; and a stained, wrinkled, pale blue shirt with a few buttons missing. He sat alone at the corner table closest to the bar. He was smoking a cigarette while rolling and unrolling a paper placemat that had sepia illustrations of different types of pasta.

I walked over to Jim's table and placed a small pizza that Iggy's mistress, the chef, had given me because someone had ordered it by mistake, and an almost full pack of Marlboros that a customer had left behind.

"You look hungry," I said, and then quickly headed to the jukebox, blushing at my boldness. I dropped ten quarters into the slot; I got busy cleaning tables and refilling salt and pepper shakers while Bob Dylan and Dionne Warwick serenaded me about ladies laying on brass beds and saying little prayers each day. When there was nothing left to clean, I sat at the waitress table, quietly mouthing lyrics about troubled waters and parsley, sage, rosemary, and thyme, waiting for the last customer to leave. When Jim stood and headed to the cash register near the front door, I jumped up and slowly walked toward him. He pointed to his check, which he'd piled with a couple of dollars and stacks of nickels, said, "You look reckless," and walked out the door.

Days later, Linda and I were walking past Edwards Hall and saw a group of students gathered on the sidewalk. Two men in gray suits were standing beside a black car that had official-looking plates. Behind the vehicle was a new white VW van. Three bumper stickers positioned across the back bumper read: "Question Authority," "Shakespeare Lives," and "You Need

Leather Balls to Play Rugby." The two suits jotted down notes as they circled the vehicle that was drawing the growing crowd's attention. Then the front door to Edwards Hall opened; a man stood on the top step and paused to light a cigarette. He was dressed as the Marquis de Sade in a costume of purple satin knickers, white stockings, a white wig circa 1800, and black patent leather buckled shoes. Despite the costume, Linda and I recognized Jim. He was playing a lead role in *Marat/Sade* — a play about the French Revolution, human suffering, and change. It is a play within a play, in which the Marquis oversees the inmates in an insane asylum, and the inmates perform a play about the revolution and whether change is even possible. And there on the steps of the college building, in front of a crowd, Jim was in costume performing his own play within a play.

He walked confidently toward the van and the suits and assessed the situation. He unlocked the driver's door, leaned inside and rummaged through the glove compartment. Then he paused on the sidewalk, jammed a small package under his arm, stepped on the remainder of his cigarette, and walked to the back of the van. One of the two men in suits said, "Mr. Walsh, do you know why we're here?"

"Yeah, 'cause you assholes don't have anything better to do." The crowd broke into laugher. Linda and I looked at each other and laughed, too.

"Mr. Walsh, there is no need for hostility. You've been fairly warned, and you've ignored the notices. You are very delinquent on your payment. We're here to repossess the vehicle."

"Yeah, yeah," Jim grunted as he opened the back doors, pulled out a paper bag, and shoved the package from the glove compartment into it.

Linda turned to me and said, "You two are kind of dressed alike." I was wearing my favorite clothes: a purple suede miniskirt, a white silk blouse with ruffles that covered the front button panel, and knee-high black leather boots—all of which were partially covered by a long charcoal "great coat." We laughed again and that time, Jim looked over at us. He walked in front of me and said, "Will you take care of my books?" He pushed the paper bag into my surprised arms.

"Ah, okay, I, uh . . . uh . . . I live. . . ."

"I know where you live," he said, then turned back to the van and slammed the rear doors.

"Now, Mr. Walsh, there's no reason to get hostile," one of the suits said again.

Jim gave him a hostile sneer then looked at me, winked, and walked back into the building to continue the dress rehearsal.

On Valentine's Day 1970, several days before my twenty-first birthday, Jim knocked on the front door of our rental house on King Phillips Road. Moose, my German Shepard, whimpered a bark. I turned down the radio, and Moose followed me to welcome the unexpected visitor.

"Hey, hi," I said. "Did you come for your books?" He walked past me and went into the kitchen, which was filled with the aroma of Arab rice that I'd made from my roommate Linda's recipe. She had grown up in Saudi Arabia, where her father worked for Aramco; she'd decided to attend URI because her grandmother lived in Newport, where Linda spent holidays. When not at her grandmother's house, Linda came home with me, and now our house was becoming a real home to both of us.

"No," he replied. "I brought another one, but it's for you." He handed me a small, shiny white book. The title was printed in sky blue letters: *The Days Run Away Like Wild Horses over the Hills*. The author's name was beneath it in bold orange: Charles Bukowski. I kept looking at the book, speechless. No one I knew read poetry except in English class. It felt like the most exotic gift I had ever received.

"I have more books where I'm staying," he said, pointing toward the house down the hill. "I wonder if you could take care of them, too. My room got flooded, and it's still damp." He walked over to the sink, turned on the faucet, and leaned down to take a drink. Moose sniffed at his leg, walked back to me, and lay down at my feet.

"Sure," I said. I noticed he was wearing the same unwashed clothes that he had on when I first saw him at Iggy's. "I was just going to give my dog a bath. He keeps running down to the water and chasing the seagulls, and he's all salty. No one's here: My roommates are on campus at the library, then they're going to a fraternity party."

"Guten Tag, Herr Moose," Jim said in a perfect German accent and leaned down to pet Moose, who cowered close to me. "He doesn't act like a moose or a German. He seems kind of scared."

I chuckled and leaned over the dog, too. "I got him from the gas station attendant up the road who thinks he was abused and abandoned, and that he's still scared. He's more like a lapdog than a watchdog. Wanna help me give him a bath?"

"Hey, I might get my clothes dirty." We both laughed.

"If you help me with Moose, I'll wash and dry your clothes. I can fix your coat lining, too. If you're hungry we can have Arab rice. I just made a big batch for the house."

We lifted the cowering Moose into the tub, shampooed him, then rinsed him off. Jim took off his clothes and wrapped a towel around his waist while I went to the basement to stuff his clothes into the washing machine. When I came back, I found him wandering around the kitchen. He mentioned his books. I brought him into my room and showed him the bag of books I was storing for him. He pulled out the package that he had jammed into the bag from his glove compartment—he called it his drug compartment—and returned to the kitchen.

We ate the aromatic meal while he told me things about his life that I'd already heard from my roommate Margie. A new bit of his biography emerged about his student days at Clongowes Wood College, a secondary school in Ireland, run by Jesuits.

"I hated the school, but my father thought the discipline would be good for me. The food was horrible, lots of mashed potatoes covered in gravy. We fought over it, though, because it was better than the stuff that was supposed to be meat."

As I looked at his half-naked body, which was a little pudgy, very white, and kind of hairy, I felt exposed as I looked down at my olive-green turtleneck, faded bell bottoms, and bare feet. The moment felt sexier than the sex I'd had with the three other men in my life. He looked at me and continued. I tried to focus on his words.

"The worst part was, there was corporal punishment. I know a lot about that because the priests used it on me—too much, if you ask me. See, I was abused, too, like Moose." He laughed and leaned down to stroke the dog's head again.

He went on to tell me that the school is prominently featured in the Irish writer James Joyce's *A Portrait of an Artist as a Young Man*. I was a good listener and ate his stories up hungrily, feeling as if my life was getting richer with each word he spoke, his every shrug or short laugh seasoning the room.

"This was delicious," he said, as he moved his empty plate aside. He opened the package from the book bag, pulled out some grass and ZigZag papers, and rolled a joint. "Where did you learn to cook?" I was nervous as the sweet smell of smoke surrounded us. I hoped I wouldn't cough like I had done the few times I'd smoked with my roommates.

"I taught myself to cook. I pretty much taught myself everything," I said. "My mother was always busy, and my father, who is twenty-five years older than my mother, is more like a grandfather. I do remember watching my aunt make soup with the vegetables and herbs from her garden, along with a chicken that she got from her neighbor."

I took a deep breath and watched him finish rolling the joint. Then I nervously added, "I usually throw ingredients together and try not to overcook them, except for this Arab rice. I followed the recipe because it was complicated, and I'm not Arab."

We both laughed as he handed me the joint and said, "Take a small hit, it's really good stuff." As I took it, he touched the top of my hand and said, "Relax."

Relax, I did, and started telling him more. I hoped he would find me as interesting as I found him.

"I was born during a blizzard, on my due date, and I think that's why I'm always on time. My mother took the first cab of her life. She went to the Providence Lying-In Hospital alone because my father stayed home with my three siblings and because of the snowy roads. The cab driver was very kind to her. After he dropped her off, he went into the gift shop and bought the only balloon left, a pink one, with—according to the volunteer who delivered it to my mother—a note that read: 'I hope it's a girl.'"

Jim laughed. I was encouraged to go on. He helped himself to more rice and listened to me between bites.

"My mother's milk dried up when I was three weeks old, when her father died. She said she was grieving so much she couldn't nurse me. Maybe that's why I cook so much food, because my mother couldn't nourish me." I sighed. "I think I have a reckless hunger."

Jim reached over, took my hand, and kissed it. "See, Susie? I knew there was something reckless about you when I saw you at Iggy's."

No one had ever called me Susie. I felt special, like we already knew each other because he'd given me a playful nickname. I kept going. "I was born the month that *Death of a Salesman* opened on Broadway. My father was a successful salesman and had a thriving business as a 'Tin Man' for aluminum siding. He made the sales; his partner, Rod, managed the installation. My sister remembers that my mother was happy then—for a while. But one Friday night, Rod took all the money out of their business account and gambled it away at the Narragansett Racetrack. He left town and left my parents in debt for years. That happened just before I was born. I think something died in my father, because he wasn't very present in my life." I took a deep breath and leaned back in my chair.

"My father died when I was in college in Germany," Jim said. "I'll never forget the night I got the news. I had my drunken arms wrapped around a toilet bowl; I was throwing up during a party when a professor came into the bathroom and told me." He stood up, breaking the seriousness of the moment. Then he came over to where I was sitting, hugged me from behind, and kissed the top of my head. He lifted me out of the chair, then turned me around and held me. We swayed slowly to the soft radio music.

"Wanna dance?" he asked as he slipped one foot then the other under my bare feet, so I was standing on his. We slow-danced around the kitchen. I told him about the times when I had been left alone as a little girl at my aunt's house when my uncle died. How, after playing in her garden and picking blueberries, I would slip the elastic bands on the feet of my life-size Pinocchio doll over mine and dance with him because I was lonely and sad. Luckily, the tears in my heart didn't make it to my eyes. Jim held me closer and closer. I didn't feel lonely dancing with Jim.

When he finally said something silly like, "What a waste to be naked around you." I relied with a flip comment like, "What a waste not to take advantage of the birth control pills I just got." We slow-danced down the short hallway to my room. Moose looked up at us, sighed, then returned to sleep under the table.

— 3 —

Dancing with Pinocchio

DAYS LATER, Jim moved into my tinsel-papered room along with his books and his mother's desk. My roommates were as charmed as I was by his intelligence, humor, and endless stories. They thought he was a shiny balloon in our down-the-line party, just another guy I was dating. I happily moved out of my familiar activities and danced alongside Jim, feeling like I had won life's lottery. It was as if I'd slipped into his coat pocket, emerging only to celebrate his creativity and his intelligence. I lived to take care of him; I thought I must be special if someone as charismatic as he was loved me.

When I saw him perform in *The Marquis De Sade*, I became even more convinced of his talents and creativity. A crazy thing happened as I watched the play: I thought of my father sitting quietly in his rocking chair during my childhood, watching as my mother's bizarre bipolar behavior restricted my siblings and me from being children, as he lived with the only goal of not upsetting her. We were not allowed to be children but were puppets to my mother's mood swings. My father sat silently like Jim's character, the Marquis, watching as the inmates rebelled in prison.

Life with Jim was fun. I felt liberated from my unchildish childhood, and I was making up for lost time. The early days with him were so terrific. My rebellion against my mother was to live—unmarried—with Jim even if it was "killing her," and to not worry about what I was going to do after college. I think I thought that way I would be safe from the unhealthy patterns I'd developed in order to survive as a child.

Walter's calls went unanswered, and Bill went back to circling sororities for Saturday night dates. Jim and I became inseparable; he came to campus with me every day in the gold Mercedes. When I was in class, he spent hours in the student union talking with friends and arguing about politics. Between classes I sat beside him in silent adoration. He and his friends smoked grass, drank Irish whiskey, and dropped acid. Eventually, I did, too. When we were tripping, I became the designated driver, long before that was a trendy term. One day, when we were coming down from a trip, I drove Jim and a friend to a local restaurant for breakfast. There was only one open parking space right in front of the restaurant, and two policemen were standing in it, talking. I pulled halfway into the space and sat there waiting. The policeman looked over at us and stepped back onto the curb. Jim's friend in the back seat got agitated and said, "What the f___? Are you crazy getting so close to cops?" Jim took a drag on his cigarette, leaned over and stroked my arm, and said, "That's my reckless Susie." Although I took drugs, I really was high on Jim. He was my drug of choice. I wanted to dance with him until the end of time.

Gradually, my friendships with Linda and Margie became less important to me. Although we all partied and lived an exciting off-campus life, they were serious students and were in serious relationships; they both eventually married their sports-star boyfriends. As Linda and I were painfully drifting apart, she said to me, "Suze, he's not someone to get serious with. He's lots of fun, but he'll do a José Greco on your heart. It's like a giant bird has come and taken you away." Linda was the best friend I'd ever had. We took care of each other like sisters. When we'd still been living on campus, she would sneak down and open the door for me when I was out after curfew. I got us front row tickets at Rhodes on the Pawtucket to see Janis Joplin because she was one of Linda's favorite singers. We were inseparable, totally in sync with each other from when we'd first met in freshman year. Linda was one of the most popular young women on campus, and I was her wild, reckless sidekick.

José Greco was a famous, energetic Spanish flamenco dancer. And while I didn't like the imagery of Jim dancing fast and hard on my heart, I didn't believe her. But though I thought my life was getting bigger, it was actually shrinking. I invested even less time in my studies and more time in Jim. By the end of my junior year, when I was supposed to return to Plattsburg to be with Manzie, I called to tell him that I wasn't going to marry him. He came to take his car away; I never saw him again, but years later I made amends to him via a Facebook message. He was so kind and wrote a moving message to the effect that we all grow up at different times; that he grew up in the Air Force, and it just took me longer.

Jim—whose credit rating got bad reviews after his van was repossessed—made a $500 cash deposit on a new VW Beetle. When not performing at the university theater, he was working at a steak house where many of his friends worked, making fabulous tips. I finished my senior year with a very undistinguished academic record with a major in English and a minor in philosophy, unlike my former roommates who had excelled. My parents gave me a sewing machine for graduation, and I taught myself how to sew. Jim and I lived in a cool house on Hundred Acres Pond, a short drive and a long walk to the campus. The house had a dock that reached out over pristine clear water; it was where I wanted to live, and I thought that being with Jim was all I needed.

After graduation, I continued to work at Iggy's, though my roommates had moved on and my parents were encouraging me to find a real job worthy of a college degree. When I finally introduced Jim to my family, they also were charmed by his personality and ability to engage them in conversation. He was interested in what they did and could carry on a conversation as easily with my sister about the kindergarten class she taught as he could with my oldest brother about negotiating with the truckers union. When Jim was on, he enlivened everyone around him—his attention made everyone feel special. He searched for the smallest details in a conversation that would give him a sense of the drama or the behind-the-scenes story. Even then he was gathering material for his future career as an actor. The longer I was with him, the less I wanted to be with anyone else or do anything unless it included him. It was easier for me to be alone with him because I felt insecure around his theater friends and, gradually, I didn't like being high around his other friends.

"I can't spend all my time with you," he said, often irritated. "Go out, have fun, make friends!" But though I looked good on the outside and was finally in a real relationship, I felt kind of empty inside. Jim was never at a loss for something to do or somewhere to go until he was exhausted and would collapse for days, reading books and scripts and watching *The Dick Cavett Show*. That's when I was happiest—when I was taking care of him. That's when I knew what to do and who I was.

Eventually I came down with pneumonia and spent weeks in bed, recuperating. When the antibiotics finally seemed to work, I went back to Iggy's. When I wasn't working, I hung out with

Jim and his friends, either at our house on the pond or where one of his buddies lived, a place near the beach with an ocean view. They watched football, played cards, made great food, smoked large amounts of grass, and drank until everyone fell asleep. But I hadn't fully recuperated from the pneumonia, and I often had recurring bouts of bronchitis and felt exhausted. At those times, I didn't feel like I was dancing along with Jim; I felt lost and depressed.

One of Jim's friends in the URI psychology department was living on a "farm" that was a twenty-minute drive from campus. It was really a gentleman's small estate owned by a doctor—Dr. Laskey. While Jim was visiting his friend, he helped him with a landscaping project and had coffee with Dr. Laskey. When he came home, he brought fresh vegetables from their garden and a lot of enthusiasm about the doctor.

"Susie," Jim said, "you should see this place. It's fantastic. It has beautiful gardens, woods, and a river at the back boundary. And Dr. Laskey—he's really interesting. He was trained at Harvard Medical School, but he and his wife decided to move to the country. He takes care of the local mill workers; his wife died a while ago, and he lives in the main house with his daughter. And he has cottages that he rents out."

Jim had told the doctor about my having been sick and how I hadn't fully recovered. The doctor suggested we make an appointment to see him. Jim was excited about the appointment; I was excited that Jim was taking care of me.

— 4 —

Dr. Earth

*T*HE DAY OF MY APPOINTMENT I put on my best dress—a green batik shirtwaist that I'd recently made with my new sewing machine—and headed out the door, hand-in-hand with Jim. Moose walked us to our white VW Beetle, licked my fingers, then turned away when I didn't push the front seat forward and invite him to jump in. We drove along Route 2 and took a slight right onto Shannock Hill Road, a street I'd never been on before. Trees lined both sides of the road, which suddenly took an almost ninety-degree turn that snaked down a steep incline. Jim downshifted to second gear around the curve, then quickly shifted into neutral once the road straightened again. We coasted along laughing as though we were on an amusement park ride. Shannock Hill ended at Main Street in the town of Carolina. The Albert S. Potter Octagon House (known simply as the Octagon House) was on the corner; it was the first octagon building I'd ever seen. Another first with Jim. Although we were less than ten miles from home, it felt as if we'd gone on a long journey.

At the eight-sided house, we turned left, drove a short distance, then turned left again after a Catholic church. We saw two houses set back from the road with a large pond of gray gravel in front of them. I instantly noticed how well cared-for everything looked. It was apparent why Jim had been so excited after his first visit. The origin of the farm's name, Black Acre, was never clear but had been used by several tenants over the years. Some speculated that "black" referred to the fertility of the soil. Some said it was because the doctor had once invited a Narragansett Indian elder to perform a healing ceremony or a kind of exorcism to quiet a mysterious dark spirit that lingered from a past wrong that had happened there. Dr. Laskey had been caring for and cultivating the land since the 1950s. I immediately felt that the farm had a presence, a unique personality that was more than the collection of buildings, meadows, and gardens. I knew it was a special place.

Jim led me to the doctor's office on the ground level of a small shingled house, which was separated from the main family dwelling by a narrow graveled drive. He introduced me to the doctor and left to find his friend.

Dr. Laskey was an older man, much like my father, with glasses and white hair. He was wearing a bow tie. He sat at a large desk and asked me questions about my current health. I was surprised when he asked about any illnesses I'd had as a child, about how many siblings I had, and where I fit in with them age-wise. He listened to my heart, took my temperature, examined my throat, and told me to cough while he listened to my lungs. Then he sat quietly and wrote notes in my file. I looked around his simple office and focused on a large green fern that hung in the window. I thought he was writing me a prescription. Instead he leaned over his notes and looked at me.

"Do you want to heal or deal with the condition you now have?" he asked.

His question surprised me; I didn't know how to answer. I was mute for what seemed a long time. Then something surfaced through my shyness, and I said, "I want to heal."

He wrote something on another piece of paper then handed it to me. It read: Coltea from Meadowbrook Herb Garden, a nap each day at the same time for the next three weeks, a good night's sleep. He also recommended a very high-quality brand of several vitamins from Mother Nature's Health Shop over in Wakefield, and he gave me a brown bottle of little white pellets, which I later learned was Anthroposophic Medicine. He instructed me to place six pellets under my tongue three times a day.

"It's important to consciously establish rhythm in one's life. We are beings of rhythm. The most obvious rhythm in our bodies is the relationship between the heart and lungs—one breath to four heartbeats. The medicine will be more effective if you take it at the same times each day." Then he stood, put on a straw hat, and opened the door for me.

I followed him like a puppy—I thought we were going to find his daughter's boyfriend and Jim. We walked along the narrow road, past the main house and his office, toward the meadows and woods and stopped at a small garden in front of two cozy cottages. Morning glories beamed their blueness from where they climbed along the fence bordered with purple asters and deep yellow mums. Tomato and pepper plants added yellow, red, and orange to the leafy shades of fading fall greens; stalks of brussels sprouts stood tall.

"It's beautiful," I said.

"You have to eat like this if you want to heal," he said and moved his arm in an arc in front of him toward the garden. "Healthy food is medicine; nature is our pharmacy."

Until then I had never thought of food as being healthy or not, beyond knowing that you shouldn't eat too many sweets. We continued to slowly walk along the path farther into the property toward the river. Several times I whispered into the silence how beautiful everything was, and how he must enjoy living there. He finally spoke again.

"What are you going to do with your life?" he asked. No one had ever posed that question to me before. I told him about my English/philosophy education and admitted that I didn't know what I wanted to do, but that I was waitressing because no one was hiring philosophers these days. I kind of laughed.

We came to a small fenced-in apple orchard with a tool shed at the far end. He opened the gate and we walked slowly among the small trees. I could smell wild grapes whose vines covered the fencing that was strung between wood posts. The doctor told me to help myself to the apples, so I picked one for Jim and one for me. I bit into it; the taste was delicious, sweet, and a little tart. "Eve bit into an apple and it led her out of the garden," I said. "I'm biting into one and it's leading me into one." I smiled. He smiled, too.

We left the orchard and went around a curve to a small field where vibrant green plants about eighteen inches tall stood in rows a foot apart. Their aromatic, sweet scent reminded me of mint, pepper, and licorice. I breathed in the earthy fragrance, which I soon learned was from basil.

A middle-aged man in a green felted wool fedora and wearing light colored slacks, a white shirt, and a faded corduroy jacket, was stooping down, pinching off flower blossoms that grew at the tip of the stems. He stood up as we approached, then said to Dr. Laskey, "I think we can get another cutting in if the weather stays like this all September. I have a good crop in the drying house now."

The doctor nodded and said, "Heinz, I'd like you to meet Susan West."

The man tipped his hat, revealing his balding head; we shook hands. His eyes were very blue, and his smile was easy.

"Heinz owns Meadowbrook Herb Garden. He's been trying to grow basil and savory here using biodynamic methods. But the project seems inefficient, business-wise, because of the five-mile drive back and forth to Meadowbrook, the timing of harvesting, and driving crops back to Meadowbrook."

Heinz shook his head and said with a sigh, "Yaaaah. It adds extra time to an already labor-intensive process."

"What's biodynamics?" I asked.

Heinz chuckled. "That's a big question."

"Is it organic?"

"Yes, some, but it's more. We are a little like doctors for the earth. We heal the earth and the earth heals us. Yah, so it is good to meet you, Susan West. Come see what we do at the herb garden if you want to know about biodynamics."

Then Jim and his friend Bob walked toward us. They were both smoking cigarettes. The doctor told me to check in with him in three weeks; then he and Heinz meandered away. Jim, Bob, and I continued on. We walked to a beautiful large meadow filled with golden grasses; a narrow path through the center of the area led to the back boundary of the property along the Pawcatuck River. We stood quietly and listened to the river sing its drifting song; we watched birds and bees dart among tall purple flowers that were scattered along the riverbank. Bob took us on a tour around the three cottages—one set deeper into the woods and two that were very close together along the path where I'd walked with the doctor.

"That's the mouse house," Bob said, pointing at the smaller building. "The other is a converted hay barn that might be available to rent soon."

We walked behind the converted barn where five ponies had gathered behind a fence. They stood near a small shelter, eating grain from a feeding trough. They snickered and snorted as we approached, then they filed past us, kicking and dancing down a sloping meadow that looked to be about two acres or more. We watched them run and play. I recalled how much I had loved riding the ponies in Roger Williams Park as a child and thought how amazing it must be to have ponies of your own. The house that might be available to rent looked over the stable and fields from the back. I saw beauty everywhere; I dared to wonder if we might live there at some point.

While I'd been with the doctor, Jim had harvested a big box of vegetables: tomatoes, peppers, eggplant, leafy greens, and some apples and raspberries. We sampled a few and decided they were better than any produce either of us had ever eaten. It was an amazing experience for me to taste such delicious food; it reminded me of when I'd been alone in my aunt's garden, eating tomatoes fresh and warm from the plants. And now, with Jim, the apples and raspberries I ate tasted like summer and childhood. I thought I'd never feel alone again as long as I was with him.

As a diligent patient, I was eager to follow all of Dr. Laskey's suggestions. And when I went to the Herb Garden for my tea, I fell in love with the place. The greenhouses were filled with culinary and medicinal herbs; aromatic herbs and spices filled the shelves of the little shop. Almost a dozen young people worked in the greenhouse, in the packing and drying rooms, and in the building where jars were being filled with exotic spices from around the world. Everyone was friendly and seemed happy.

When I asked to speak with Heinz, he came over from his house. He remembered meeting me at Dr. Laskey's.

"I'd like to work here," I said. "Especially in the greenhouse. Do you have any openings?"

"Unfortunately, it's the end of the growing season," he said, "but if anything opens up, I will call you."

I was disappointed but pleased to find such a little treasure to visit whenever I could.

My health soon improved, my energy returned, and I felt better than I could remember ever feeling. My hair grew shiny and full and my skin glowed. Jim and I researched the vitamins that Dr. Laskey had prescribed and began to research others for my family. It wasn't long before we recommended that my father take certain vitamins for his heart condition. By then he was eighty-two and was taking nitroglycerin several times a day. My mother checked with his doctor to make sure the vitamins would be okay. His doctor said, "It can't hurt, but he's old, so don't expect much."

After two months of the vitamin therapy, my father felt stronger. And he'd reduced his intake of nitro to almost none. His doctor asked my mother what we'd recommended; even he was impressed. Also, after much study, we gave my sister a vitamin protocol for the psoriasis that she'd developed as a young teen after taking thyroid medication. Within a month, her condition started to improve and five months later was completely gone.

In March 1972, Dr. Laskey died. I had been his last new patient. Six months later, Jim and I moved into the converted hay barn at Black Acre Farm—it was our first year-round rental together. On January 2, 1973, Heinz called to say there was an opening at the garden. It wasn't in the greenhouse, but in the filling department. Still, I jumped at the chance to be on my way *back to the garden*, as the music of Crosby, Stills, Nash & Young affirmed, magically blaring throughout the hay barn over Jim's state-of-the-art speakers.

My first day at Meadowbrook Herb Garden was the beginning of my first and last eight-to-five job. I pushed my purple suede miniskirt to the back of the closet and revamped my wardrobe around Jim's Christmas present: a pair of Frye boots. New Levi's denim overalls and flannel shirts complemented the boots and became my signature look. Heinz met me in the shop and introduced me to his wife, Ines, a slim, attractive woman with ash brown hair, who groomed and guarded her domain with crisp friendliness from behind the counter. I commented on a magnificent stained-glass panel of a man slaying a dragon; it hung at the top of a large window that provided a view of an enclosed showcase garden.

"That is Saint Michael casting the dragon out of heaven," Heinz explained in a theatrical voice. "The dragon lives invisible among us on the earth and within us, too. We must find the courage within to slay the darkness in the world and within ourselves."

We left the shop through a small door that led down three wooden stairs into the magic of the greenhouse. A six-foot-tall fig tree grew on one side of the steps; on the other side, cardboard boxes had been neatly stacked, ready for customers to fill with plants. The warmth of the greenhouse, in contrast to the cold January day, released intoxicating fragrances of the hundreds of well-cared-for herbs that were used for medicinal, culinary, and cosmetic purposes. They flourished happily in the velvety brown soil and moist, warm atmosphere.

"This is Kassie," Heinz said.

I smiled at the short young woman who was watering the plants. Her brown hair matched her eyes, a happy glow punctuated by her wide smile.

"Susan West is starting in the filling department but would like to work in the greenhouse someday."

"I understand why. I love being here." Kassie laughed and continued with her task.

We moved on, into the shipping department at the end of the second greenhouse. Heinz pointed out small wooden drawers lined up on one wall. He said they contained envelopes of herbal seeds that were for sale. Then I met Karen, another brunette, who worked beside a bearded man named Neil. Later, I learned that Neil was famous for using the same paper bag to hold his lunch for almost six months.

Heinz then led me across the path to a free-standing building where Anne, the spice lady, and Sally, the tea lady, filled jars and boxes of teas, spices, and dried herbs to be sold in the shop or through the mail-order catalogue. He told me I'd be working next to Anne, filling small glass jars with spices. Beyond the filling area, which shimmered in the light from windows on three sides of the room, was a larger area of the building—that one was cool and dark. It was where the inventory was kept, the jars and boxes that had been packed and branded with the Meadowbrook logo.

We went down to the basement where the large bins of herbs grown on the farm were stored, along with precious spices like saffron that had been imported from Spain and cost $300 a pound. Heinz told me that everyone wanted the colorful metal box that the saffron came in. I noticed one of the large rounded containers was labeled Coltea, the blend I had been drinking daily for several months at Dr. Laskey's suggestion. Beyond the bins of tea blends, tall columns of boxes stood on wooden pallets that kept the products off the floor.

"We have to keep the temperature and humidity stable year-round," Heinz explained. "It's important, because it maintains the vitality of the herbs and the integrity of the cosmetics."

I walked to the shelves of cosmetics that I'd noticed earlier in the shop but hadn't paid much attention to. I picked a box off the metal frame; the front panel read: *Dr. Hauschka Cosmetics*. Below the brand, a descriptive line read: *Rose Cream*. A side panel defined: Healing Preparations from Elisabeth Sigmund. On another side, the ingredients were listed along with directions to "apply sparingly to the face during the day." My mother only used night creams and makeup during the day. I only used soap to cleanse my skin and only eye makeup and blush.

When I told my parents about my new job, and its pay rate of $1.25 an hour—$0.35 below the minimum wage because I was considered an agricultural worker—they were shocked. "And you don't even get benefits?" my mother asked, the pitch of her voice rising in agitation. Their disappointment and confusion were obvious. After all, my mother's life goal had been to ensure that her four children received a college education, good dental care, and secure jobs.

"Yes, I do get benefits," I argued. "I get a ten percent discount off everything in the greenhouses and shop, except for the books. And when the weather improves, I can ride my bike to work." My belief was that I was getting a post-graduate degree in sustainable farming at a university that didn't have any walls. I would eventually discover that I was being introduced to a holistic philosophy, a spiritual philosophy, and, after all, I had minored in philosophy, so it made sense. To me.

During the winter months while my hands were busy filling jars with spices, my mind and heart were engaged with getting to know the biographies and life stories of my coworkers. We also spent hours discussing the books we read: books on nutrition, sustainable agriculture, spirituality, and the occult. Several of the titles I recall are: *Autobiography of a Yogi* by Paramhansa Yogananda; *Let's Get Well* by Adelle Davis; *Knowledge of Higher Worlds and Its Attainment* and *The Agricultural Course*, both by Rudolf Steiner; and *Back to Eden* by Jethro Kloss.

The Herb Garden was closed from twelve to one for lunch each day, when all the workers gathered in the filling room. If the weather was warm, we ate outside at a picnic table near a cedar tree. We discussed the politics of a Richard Nixon-led country, Bergman films like *Cries and Whispers*, the personal results of a new dietary choice, and the benefits of chiropractic adjustments. On Thursday nights a group of us went to shop at the local wholefood co-op for granola and brown rice, and then to get an adjustment at Back to Health, a chiropractic clinic.

It was a magical time for me as I connected to my fellow workers—all college educated, all looking for a road less travelled at this six-acre oasis located at an obscure bend in the road. Every Friday we each bought a German chocolate bar from the shop and savored it throughout the afternoon. I bought two, one for me and one for Jim. The chocolate was a far cry from the Hershey's of my youth. On the last Friday of the month, I also bought a book by Rudolf Steiner, a jar of either a spice or an herb, and a houseplant, usually a scented geranium or a fern. I considered my houseplants some of my most prized possessions.

When spring arrived, the schedules changed. I still spent mornings in the filling room, but after lunch I went either to the greenhouses to help Kassie make cuttings and sow seeds in flats of potting soil, or out to the fields if more help was needed. Out there I learned to turn compost piles, spray biodynamic preps instead of synthetic pesticides and fertilizers on the fields and plants, cultivate, plant, weed, mulch, and eventually harvest crops of vibrant healing herbs.

When the weather warmed, I traded my overalls for short denim cutoffs, colorful tomato red and periwinkle blue T-shirts, and Timberland boots. I stopped bleaching my hair blonde and let the sun highlight it instead with caramel streaks among my natural light brown locks. The blonde/black eyeliner look that I'd hidden behind for years was slowly changing as I found new beauty, more inner than outer, as a natural woman. Not wanting to pollute my body's functions with hormones and chemicals, I threw away my birth control pills and paid close attention to my menstrual cycle to avoid pregnancy by using the rhythm method.

Along with my coworkers, I also studied the rhythms of the moon. We tried to plant the seeds and make cuttings as it waxed, to harvest crops when it was full, and to weed and mulch as it waned. One of the side effects of learning to doctor the earth was that I was beginning to understand what Dr. Laskey had meant when he'd asked if I wanted to heal or to simply cure my bronchitis. Healing went far beyond taking pills. It was a lifestyle choice for a lifetime that would lead me toward wholeness, one day at a time.

— 5 —

Sex, Drugs, and Rudolf Steiner

"NUTMEG IS HALLUCINOGENIC," I said proudly one morning as I grated the fresh spice over John McCann's Steel Cut Irish Oatmeal, while using my new microplane grater, a gift from Jim. "It contains myristicin, just like LSD, but you need to consume large quantities to get high." I loved to tell Jim things I was learning at the Garden. We poured raw organic milk into our bowls; the steam rose, fragrant with the nutmeg and cinnamon, enhancing the porridge as it mingled with the smoke of his ever-present cigarette.

He grated some nutmeg into his coffee and said, "Mind-expanding spice! Are there others? I like it. I wonder if it would go well with grass. Can I smoke it?"

"You're a nut, like nutmeg," I said. "A hard shell on the outside but intoxicating when open."

We both laughed. We laughed a lot that first year when we lived at Black Acre. We laughed and we made love—mornings, evenings, after a walk in the middle of the day. I discovered that, while I'd had sex with other men before Jim, this was different— at least it was for me. Our whole beings merged when we made love. I held back nothing of my twenty-two-year-old self with

Jim. He seemed to do the same. We also could be silent together, and we often sat quietly, especially when drinking morning coffee in the tiny kitchen off our bedroom at the front of the house. I usually wore a linen caftan at home—it made me feel romantic, like a character in our special story of living in a cottage in the woods. Jim, always in jeans and usually just an undershirt at home, had little regard for his appearance.

These were some of my favorite times with Jim. The sun arrived, like an early guest, finding a path through the trees outside the window. It cast shafts of warmth and held us in its light. I was happier than I had ever been. Between the Herb Garden, basking in Jim's loving arms, and being high with Jim as a brilliant guide, life seemed perfect. I was also opening to a new world through the books I was reading. For the first time in my life, I felt whole. Jim and I had each other, and I hoped that our life together would be enough for him. If a cloud of doubt entered my mind, he would surprise in a way I never expected. And I would trust that we were meant to be together.

One particular day was very memorable for me. Jim woke me up in what felt like the middle of the night. He said he had a surprise for me. Then he handed me a flannel shirt to put on over my nightgown and tied a red calico scarf like a mask over my eyes. He guided me to our VW Bug. We drove for about fifteen minutes before he parked and opened my door. We then stumbled laughing through velvety cold sand; I heard waves breaking and guessed we must be at Moonstone, my favorite beach. We held hands; the cold water circled around my feet. Jim untied the scarf from my eyes just as the sun rose between the top sheet of the sky and the wrinkled bottom sheet of the ocean. I was deeply moved by this small adventure, which was amplified by the beauty of the sun's majesty.

"I wanted you to see the sunrise with me. It was the only thing that made that lousy job as a beachcomber last summer bearable."

It was a powerful moment for me because I felt that Jim was really sharing himself with me. We stood quietly watching the sun as it became fully visible, a mysterious sphere lighting the world.

"It's so beautiful it would be a perfect place to get married," I said, surprised by my own words.

"We're as married as we want to be don't you think? Who needs a piece of paper to prove it?" He pulled me closer to him. I felt as if I knew what he meant, and I glowed blissfully inside. My new narrative to myself was that we married that day, and the sun was our witness.

As Jim introduced me to drugs like hash, LSD, and "magic mushrooms," I felt that I had experienced then what I later learned Steiner described as a higher consciousness, a world that existed beyond matter, matter that was spirit come to rest. When high, I perceived the movement and the forces that surrounded matter, and everything I looked at—a tree, an animal, a thought, or a chair—had many more dimensions. Everything was alive, and I wasn't trapped in my head and my fears. Sex, food, and especially music came to life in a profoundly new way. Music resonated through me as if my body was an instrument that was part of the sound. I felt porous, without boundaries. The silky sounds filled the upstairs room of our house, our room with a view.

One set of windows overlooked the pony barn where Licorice and Sassafras, two of my favorite ponies, returned to their shelter after a day of grazing in the high meadow. While Bob Dylan sang about "All the Tired Horses" on our stereo, the horses returning to their shelter seemed to be in sync with the music. So were Jim and I as he held me in his arms, and we slow-swayed to the music as if Bob Dylan was singing us his song. From our other set of windows, our view was of expansive lawns, stone walls, and dogwood trees. When not inside, Jim and I walked together through the golden fields, past where Dr. Laskey had offered me an apple, and through the woods to the back meadow, and then down to the river. We walked in all weather and in all seasons, each season sharing its unique beauty of the year.

We loved the upstairs room. It had large windows on both sides of the cathedral-like space, with built in window seats that overflowed with soft pillows. The room was spacious, the full size of the three small rooms downstairs combined. French doors at either end opened out to two small balconies; wisteria climbed and tendrilled around the railings and rustled with clusters of purple in early summer. A fire burned or smoldered in our black Jøtul woodstove from late autumn until early spring. Now when I looked out windows, I did so as a student of life who had been lifted out of time, carried by all the new spiritual ideas I was reading, and embraced by Jim's love.

Whatever I learned at the Garden, I eagerly shared with Jim. The longer I worked there, the more confidence I gained. Slowly, I was climbing out of his pocket and gaining a worldview beyond his. Not only did he find my new life interesting, but he added my experiences to his repertoire of knowledge, which highlighted his already enormous charisma, especially to his theater friends. Most especially, his women theater friends. Jim seemed proud of how much I was learning not only as a gardener but also about nutrition and the work of Rudolf Steiner, which included topics like karma and reincarnation. My life felt exotic and full, as my inner student had finally awoken.

While I had spent years daydreaming while gazing out of many a classroom window and barely getting by scholastically, I now was becoming a student of all things spiritual. The first Steiner book I purchased from the shop was titled *Knowledge of the Higher Worlds and Its Attainment.* It described how a slumbering seed was within every human being, a seed that we are each able to nurture and awaken to higher worlds and a higher consciousness. As I read more and more works by Steiner, I began to notice a subtle shift in my feelings about using drugs and getting high. Where once it felt good and right, slowly it began to feel uncomfortable and unhealthy.

Jim often invited his theater friends, his friends from the steak house (where he still worked when not performing at the URI Theater Department), and another tenant, a psychologist who lived on the farm, to visit us. They all got high, listened to music, drank herbal tea, and ate the homemade bread I'd crafted using flour ground in my manual cast iron grain mill. I served it warm, spread thick with local honey.

I began to withdraw into myself when his friends were around. They stayed too long, laughed about things I didn't find funny, and often fell asleep on the window seats, where they remained till morning. The more conflicted I became about drugs, the more I took solace in my spiritual studies and getting high on my life of studying and growing herbs. I occasionally smoked a little grass with Jim when we were alone, but inwardly I hoped he would find our life together enough without always getting high.

However, Jim always wanted to get stoned, whether we were going to a movie or to visit family and friends. He was even more entertaining when he was doing drugs, and we all got high on him.

And, though intuitively I felt that the drugs weren't healthy, I used caution when I approached the topic with him. "I don't want to put synthetic chemicals into my body anymore," I said. "I don't think it's healthy for us."

Jim laughed. "What's happening to the reckless Susie in purple suede miniskirts that I fell in love with? Guess you'll have to stick to marijuana. It's natural."

My days at the Herb Garden continued to be filled with discussions about spirituality, consciousness, food as medicine, and transforming the world through peace and love. One friend told me that Steiner said that mind-expanding drugs were from the past, that it was important for modern human beings to develop their consciousness by meditation and inner development, that drugs were a false and dated path. That made sense to me, as I knew that a natural shift had occurred in me about using them.

I realized that, though, while high, I seemed to see and perceive new dimensions of reality, the feelings and the insights never lasted. There was always a "down," accompanied by a sense that I needed to recover my energy. The drugs were not really transforming me in a positive way.

I did start to notice that, with meditation and spiritual exercises like observing my thoughts, speech, and feelings—each on a different day of the week—I became calmer. The practical work of growing plants and studying their medicinal properties also gave me a sense of a heightened awareness, a sense that I was connected to nature. I began to feel much healthier. My focus shifted from how I looked outwardly to how I was feeling inwardly.

Our romantic, natural life together at Black Acre changed rather dramatically in June 1973. I was twenty-four years old, and Jim was about to turn thirty. Six months after I'd started working at Meadowbrook, Kassie and her boyfriend decided to move to New Hampshire to start their own garden center. Suddenly a job in the greenhouse was available. Heinz offered me the position. I was very excited to move from the filling department to the greenhouse. It meant that I'd work closely with Heinz, who I had come to learn was a master biodynamic herb grower. He would teach me all that he'd taught Kassie about growing herbs. The job also included covering the shop each morning from ten until noon, when we closed for lunch. The move to the greenhouse and shop brought me close to customers and sales. It also meant that I had to work weekend mornings for a few hours watering the plants. I didn't mind at all.

Around the same time, Jim and several of his friends who worked at the steak house walked out on the job one night because they felt that they were being treated unfairly. Jim had initiated the walkout. They were all fired and, as a response to their dismissal, they brought a lawsuit—also initiated by Jim—against the owners. After a months-long mediation process, each waiter received a small settlement for back wages and tips, and they were offered their jobs back. By then Jim was coming to the realization that he wanted to pursue acting as a career. And he wanted to find theater work in New York.

We decided that I would remain at Black Acre and work at the Garden, since I had been promoted. Jim would come and go between auditions until he got a job and, hopefully, acting work.

He slept on the couch of a friend while he auditioned for off- and off-off-Broadway parts, landing a small role now and then. He also worked as a bartender between gigs. Whenever possible, he returned to our oasis, my loving arms, and good food.

On one train trip home from New York, he brought me a Siamese kitten, which he hid in his Danish School Bag, his only fashion indulgence. Along with the kitten came a story. A new acting friend, purported to be related by a cousin's marriage to Sir John Gielgud, whom Jim held in high esteem, invited Jim to visit him at his Brooklyn apartment.

"He said, 'Jimmy, I have a gift for you, a very precious gift, come for brunch on Sunday.'

"I thought maybe he was going to give me a jewel or some gold, as he was from a very wealthy royal Indian family." Jim laughed when telling the story, repeating it with a perfect Indian accent.

"So, I took some of my best grass and jumped on the M train to pick up my treasure. When I got there, he showed me a box of kittens. They didn't even all look like their purebred mother.

"I said, 'What the f___! This is the gift?'

"He said, 'Jimmy, the mother has the purest blood. She was a gift from a member of the royal family. I brought her all the way from my home in Mumbai. Sadly, she got out one night, went down the fire escape, and met a cool Brooklyn tomcat. It's so New York.'"

I loved the kitten and named her Nutmeg because of her dark brown point colorations. Jim called her Dummy; she eventually became Miss Dummy. She meant the world to me and became a wonderful companion when I was alone. Although Jim laughed about it, I thought it was a sign that we were really a family, even though he was coming and going. When Jim called once a week from the city, I always included stories about Nutmeg and the cute things she did, including when she killed her first mouse.

Whenever Jim was in a play, I went to New York to watch him perform. At those times, I pulled out my old miniskirts and lace blouses, polished my Frye boots, and caught a bus from Kingston to Penn Station. Enclosed in Jim's arms, I slept on couches or next to him on the floor in the apartment of one his growing community of theater friends. He introduced me to my first falafel on pita bread that he bought from a small truck on the Upper West Side. Jim's world continued to offer me everything I thought I needed.

At small, intimate theaters on the West Side, I watched him apply makeup in the dressing room, and then I sat in the front row and applauded his talent, amazed at the range of characters he embodied. We went to eat with the cast after the play ended. Joints were passed. I noticed that, while I nursed a glass of wine all night, Jim drank shot after shot of top-shelf Irish whiskey. But because he entertained us with amusing stories of quirky directors and slipped in and out of roles with foreign dialects, I ignored my concerns.

In early December 1973, soon after one of my trips to New York, I realized I was pregnant. I didn't tell anyone but Nutmeg; I reported the results of the home pregnancy test that I'd gotten from Planned Parenthood only to her. The cat, after all, was my closest companion at night and on weekends when Jim was away.

When we'd moved to Black Acre, I'd given Moose to my parents because the landlady had several dogs and didn't think it wise to let the renters bring new dogs onto the property. When my parents moved from Providence to Newport to be closer to my cousin, who was my father's doctor, they gave Moose to the gas station owner at the top of their street. The owner was happy to have such a beautiful German Shepherd that he expected would protect his business at night when the station was closed. He assured my mother that he'd take Moose to Roger Williams Park each day for a good run. Little did he know that Moose didn't have the watchdog gene.

Nutmeg was the smartest cat I'd ever had. Though we'd had cats when I was growing up, they mostly lived in the cellar to keep mice away or outside when it was warm. Tiger, the one cat that I remember loving, holding, and sneaking into my room at night to sleep on my bed, had been killed by a car. I remember lying on the couch, uncomforted by my family, and crying for days. It was my earliest memory of experiencing grief.

Nutmeg followed me wherever I went in the house and even went for walks with me to the back meadow. When I came home from work, she was waiting for me at the door. Although she could come and go freely inside and out, she really preferred to be an indoor cat.

I decided to wait to tell Jim that I was pregnant until he came home for Christmas. The play he was performing in was closing soon, and he had found a friend to cover his shift at the bar for the week between Christmas and New Year's. During the time before his return, I submerged myself into a book by Steiner titled *The Kingdom of Childhood* and another one about the cycles of human life.

According to Steiner, a child didn't grow up; it grew down into the earth from the spiritual world. Each seven-year cycle was related to the planets. I quickly read about the cycle I was in—the one between the ages of twenty-one and twenty-eight. It was called the sentient soul time part of the sun cycle. It was a time when we asked what the world has to offer us. It was titled *Play That Turns to Responsibility*. I was in rhythm, playing with love, with a new spiritual view, with plants and gardens, all with total abandonment, on the arm of a talented actor. I felt that I was ready for the responsibility of a child.

Nutmeg curled up beside me as I sat on the mattress on the floor, propped against the bedroom wall. I read passages aloud to the cat and repeated ideas to her that caught my attention.

"Wow—it says here that a child chooses their parents when in the spiritual world. Along with their angels, they bring the parents that they need together in order to learn the lessons they need to learn in their life. Wait till I tell Jim." The cat loved it when I talked to her and would stroke her nose against my hand and purr.

The idea that the child growing inside of me had chosen me to be his or her mother resonated very deeply. It seemed really true to me. When the woman at Planned Parenthood had asked me what I intended to do, if I was going to have the child, I answered, "Yes, absolutely, yes." Even though I wasn't married, I felt that having this child was absolutely right. I felt even closer to Jim as I wondered what he was going to say.

The thought of me having chosen my parents was more challenging for me. I pondered over why I had needed my parents in particular, and what lessons I still needed to learn. I didn't look forward to telling them that I was pregnant, but I felt I would be strong with Jim at my side.

With Nutmeg curled up next to me, I drifted into sleep each night eager, though admittedly a little nervous, as Christmas approached.

— 6 —
Mother and Child

I LOVED BEING PREGNANT. It felt like something mysterious yet familiar was happening to me. It seemed like further confirmation that Jim and I belonged together, and that we were truly now on a lifelong journey together.

Leading up to Christmas, I took every opportunity to learn how to have a healthy pregnancy. After reading *Let's Have Healthy Children* by Adele Davis, I started to follow her diet for expectant mothers, took her recommended vitamins and brewer's yeast, and even acquired a taste for organic chicken livers after I sautéed them with onions and apples. I eliminated even an occasional glass of wine and was determined never to smoke grass again.

I was also reading about Esoteric Christianity, a little-known version of Christianity that speaks of Christianity as an inner event that, through an individual awakening, leads to less of a traditional religion and more of a new consciousness of freedom and love. Unlike what the Catholic church claims—namely, that human beings only have a soul and not an individual spirit and therefore need the Church to have a direct relationship to the spiritual world—this view states that human beings can develop a direct relationship to the spiritual world. It also advocates that the event of Christ happens continuously within each human being on earth throughout the cycle and the seasons of the year.

These thoughts resonated with me as I opened a flap of my Advent calendar each morning and prepared for Christmas and Jim's return. Inwardly, I saw myself becoming more like Mary and less like the Magdalene of my childhood Sunday School days; I was happy to leave my wild nature behind. Now that we were to become parents, I thought Jim would realize that we needed to create a healthy environment for our baby.

Working each day at the Herb Garden in the greenhouse, I felt like I was in a wonderful womb-like place, a small Garden of Eden, the perfect place to be pregnant. The warm, moist air, filled with the fragrances of the plants I tended, enveloped me in an aura of well-being. My body absorbed the atmosphere like food. In the shop, I browsed through the fairy tales and children's books while trying to decide which one to buy first. The Steiff stuffed animals beckoned me: I chose one after another to hold, kiss, and snuggle to my heart when no one was looking. The bear was my favorite, and the first one that I bought. I named him Zephir after a character in the children's book *Babar the Elephant*.

My parents sent me a check for one hundred dollars after Thanksgiving. Every year, they received a Christmas check from my father's wealthy sister, and they shared it with their children. I took the opportunity to buy the beginnings of a wooden Christmas nativity set that we sold in the shop. I started with the hand-carved wooden crèche, the baby Jesus, the manger, and Mary; Joseph was out of stock. I made a seasonal table for the crèche upstairs next to the window seat that faced the pony barn. I surrounded it with green moss and boughs from the woods and with crystals that I was slowly collecting. I decided that I would add to the nativity set each year and buy the wooden animals, trees, shepherds, and wise men that were part of the fifteen-piece collection, and, of course, Joseph as soon as he was available. I was eager for Jim to see it.

I did finally tell my friend Anne, who had a young child, that I was pregnant. But I wanted Jim to know before I told anyone else.

My coworkers, however, said I glowed and looked beautiful. "It must be your new diet and all the vitamins and herbs you take," they remarked. I smiled, beaming. I was eager to return after my Christmas vacation and share my good news with them.

When I met Jim at the Kingston train station two days before Christmas, he slid onto the passenger seat of my sister's hand-me-down Plymouth Valiant convertible that she'd recently given me when she bought a new car. Jim's Danish School Bag was at his feet. He leaned over and hugged me. I thought about the leather backpack that I had bought him for Christmas; I looked forward to seeing him open it on Christmas morning.

"Wow, it's good to be home. New York is a trip," he said, accentuating the word *trip*. He lit a Marlboro with the cigarette lighter that was built into the dashboard. I opened my window and took a deep breath. I kept the air circulating a few minutes to clear out his cigarette smoke. During the twenty-minute drive home, past the open fields and over Shannock Hill, the nervousness crept in.

"I baked five fruitcakes: one for my parents, one for Rae, one for your mother—without the cognac of course—one for Scott and Vicki, and one for your brother and Lois. I bought herbs, teas, and spices for your sisters. And I made plum pudding for you to have while you're home." I chatted about where we would spend Christmas Eve, Christmas Day, and Christmas night, and who was going where and when. I told him that my parents and sister would be visiting my brother in Marlboro, Massachusetts, for Christmas, and that we wouldn't see them until after the holiday.

"I took the whole time off from work while you're home," I said. My stomach felt jumpy. I wanted to tell him the news but thought it would be best to wait until we got home. He didn't seem excited about my taking a week off. I thought he must be worried about my going without a week's pay.

When we finally arrived, he rummaged through the refrigerator and drank the raw milk straight out of the bottle. I showed him the plum pudding and brandy sauce; he scooped a large portion into a bowl. From the rocking chair near the warm wood stove, Nutmeg greeted us with a yawn and a flick of her tail. We stood in front of the stove and Jim hugged me. "I love this place. What a relief after New York."

I held him tightly. "I love you," I said. "Look what I got for us." I showed him the nativity set.

"Hmmm, I remember seeing ones like that when my family lived in Germany."

I didn't want to talk about his family or his life in Germany. So, with my eyes focused on the crèche, I said, "I've got something to tell you."

We sat on the window seat couch; Nutmeg jumped off the rocking chair and joined us. She nuzzled in my lap, and then leaned over to sniff at the bowl of plum pudding that Jim was holding.

"What?" he asked. "Did Herr Heinz give you a raise or a bigger discount on all the stuff you buy?" He nodded toward the wooden manger.

I laughed a little. "No. I'm pregnant. We're going to have a baby."

He looked at me but didn't say a word.

I kept talking. "It happened when I saw you in New York. I'm about six weeks pregnant. I feel really good, but I get tired. And I'm excited."

Jim, however, didn't look excited; he looked agitated. He stood up, lit a cigarette, walked to the end of the room, and looked out the French door window. I felt a chill; I got up and added a log to the blazing fire. I held my breath and waited for him to say something. Anything. He went over to his school bag, took out a bag of grass, rolled a joint, and lit it. He inhaled deeply, and then offered it to me. I declined. I hoped he would relax and that his mood would change.

"Pregnant," he said loudly at last. "That's crazy. It costs a lot of money to have a kid. I'm just starting to get roles, and we don't have any money."

I quickly said, "I can waitress again for a couple of months on the weekends to make extra money when I'm not at the Garden. Prenatal care is almost free at Planned Parenthood because I don't have insurance. And they told me it only costs about $700 if we go to a birthing center. Maybe I could even find out about midwives."

"Do you really want so much responsibility so young? You agreed that we're not getting married — right?"

I knew he had been married for a short time several years before we'd met. It had been a difficult time for him. I didn't want to get married either, because I thought of us as free spirits, especially after watching the sunrise on Moonstone Beach, and that our special relationship was much better than marriage.

"We don't need to get married," I said. "But yes, I want this baby. I don't mind the responsibility; I'm excited. I love you; it will be great."

He sat down beside me and, between drags on the joint, shoveled spoonfuls of the pudding into his mouth. I quietly hugged Nutmeg, hoping Jim would say something else. Then he looked at me sideways and said, "Nothing's going to come between me and my career. Got that?"

I read that as an *okay*—not a complete rejection. "Don't worry, I'll take care of everything," I replied happily. "We won't get in your way or hold you back from being a successful actor. It will all work out." I was relieved.

The story I told myself was that his career was important: it wasn't that he didn't want a child, he was just afraid that one would get in the way. I figured that, if I took care of everything, he would eventually see how wonderful a family would be.

On Christmas Eve, we spent the night with close friends of Jim's. They were the backbone of a large liberal family: a university physics professor named Scott; his second wife, Vicki; and five children ranging in ages from five to thirty. Jim's friend John was married to the eldest daughter, Toby. The family home was a big old house that was always filled with lots of relatives and friends. There were several couches that were always available for guests who didn't want to—or shouldn't—drive home. After delicious food, lots of drinking, and discussions about the theater, the politics of Richard Nixon, and the innovative *Roe v Wade* bill that would enable a woman to have a legal abortion in the United States, the room quieted. Sitting in front of the fire, we all yawned. Then Jim said: "Susie's going to have a baby."

I was surprised but happy that he'd announced the news.

Drinks were raised and cheers were made.

"What wonderful news to share on Christmas Eve," Vicki said. "A young mother waiting for her child to be born."

I felt as if we were part of the family; I looked forward to going to future gatherings there with a child of my own.

The next morning, after breakfast, we opened presents with them. Jim really liked the cognac leather backpack, and I loved the off-white Irish knit cardigan sweater that he'd bought me in New York.

After clearing away the wrapping paper, saying thank you and good-bye, Jim and I went to his mother's apartment for more Christmas celebration. We didn't talk about having the baby while we were alone, but he made the announcement at his mother's house. His mother seemed happy and surprised; she and his siblings congratulated us. I became more relaxed and believed that Jim was warming to the idea of being a father. And yet, after his initial announcements at Scott and Vicki's and his mother's, he never said anything more about the baby. Instead, he talked about New York, and he entertained us with amusing theater stories and new character impersonations that he slipped into seamlessly. He was the center of his family's attention and the center of my world. It was intoxicating to be with him on any terms that made him comfortable.

Several days later, we drove to Newport to visit my parents, who had returned from visiting my brother. They had rented a small bungalow on Burdick Avenue from my mother's niece Colleen so my father could be closer to Colleen's husband, Richard, who was also my father's doctor. It was a beautiful drive; I loved going over Narragansett Bay on the two bridges and looking out at the small islands and farms that sloped down to the water. Once at the house, however, I felt more like a guest than like my parents' child who had grown up in our home on Alabama Avenue in Providence.

Jim and I sat in the living room in front of their glass-covered mahogany coffee table that, like them, had been transplanted from Providence. We listened to the stories of how successful my brother was, how delicious their Christmas dinner had been, how adorable their little girl was, and how tastefully Nancy, my sister-in-law, had decorated their house. As I sat there listening, I realized that the wooden manger and ceramic characters in the nativity scene on the coffee table were the only familiar remnants of Christmases from my childhood.

I gave them the fruitcake and fresh herbs—rosemary, thyme, sage, parsley, and chives—that I'd planted in a large red pot. I also gave my mother the novel *Captains and the Kings* by Taylor Caldwell, and I presented my father with several used books that contained a variety of detective stories. "I'll come in the spring," I said, "and make a little garden for you. I'll plant the herbs outside your door."

My mother handed me a card. "It's a check," she said. "I never know what to get you."

There were several wrapped packages from my sister. I knew they would be clothes, and, though we had different styles, they were always very nice. That year's gifts were a green wool turtleneck sweater and red-white-and-green-plaid wool bell-bottomed hip-hugger pants to go with it. Jim got a charcoal gray scarf.

When I had moved in with Jim during college, my parents hadn't said much. By then I was supporting myself, and they'd found Jim as charismatic as everyone else had. I didn't really know what to expect when I finally said, "We're going to have a baby. It's due in August, and I'm sure it's a boy."

Jim lit a cigarette and my father relit a half-smoked cigar. He was down to two a week because of his heart problems, and he nursed one along for days at a time.

My mother jumped out of her chair. "Well, you'll have to get married now! You can't have a child without being married."

"Um, we're not getting married," I said quietly. "I told you before, we don't need a piece of paper to say we're married." I felt very anxious inside, even though I tried to look calm.

"But it's different when you have a child. What will people say?"

I boldly said, "I don't care what people say. Who cares about that? We love each other. That's what really matters.

"Your sister and brothers were all married before they had children. Why won't you get married?" My mother's voice got louder and higher, just short of shrieking. I was waiting for her to tell me that I was putting another nail in her coffin.

"Hon, hon, sit down," my father gently told my mother. I was hoping he would say it was okay. Jim's family and friends had been so happy and supportive; I didn't want my parents to make a scene that might scare Jim away.

Then my father said, "If you live together and are going to have a child, I don't understand why you don't want to get married."

I repeated my argument that we didn't need an institution like the Church to tell us we were married. The Church had done some sketchy things over the years that I didn't believe in. "I haven't been to church for years, and I'm not a Catholic anymore. They lost me a long time ago when they turned our movie theater into a satellite chapel and told us to go there instead of beautiful St. Paul's Church."

Jim sat quietly beside me, smoking. I felt that his presence gave me the support I needed to ignore my parent's wishes. I actually thought my confidence convinced them.

The following week, I received a letter from my mother that captured the brunt of our visit. In it, she said that my father was heartsick and that I was killing him, that I was killing both of them, and that I was selfish. *Your father needs extra oxygen each day since you told him about being pregnant.* That is the sentence I remember most.

When I called my sister to tell her about the letter, I realized she also felt I was making the wrong decision and was on my parents' side of the argument. She resented that I was creating chaos in the family because she was the one who had to deal with my mother on a regular basis. My sister was divorced, had two young boys, and relied on my parents to help with childcare while she worked and studied for a master's degree. She was also the one my mother called daily to unload her burdens. Each Sunday, my sister went to dinner at their Newport bungalow. Between the letter and my sister's reaction, I began to feel defensive about my relationship with Jim, and even more committed to not getting legally married.

I stopped being on speaking terms with my mother and sister. I did, however, stay in touch with my father. I went to visit him on my day off every Thursday when my mother was at Bostitch, the company known for desktop staplers and other tools. She was the executive secretary for the president of international sales. One of my regrets later in life was that I never took the time to visit her where she spent so much of her life.

The first time I went after that awful Christmas debacle, I brought my father an expensive cigar, a chocolate bar from the shop, and thoughts from the latest book on spirituality that I was reading.

When I talked to him about the letter from my mother, he responded, "Oh, sweets, don't worry. Your mother and sister watch too many soap operas. You're not killing me. The odds are in her favor. I'm eighty-five and probably am dying anyway. Your mother is crazy but means well. She just wants what's best for you."

Although I felt close to my father, he was no match for my mother's anger. I really needed to be comforted, not reminded of the family commandment: "Don't upset your mother." Wasn't a mother supposed to nurture her child, especially when she's pregnant?

That day, however, he added, "What I don't understand is how you and Jim will replace a two-thousand-year-old tradition." His concern was for me, and not about what people would think.

I assured him that we would be fine. It reminded me of the time I'd told him I was taking mind-expanding drugs, and his reply was that he thought drugs were for people who were sick. He didn't always understand my decisions, but he was still kind to me.

The Thursday visits with my father meant so much to me. Jim was in New York most of the time and only came home once or twice during my pregnancy. My life at the Garden was very full, but I was awfully lonely. When I wasn't waitressing, I spent most evenings and weekends alone, reading and preparing to have the baby.

Nutmeg and I, along with the child growing in my womb, became our own little family. As my baby grew and my abdomen got bigger, I took warm lavender baths, watched my body expand, and rubbed rose oil over my baby hill, soothing and welcoming the child within. Each evening I read passages aloud to my baby and to Nutmeg from my Steiner books and from books on natural childbirth and breastfeeding. I also drank cups of chamomile tea that had been grown biodynamically.

I traded in my very faded tight jeans for an old pair of overalls that Jim had used in a theater production and paired them with a green wool cardigan sweater from my father. My understanding of plants was growing as I was blossoming among the umbelliferae—plants of the air element—and the labiatae—plants of warmth. Each herbal plant has a strong connection to one of the four elements—earth, air, water, and fire—and each plant also has the four elements represented in its form. The roots relate to the earth, the stem and leaves to water, the fruit or ripened ovary relates to fire, and the flower to the air element. An airy plant such as chamomile, whose leaves and flowers are used for tea, helps direct the air in the intestines back to where it belongs, thus bringing relief from indigestion. Chamomile is also good to drink before bedtime to relax.

As my pregnancy went forward, it became less appealing to me to run to New York to visit Jim. He was now called J. T. Walsh, as he'd needed a new name because there was already a James Walsh in SAG—the Screen Actors Guild. He was becoming a working actor, but he still bartended whenever possible and occasionally sent me a check that I deposited in the bank. It didn't take much on his part to keep me hopeful.

He was getting better parts in the theater, but he said he could probably come home for the summer because there wasn't much theater going on when it was so hot. He agreed to take an intensive natural childbirth class with me sometime in the summer. Again, I felt relieved and confident that, if I took care of as much as possible, everything would be fine, and we would have enough money saved.

In May, my sister called, a sign that there was bad news. She told me my father was in the hospital for tests and that he might need surgery. I took the next day off and went to visit him. I brought a basket filled with homemade bread, fresh carrot juice, and sorrel soup. He tasted a little of everything. When his nurse came by to check on him, he introduced me to her as "My daughter Miss West."

"When are you expecting?" the nurse asked.

"Early August, so it's a Leo. And I'm sure it's a boy."

She nodded toward my father's plate. "Looks like he likes your food better than ours." Then she smiled and said, "Good luck with the baby," and she left the room.

I stayed with my father all afternoon and told him about my friends at the Garden, about Jim getting steady work, and about our plans to take natural childbirth classes together when he eventually returned in the summer.

My father told me that he was feeling weaker, and that he didn't have much energy even for the things he liked to do, like drawing on the porch. "I've had a pretty good life, though," he added. "I can't complain."

"Are you afraid of dying?" I asked, suddenly feeling very sad.

"No, I'm not afraid. But don't talk about death around here, because everyone pretends it's never going to happen, especially your mother."

I leaned close to him and felt my heart swell with emotion. I loved him so much. He was sweet, and I was grateful that he wasn't angry with me like my mother was. I knew I was his favorite child. I wanted to be there for him, but not to be so sad that my baby would feel the sadness. I wanted to give him something that would connect us and help him. "Remember how you felt better after we recommended vitamins to you several years ago?" I asked. "And how the breathing exercises I showed you helped when you struggled to breathe and when you felt anxious?"

He nodded.

"Now I want to show you how to meditate. It's easy, Dad. Close your eyes and relax. Take a few gentle breaths and say to yourself: 'Wisdom lives in the light.' If your mind wanders, go back to that mantra, 'Wisdom lives in the light.' I meditate every day before I go to work. I'll think of you when I mediate, and you try it, too. Okay?" He nodded again. "Try to choose the same time every day to meditate. And start with fifteen minutes if you can."

Late that afternoon, my mother arrived at the hospital after getting out of work. She kissed my father and seemed relieved that I had spent the afternoon with him. She was happy to hear that he had eaten a nice lunch. When the doctor came into the room to report on the status of my father's tests, my mother simply said, "This is our daughter Susan." She acted as though I wasn't pregnant and that everything was normal.

Nice dodge, I thought to myself. *He won't know I'm not married.*

We learned that there were some suspicious growths on my father's spine, and that he needed to get some rest and build himself up for exploratory surgery later in the month.

Spring was very busy for me between my job at the Herb Garden preparing volumes of herbs to be sold at local flower shows and putting in a small vegetable garden behind our house. By then I was also waitressing the lunch shift on weekends; lunch was a slower shift than dinner and less physically demanding. I also went to visit my parents on Sundays for dinner, always bringing along herbal teas, brown rice pudding, and hearty soups. My condition was no longer the topic of concern for my mother and sister; my father's health consumed my mother, and she was in a state of panic about losing him. My sister and I did what we always did as children; we took care of her. My father's operation had gone well, but the pathologist had determined that the growths were cancerous, and the doctors couldn't assure my parents that more wouldn't appear. For the moment, however, we held onto the hope that he would be okay. I was grateful to be on speaking terms again with my mother and sister and prayed that my father would regain his health.

Nutmeg had been busy, too — she delivered a litter of five kittens. I found homes for four of them, but I kept her son. I named him Mutzeputz after a cat in a fairy tale titled *The Three Candles of Little Veronica,* a story about how a child lives between two worlds: heaven and earth. He looked Siamese in all ways except for a white patch around his left eye. He was very cute, but a little ornery. There was no cuddling with Mutzeputz.

On June twenty-fourth, we had our traditional St. John's Festival at the Herb Garden. Seven months pregnant, I stepped, rather than jumped, over the remaining embers of the fire and wished for blessings on my baby's arrival and on my father's health. Several days after the festival, my baby was busy too: he decided to arrive five weeks early. On June 28, 1974, I drove to the Garden with the top down on the convertible. As I was watering the wooden racks filled with plants that now seemed to be pleading to get out of the greenhouse and into the ground, I felt warm moisture run down my legs. I walked into the gift shop to the phone on the wall behind the counter and called Dr. LePere: he told me he'd meet me at Westerly Hospital as soon as he could. On the way, I stopped at our house to call St. Clement's Theater in New York City, where Jim was then performing. I left a message for him and rubbed some essential oil of rose on my stomach. Then I went back outside, put the top up on the car, and drove to the hospital. Alone.

Beginnings

"H I, MY NAME IS Cathy. I'm here to shave your pubic hair."

I sat, startled, and watched as a young woman in blue scrubs placed a metal bowl of water on the stand beside me. She pulled the curtain closed around my hospital bed.

"We want to make sure everything is fresh and clean for the delivery." She ripped open the plastic bag of a disposable razor.

"How are you doin'?" she asked as she lifted my hospital gown and gently rubbed some soapy foam on the soft hair beneath my pregnant stomach.

"Well it's kind of sudden, five weeks before my due date. I was going to take natural childbirth classes and maybe find a midwife." I watched her quickly shave the small area around my vagina.

"Well, don't worry. We're all here to help you. And babies have a way of changing our plans. Just relax and save your strength for the labor." She left the curtains closed.

I took a deep breath and adjusted the pillow lower down my back. An older woman in a black skirt and white blouse came in and stood beside my bed. She was carrying a clipboard.

"Susan Margaret West?"

I nodded.

"It says here that your status is single, and you have no health insurance. Is that correct?"

"Yes."

She confirmed my date of birth, social security number, address, and telephone number.

"We're going to enroll you for public assistance to cover the hospital costs, please sign here." She handed me the clipboard. I signed beside the X. "A case worker will follow up in six to eight weeks to review your status. Any questions?"

I gulped and shook my head no, feeling as if I'd just done something wrong.

"Good luck with the delivery." She opened the curtains around the bed, and quickly left.

I looked around the rectangular room. Two more of the beds had filled with very pregnant women since I'd arrived. I watched as the nurse in blue scrubs came and went to perform the hygienic protocol, but no social worker followed. I closed my eyes; warm tears surprised me and slowly ran down my cheeks. *Had I called the right number at the theater to leave a message? Would Jim even get it before the theater opened for rehearsal? Would he get to the hospital?*

Dr. LePere came to examine me. He had been a friend of Dr. Laskey's and was still friends with the doctor's daughter Patti, our landlord. Patti had recommended that I see Dr. LePere, even though I was going to Planned Parenthood and had been planning to go to a birthing center or find a midwife. I wondered if he knew that I had been enrolled in public assistance.

"You've got some time to go; your cervix is just beginning to dilate. Any cramps yet?"

"Just a few. Not bad, though."

"It'll be awhile, late tonight or even tomorrow, so relax and try to rest before the work really begins. I'll check on you later. The nurses are here to help whenever you need them."

While I waited for my labor to begin, I thought of my mother. She often said that, if she had to do it again, she would have gone on welfare rather than leave her newborn babies after only two weeks to return to a full-time job. But, somehow, I didn't believe that she would sympathize with my being an unwed welfare recipient.

By late afternoon the cramps increased and came more frequently. I thought about nothing but preparing for the next round. It was scary and painful. Nurses came and went; they walked me around the room and told me to breathe deeply. I remember hoping that they would give me something for the pain, but I still wanted to have a natural childbirth as I'd originally planned.

"The baby is almost five weeks premature," a nurse told me. "It will be better for the baby if you don't have any drugs."

Then everything became a blur as the contractions increased in intensity and came faster and faster. The doctor appeared and said that I was on my way to the delivery room.

"And you have a visitor," he said.

As I was being rolled down the corridor, Jim was suddenly beside me.

"I made it. That wasn't so bad was it? You're almost ready to deliver. I'll see you later in the recovery room."

I was so happy to see him and would later joke to everyone about Jim showing up fifteen minutes before my delivery and saying that it wasn't so bad. Covering up my pain with humor became a fine-tuned defense mechanism of mine for many years.

John Alan West was born at 12:10 AM on June 29, 1974. The doctor told me they were going to give him a little oxygen and that I should rest. I felt too weak to ask questions before they whisked him away.

Jim was waiting for me in the recovery room. He had seen John and told me that he was beautiful but was having difficulty breathing. We shared the ginger ale and ham and cheese sandwich that an aide brought me. Jim told me about his dramatic exit from the city: finding a replacement at the bar where he worked, getting a friend to cover for a script reading, catching a train from Penn Station to Kingston, hitchhiking to Black Acre Farm to get his car, and arriving just in time.

Like the experience of labor, Jim became a blur. I fell into a deep sleep but was soon awakened by a young doctor who said my baby had a rare disease. I needed to make a decision right away: did I want to authorize the hospital to have John transferred to Women's and Children's Hospital in Providence?

"'They might have more experience with this kind of condition," the doctor said.

"I thought he just needed some oxygen since he was early," I said.

"We've done everything we can do and he's still struggling to breathe. Do you want us to transfer him to Providence?"

"Yes. Of course," I said and signed the authorization form.

It was a condition called Hyaline Membrane Syndrome, which meant that John's lungs were functioning as if he were still in the womb. His lungs didn't expand and contract easily, so he needed assistance breathing. The doctors in Providence didn't know how long he'd be in the ICU.

Jim went back to New York.

And, for the next twelve days, I went to the hospital and sat beside the small incubator where John slept with tubes coming out of his arms and oxygen being pumped in so he could breathe without struggling. The nurses let me open the incubator and stroke his little arms and hold his tiny hands. I felt so sad that I couldn't hold him; I longed to be able to nurse him. I had read about how important it is to nurse your baby in order to bond with them, and how nutritious a mother's milk is. I felt discouraged, but sat quietly beside him, meditating, praying, and trying to let him know that I was there.

Finally. a nurse let me hold him.

He was so small, so vulnerable. I held back my tears and whispered in his tiny ear, "Come on, John, please get better so I can take you to our beautiful home in the country and get you out of this noisy city. You need my milk — not that stuff that's in those tubes."

The next day a nurse called to say that John was breathing on his own and that I could take him home. It felt to me like he had heard me. I was happy and scared at the same time. Jim couldn't get back for several days, so I asked my friend Anne to go with me to the hospital.

"I'll go but I'm afraid to drive in the city, so if you drive my car, I'll hold the baby."

The whole process seemed to take forever. But at last we made it home. As soon as Anne left, I sat at the kitchen table, guided John to a breast that was swollen with milk and prayed that the La Leche League was right and that it wasn't too late to nurse. I took another step on the journey of motherhood, alone in my kitchen with my tiny baby.

And that was how things were for the next few years: John and I most often alone, Jim coming home once in a while, then leaving again. Somehow, our lifestyle almost felt normal.

"I think Heinz has more under his hat than you think," Jim said late in the summer of 1977. He leaned against the doorway to our bedroom. Never one for shorts, even in summer heat, he wore white jeans and a long-sleeved, pale blue paisley shirt that I'd found for him at the local consignment shop. I slipped into a fringeless denim miniskirt, gold peasant blouse, and sandals, preparing to meet with the owner of Meadowbrook Herb Garden.

We had recently returned to Black Acre Farm after spending time on the road while Jim toured for a year with the Acting Company. It had been his first full-time acting job. The company was a highly respected repertory group that gave him the opportunity to perform in Shakespeare's *Love's Labour's Lost* and *The Kitchen* in theaters and universities all over the country. When the company spent several weeks in one location like Chicago, Denver, or Los Angeles at a theater festival or a university theater, I packed John into our "newer, better car"—the white VW Beatle—and drove to meet them. Jim had installed a CB radio in the car for me to use for directions or to get help if needed. My handle was *The Pedal Pusher*, and I became very good at asking for directions as I drove with John to meet Jim. The company's final performances of the year were in Los Angeles. We drove home across the country together.

Soon after our return, I'd stopped to visit everyone at the Herb Garden. Heinz had invited me to his house that night to discuss a plan.

"What do you mean what's 'under his hat'? He probably wants to know if and when I'm going back to work full time." I picked up Little Man (my nickname for John) who was holding on to both my legs as I stood by the door. When I'd first seen him in the incubator at the hospital, he'd looked like a wise little man, a being from a faraway place. Now, three years later, he was a beautiful boy who was learning to talk about the world and using lots of new vocabulary that he'd learned while we were traveling.

"Mommy, the green room isn't green—that's so silly," he said one day when we were backstage in a theater. "And I don't like when Judson tells daddy to break a leg." One of his special lines was, "The theater's dark today, so can we go to the zoo?"

Our time on the road with Jim had been mixed. On the positive side, it was great to travel and see new places. When Jim was rehearsing, John and I would visit local museums, parks, health food stores, and the occasional Waldorf School. We stayed up late in order to spend time with Jim and his friends, and often went to noisy bars for late dinners and drinks. There was little rhythm to our life on the road. John got ill once with a bronchial-like cold. I took him to the emergency room and was told to get a vaporizer, let him rest, and keep him warm. After his compromised beginning, I was insecure about his health and worried at the first sign of a sniffle. In addition, I felt conflicted between being a good mother and being with Jim. Now that we were home again, I hoped my fears would finally subside.

Nutmeg rubbed up against my legs and John squirmed out of my arms, grabbed her, then toted her up onto the kitchen chair with him. We had rented out our house to a young couple when we were on the road, and they had taken good care of Nutmeg. Nutmeg let John carry her around like a rag doll, while Mutzeputz stayed clear of him. Jim lit a cigarette and stepped outside the screen door to smoke.

"That Heinz is pretty shrewd, surrounding himself with beautiful women wearing cutoffs and bikini tops and paying them minimum wage. While he and the lovely Ines drive a new Mercedes."

I smirked inwardly, wondering if he might be a little jealous. *How ironic*, I thought, since he had so many female theater friends.

I opened the door, and Nutmeg jumped out of John's arms and ran out the door. John started after her. In an instant, Jim bent down, scooped John up in one arm, dropped his cigarette, and crushed it under his foot. Then he stopped to pick it up and put it in the can of sand that I'd placed outside the door.

"They're halter tops, not bikinis," I said. "Maybe you just don't want to be left alone to put Little Man to bed and clean up the dishes." My voice was an octave higher than usual. I hoped to emphasize that I could use a little help from Jim on the occasions when he was home and not performing Off-Broadway. And getting closer—and closer—to Broadway.

"Tbo and Jaybo are coming by later. Don't worry, we'll take good care of Little Man."

When I first met Jim and he was living down the line with several guys, Ted and Jay were the ones that he'd hung out with most. The housemates added "bo" to their names. They called Jim, Jimbo. It reminded me of hobo, which is short for homeward bound. I romantically thought he was a hobo, and I was his home. Everyone in their house joked about Tbo being a business major and a success at selling the best drugs on campus.

Halfway to the car, I turned back and said, "Please don't smoke in the house and certainly not close to John. Please don't smoke anything around him. And be sure to bring the cat in before it gets dark. There are coyotes around."

Jim took John's hand, and together they waved good-bye to me, John laughing and bouncing in Jim's arms. Then Jim called out his now favorite refrain: "What happened to my wild, carefree Susie?"

I pulled away in my old Valiant, knowing that with its 140,000 miles, its days were numbered. Jim's smoking concerned me. I did whatever I thought I could do to prevent it, like throwing away his cigarettes, crushing them when he wasn't looking, and emptying his ashtrays so he couldn't find any butts big enough to light up. I was also beginning to pour out small amounts of whiskey that he'd stored on the top shelf and to throw out small amounts of pot that he'd left in plastic sandwich bags around the house.

As I drove toward Heinz and Ines's house, I thought about John's birth, about his time in the hospital, and the sad months that had followed. Not only had the days after his birth been challenging, but also, during the first three months of his life, I nursed him every two hours around the clock and often cried with overwhelming fatigue. Then, as things in life sometimes do, they got worse. When John was four months old, my father died.

In my memory, his death was like a three-act play: the spiritual experience of the day he died, his funeral, and my mother's grief. Each act was intensified for me because Jim was away in Washington state, performing Stanley in *A Streetcar Named Desire*.

The day my father died, I had put John down for his morning nap and was upstairs in the large loft space. I sat in my usual chair, a hand-me-down that I had reupholstered, and the spot where I journaled and looked out at the grazing ponies. Although lonely while Jim was away, I took solace in the beauty that surrounded me. It was a daily ritual that I did before I meditated. (As a birthday gift during my senior year in college, Jim had paid for me to take a workshop in Transcendental Meditation, which had been introduced in the United States in the 1960s by Maharishi Mahesh Yogi. I had been meditating consistently since then, but instead of using the mantra that I was given in the workshop, I was now working with one from the German philosopher Rudolf Steiner's work—the same one I'd taught my father.)

After getting settled that morning, I closed my eyes, focused on relaxing, and then brought the words "Wisdom lives in the light" to my inner silence. After about thirty minutes in a deep state of calm and inner attentiveness, I slowly opened my eyes . . . and looked directly into the eyes of my father who was sitting in the rocking chair across from me. The room felt porous; light streamed through the walls as well as through the windows. A sweet sadness and warmth surrounded me. Then my intellect took over, and I realized where I was. My father disappeared.

I sat in silence, feeling filled with peace.

Then the phone rang. It was my mother, sobbing hysterically.

"He's gone," she cried. "They called me at work. I didn't get to see him again."

My father's death and funeral were difficult. My mother grieved so much that I reacted to her grief by holding back my tears. She threw herself onto his casket, weeping, "Why did he have to die?"

She told me that she'd had a dream the day after he died. In her dream, my father was trying to step over a stone wall, and she, my mother, was holding onto his leg. He tried to shake her off so he could cross the wall.

"What do you think it means?" she asked me as she sobbed in my arms.

I think your grief is holding him back, I thought, but didn't have the heart to say. Instead, I put my arm around her, hoping to console her. My spiritual studies had led me to understand that death on earth was birth or a new beginning in the spiritual world.

"Mom, he was eighty-five years old, and he died before he had to suffer with painful bone cancer. I miss him, too, but it was his time."

Luckily, I had gone to visit him about six weeks after John was born. He'd held his newest grandchild and said to me, "He's a beautiful little tyke, isn't he?"

Before Jim had left for the Playhouse Theater in Seattle, I had read lines with him because he'd wanted to get a jumpstart on rehearsal. It was his first leading role, and a well-known actress, Eva Le Gallienne, was to play Blanche. After I returned home the night of my father's funeral, I received a call from the actress who had the role of Stella in the play. She asked to speak to Jim, but he hadn't come home yet. Then she broke down, cried hysterically, and told me that she knew Jim would never leave me, but that she was in love with him. They'd had an affair and her heart was broken.

I was stunned. My feelings bounced from fear to anger to jealousy to sorrow. It frightened me to think that Jim might have left John and me. And I was angry that I didn't even know where he was or how to contact him. When he finally arrived, he assured me that he loved me, that theater affairs were common, and he had fallen into the trap. He told me would never leave us.

We made love as one emotion after another hit me. When my fear of his deserting us had lifted, I felt betrayed and lost. But I thought that I'd have to forgive him because I didn't know what else to do. I didn't want to be alone. I was beginning to think that Jim had gotten so deeply into his character that reality and fantasy had blurred. When I'd been reading lines with him, I'd felt a little like Stella, the wife who couldn't live without Stanley, but also like Blanche Du Bois. Then I found a poster of the play's performance schedule and the cast.

The last performance had ended two days before my father's death. So it was a double blow. Jim had had an affair and had decided not to come home for the funeral.

It was all so traumatic for me that I internalized my grief and moved forward with my life, thinking I had no other options. As time went on it got easier. When I felt sad, I wanted to hide my emotions from John, so I would turn on the radio and sing.

And now, driving to meet with Heinz, I turned on the radio and sang "The Best of My Love" along with The Eagles. Then I parked in front of the Herb Garden and calmly walked down the driveway to Heinz's house.

— 8 —

Thorns and Roses

IT WAS THE FIRST TIME Heinz had invited me into the main house. Ines greeted me and led me through her kitchen while asking questions about John and Jim in her lilting, singsong German-accented voice. I stole envious glances at not one but two immaculate stoves, shiny appliances, and perfectly trimmed flowering plants that lined the windowsills. Familiar stuffed animals—a dog, a bear, and a fox that I recognized as from the Steiff collection sold in the shop—sat on the cushion of the window seat. An enormous asparagus fern with red berries hung above the sink.

I followed her to Heinz's study, where two walls were lined with bookcases, a woodstove was on the third, and, on the outside wall, a large window overlooked an ornamental garden. Heinz sat in a blue swivel chair that allowed him to put a book on the shelf behind him, then swivel back toward me. He gestured for me to sit across from him.

"I'll bring you some cookies and rose petal elixir," Ines said.

I quickly learned the purpose of the meeting: Heinz wanted me to be a sales representative for the products he sold both in the shop and through a mail order catalogue. He mentioned the spices, seeds, herbs, and teas that I had become familiar with when I'd worked at the garden, but he seemed more interested in finding a way to promote the Dr. Hauschka products that he sold through the catalogue and to a select group of customers who had discovered the products while traveling in Europe.

"I think you would be good at this job, because you travel to New York and around the country to see Jim. You also understand the value of the biodynamic/organic healing element of herbs."

Ines came back into the room and offered me cookies and a rosy sparkling drink from a tray.

"Susan, you're so good in the shop, our sales have never been better," she added to Heinz's pitch.

Although I was more of an earthy garden girl, the idea of cosmetics interested me. Since I'd discovered the medicinal properties of herbs and their historic use, I had started mixing herbal extracts with oils to cleanse my face and condition my hair. I'd learned that the word cosmetic comes from the Greek word *Kosmein*, which originally meant to bring order to, to harmonize, and to adorn. It fascinated me to think that our society only focused on the adornment part, and that cosmetics had come to mean a way to cover up a woman's appearance.

"I thought if you knew a little about how Dr. Hauschka's products are made it might interest you."

Over the next two hours, Heinz explained that Dr. Rudolph Hauschka had founded a company named WALA, and that the W is pronounced like a V by the Germans and has a soothing rhythmic sound. He said the doctor's goal was to make natural remedies with no negative side effects, products that supported *health* rather than those that attacked *illness*. I thought it was a wonderful, innovative idea whose time had definitely come.

He went on to say that a similar idea was practiced in biodynamic gardening—namely to support healthy processes in nature by focusing on process instead of only on substances. For example, if there is a pest on a plant, such as larvae on broccoli, the BD approach is to question why the pest is there in the first place—not simply to spray to get rid of it. By knowing that the larvae should be in the soil, digesting nitrogen, rather than on the plant, eating leaves, the gardener learns how he can help, such as by amending the soil with certain herbal preparations that would entice the larvae to move back where they belonged.

I also learned that one of the first things that Rudolph Hauschka had done was to plant extensive herb gardens on about six acres of land in the small village of Eckwälden, Germany. His pharmacy began in the garden.

Heinz had my complete attention now.

He went on to explain that the word WALA is an acronym for "Warmth, Ash, Light, Ash," which referred to key elements in the extraction method that Hauschka developed to retain the life force of healing plants. The rose was the first plant that he successfully extracted using his seven-day rhythmical process. Heinz told me that the rose was used in both the skin care products and in the remedies. The rose is a plant with great polarity. It captures the beauty and delicacy of the petal and the resiliency of the thorns. He said that the plants, along with precious stones, minerals, and some animal products like lanolin and beeswax, are the basis for over five thousand remedies and over fifty skin care products developed during Hauschka's life.

Then Heinz showed me pictures of the company, which was close to large, wooded tracts of land and to a small mountain range called the Schwäbische Alb.

While I listened, I felt as if everything he was telling me was a story I'd longed to hear since I was born. Somewhere deep within me, my whole being was saying, *Yes*.

Everything Heinz told me sounded fascinating. I tried to remember every step of Hauschka's process, but I could only retain a few bits: the rhythmical process, alchemical, roses harvested at sunrise before the dew dries, the vitality of healing plants, early morning light, sunrise, and sunset. It all sounded amazing, and I was flattered that Heinz was taking the time to share it with me. He even said that the rose petal elixir I was drinking had been made from the very roses that grew in the WALA gardens.

He then handed me a carton filled with jars of the herbs and spices like the ones that lined the shelves in the shop. The carton held about fifty boxes of Dr. Hauschka skin care products for face and body.

"I thought it would be helpful for you to try these and show them to store owners and maybe to actresses or friends of yours," Heinz said.

I stayed a little longer, then drove home, the stars and moonlight bright above me. I was excited; I felt as if my purpose in life and sense of self were forming in a new way. I was a mother, the significant other of a talented actor, and, sitting in a box beside me, the threads of a career quietly sat, waiting for me to weave them together.

Little did I know that, from that meeting on that hot summer August night in 1977 until December 2008, Dr. Hauschka products, principles, and practices would be a beacon of light in my life.

I was eager to tell Jim.

But when I pulled into park, I saw Tbo's shiny new black-and-gray GTO. I heard smooth, silky tones of unfamiliar music, combined with men's laughter. The sound drifted through the open French doors that led to a small balcony above where I stood. Nutmeg stepped out of the shadows, greeted me with a meow, and ran through my legs as we both went into the house. I put the box of spices and cosmetics on the table and noticed the dirty dishes stacked neatly in the sink. *Well, at least they're not still on the table,* I thought.

I went to John's room. The lullaby of crickets from the small garden of herbs and salad greens that I'd planted in the back of the house chirped softly through the open windows. An unknown, fragrant vine climbed outside John's window, infusing the space with earthy goodness. He was sound asleep.

I stood, looking at him as I often did, drinking in his angelic beauty, while the mobile of fairies danced slowly above his head. It still amazed me that we'd created such a lovely child. His head was large and beautifully formed, with hair that felt like a breath of golden light. He turned, his small hands cupping upward, as I bent to kiss his soft pink cheek that I thought was as delicate as a rose petal. Then I closed his door and climbed the stairs to the loft. That's when I smelled the scent of grass, and realized that Jim and his friends had been doing what I'd asked him not to do while John was in the house. It was times like these when my love for Jim felt thorny and painful and not as if we were walking together in fields of gold. I remembered what Heinz had said that night about the polarity between the thorn and the rose. As I climbed the stairs, I felt the discomfort of that realization, and I wondered if I could live with polarity.

Letting Go and Letting Come

WE STAYED THE COURSE in spite of our differing priorities. John was growing into a beautiful, healthy child, and the carton full of herbs, spices, and cosmetics was germinating into a business. Jim was getting better roles. I decided we must be okay.

John and I moved to Manhattan in October 1979, the same day Pope John Paul II visited the city for the first time. The Pope said: "A city needs a soul if it is to become a true home for human beings." I wanted to find the soul of the city.

It took a little more than three hours for us to drive from Rhode Island to Mott Street. It had taken me almost three years to convince Jim that it was a necessary move; it took me longer to find the soul of the city—and my own.

Before moving to New York, I became an apprentice to the guiding spirits of the plants and precious stones that the Dr. Hauschka products contained. Each morning and evening, while looking in the mirror, I pressed the cleansing cream—made with sweet almond meal, calendula, and anthyllis—gently into the pores of my skin. I rinsed it off with warm, then cool water infused with lavender, and followed up with a face lotion made from anthyllis and witch hazel extracts. The Dr. Hauschka skin care preparations were delicious and nurturing to my senses. The energetic quality was striking; I felt as if I were being nourished from the outside in. People started to tell me that my skin and hair glowed. I felt beautiful for the first time in my life.

Whenever possible, I also applied the products to John: Rose Day Cream on his face and Lip Balm before going outside. His baths became an early experience in aromatherapy: lavender before bedtime, pine when congested, rosemary during the winter, and lemon in the summertime. Jim appreciated and even bragged to his theater friends about the protocol that I'd developed for him because his skin, which became dry and inflamed when he used heavy stage make up under harsh lights, was now healthy. My confidence in and commitment to the brand grew ever stronger.

The more I educated people about the fact that what they applied to their skin mattered, the greater the sales. Friends and friends of friends invited me to their homes to talk about health and Dr. Hauschka. I always arrived with a basket filled with my freshly baked bread made from organic wheat berries that I ground myself, an herbal tea blend best suited for the season, herbs like marjoram and lovage, and spices like ginger, cardamom, and cayenne that peppered my cooking. Discussion about the nutritional value of the items I brought provided a lead-in to introducing Dr. Hauschka products. As I explained to the group, healthy skin requires a combination of healthy nutrition and products with therapeutic ingredients.

I then demonstrated the three basic skin care products that were recommended as an introduction to the line. Everyone tried each of the products, sighed, and bought them all. I told them that, when used correctly, the basics would last them for six weeks to two months. Most customers wanted more. Whenever

I was invited back to replenish supplies, I introduced the next steps in the line. Soon I was earning a better living, but more importantly, I was finding a path to a bigger world.

I felt as if I'd lived in a womb in Carolina, Rhode Island, for the first five years of John's life. When Jim was away I had filled our days with visiting friends, working several hours a week at the garden, waitressing, and selling Dr. Hauschka Skin Care, but much of the time I'd lived a kind of monastic life, meditating and studying the works of Rudolf Steiner. The Seth Thomas clock I'd inherited from my godmother chimed the 168 hours in a week: John and I had usually been alone for 128 of them.

During those years, Jim's theater friends from New York often visited us in Rhode Island; I introduced them to Dr. Hauschka products, too, and I slowly began to build a network of customers. It was then that the idea of moving to Manhattan had gathered momentum for me. I often hinted to Jim that it would be wonderful for John to go to a Waldorf School and for all of us to be together. By the time John turned five, I realized that I wanted him to attend the Rudolf Steiner School in Manhattan. Though there was a small initiative to start a school in Rhode Island, I felt it was time to create a new life that included being a real family.

"I think I can sell enough products to help us afford to live in the city," I argued to Jim. "You can't keep staying on floors and couches. We could be a family. John needs to start school soon and to be with his father. I can make this work. I know I can."

"You don't know what you're saying!" he retorted. "It's expensive in New York. It's impossible to find a reasonable apartment." He tried to discourage me, but I persisted.

"I know I can figure it out. Let's try."

"Look. Nothing is going to come between me and my career" was his mantra. "I'll take care of everything" was mine.

By the summer of 1979, I had convinced Jim, or so it seemed, that the move would be great: John would go to the Steiner School; I would market Dr. Hauschka; and we would be by Jim's side, embracing his life as a struggling actor. In theory, it all sounded good to me.

We set our expected move for September. Then my friend Suzi Clarke invited me to run in the L'eggs Mini Marathon in Central Park: the race was in early June. I left John at my mother's house for the weekend. He loved to stay at Gramma's because, among other treats she gave him, there was always ice cream in the freezer, unlike at our house, where it was only for special occasions.

The day of the marathon, I ran around Central Park with six thousand other women. Jim met me at the finish line and held me in his arms, congratulating me as I finished my first and last race in the top 10 percent of the participants.

"See?" I joked. "I'm getting in shape for life with you in the city."

That night I went to see him in an Off-Broadway production, then out for drinks with one of his friends from the cast. It felt like the early magic of our relationship was back.

Later that summer, Jim got a job at the Aspen Theater Festival in Colorado. I packed up our house while he was gone; John and I (along with Nutmeg and Mutzeputz) moved in with my mother. John was happy there. He liked staying in a neighborhood and quickly made friends with a little boy named Michael who lived across the street and another boy, Chris, who lived across the backyard and over the fence. When Jim invited me to join him in Aspen for a week, I left John in Newport. It was the longest time in five years that I'd been away from him, but I knew he would be happier going to the beach and playing with children his own age.

Jim was staying in a beautiful Vail condo that belonged to one of the festival organizers. It was a week of celebration. We attended several theater productions—one of which he had a major role in—modern dance performances, and a concert in the Gerald Ford Amphitheater. We also took many walks in the Betty Ford Alpine Gardens. On my last day in Aspen, we climbed the mountain through fields of golden grasses and had a picnic as we looked out over the town. I thought the richness of the week was a good sign, that we were letting go of a lifestyle that had been mostly about John and me living alone, and that now we were moving toward a wonderful future together as a family. Then, soon after I came down from the mountains and returned to Newport, I discovered I was pregnant. It was surprise—and not a convenient time for an unexpected child.

Though initially stunned, I soon felt joyful at the thought of another child—hopefully a girl, a baby sister for John. I didn't feel joyful, however, at the thought of telling Jim. When he flew back to Rhode Island from Aspen before returning to New York, he met my news with sarcasm.

"Fuck. I guess that rhythm, rubbers, and a diaphragm aren't such a good idea after all."

When I had started working at the Herb Garden and decided that taking birth control pills and messing with my hormones wasn't healthy, it seemed right. True, I was comfortable with mind-altering drugs at the time, but hormones had been another matter. But when the momentum of moving to New York City and getting John into a Waldorf School became a beacon, the risk of becoming pregnant got filed in the "deal with that later" file.

Second Beach in Middletown, Rhode Island, is typically almost deserted on warm, Indian-summer, September weekdays. The seasonal and vacationing crowds have left after Labor Day weekend, and families are back to school schedules. John and I had no plans each day while my mother was at her job. One of the benefits of living at my mother's house was the beauty of Newport and the lovely beaches. On most sunny days in the September of our transition, I took John to the beach and taught him to body surf. We rode one wave after another, until we stood, tired and satisfied, at the water's edge. We held hands and watched the tide sweep pebbles out to sea and bring new ones to the shore. The rhythm of the waves was soothing; I assured my little man that we would always be able to come back to Gramma's house during the summer and school vacations. These days on the beach helped me prepare for all that we were leaving behind and to open our lives to the unexpected new baby.

Each evening, I waited anxiously for Jim's call to update me on the possibility of an apartment in New York. While we lived in the place of unknowing, I knew that I didn't want to return to our old life at Black Acre Farm, nor did I want to live with my mother in Newport. She never mentioned my marriage status again after John was born because she loved him and was grateful that we were so much a part of her life after my father died. However, it was difficult for me to be with my mother for very long—it was almost as if I had an allergic reaction to her: I found it hard to breathe. Her needs were so great that the thought of living with her was not an option. But she was rightly concerned that we had limited resources, that I was pregnant again, and that we were moving to New York, a city that she deemed to be filled with crime and violence.

Jim was still my mooring in life. I was anxious but confident that it would all work out. After returning from Vail, he continued to audition in small theaters and also tended bar in his free time. During a long phone conversation in late September on his birthday, my optimism trumped his pessimism about our move to New York and my pregnancy. I assured him that all would be okay. He finally told me that our friend Toby, whose couch he was living on, had invited John and me to stay there, too, until we could find our own place.

My mother helped us pack the old blue Volvo station wagon that I was driving then with our futon, Champion juicer, cartons of Dr. Hauschka, and several books by Rudolf Steiner on meditation and the path of a spiritual seeker. She continued to remind me how happy John was in Newport and that we were always welcome there. I assuaged her fears and buried mine.

At last, we arrived at 280 Mott Street and began our life in the city. Jim and I moved the futon to the floor in Toby's living room the room where Jim had been living, and John moved to the couch next to us.

Our days were full. I enrolled John in Kindergarten at the Rudolf Steiner School on East 79th Street. Driving him to and from school was a full-time job until I found a carpool and shared the commute. I talked to everyone I met about trying to find an inexpensive apartment; I also negotiated alternate-side-of-the-street parking successfully without once getting ticketed or towed. We lived on the block that was the entrance to Little Italy, a safe, protected neighborhood, as long as one remained oblivious to the "business" dealings on the street.

On days when it was my turn to drive to and from the kindergarten, John and I would return to Mott Street by 1:30 p.m. Because it wasn't legal to park on the street until after 2:00 p.m., I would double-park, which was legal while the street was being cleaned, and later I'd move the car across the street to a parking place that was good for three days. During the two days when the car was safely parked, I either took public transportation or arranged the carpool schedule around my parking space. The old men whose lives transpired between the street and their social club and grocery stores frequently watched us park. Under their scrutiny, my cheeks turned red as I learned to pull into spaces that were only inches longer than our car.

"You can do it, Mom!" John would exclaim as he stood in the backseat, encouraging me.

One day we didn't get back to Mott Street until almost 2:00 p.m. By then, the block looked filled on both sides with cars. My heart sank. Not finding a parking space on Mott meant that our car battery would most likely be stolen, or at least one tire would be slit on the more dangerous streets east of Mott. But then I spotted an opening and sped toward it.

"Damn," I said.

John gasped. "What's wrong, Mommy?"

A vegetable crate had been turned upside down like a cone and was blocking the space. I was angry. *It's so unfair*, I thought. After all, no one was allowed to save a parking place. I rolled down my window and shouted to the familiar group of old men who were leaning against the window of a storefront.

"What's going on?" I asked, feeling very aggressive. "Is somebody taking this spot?"

One of the men sauntered over to the space, lifted the basket, placed it on the curb, and said, "Ya' late today. We saved it for ya'."

I started to laugh and cry at the same time. It was the first time I felt that I, indeed, was finding New York's soul.

Soon, Toby heard about a vacant apartment on the floor beneath her. The city had taken over the building because it had had been in arrears for many years. Several of the current tenants were forming a group to try to buy the building. The occupancy was very diverse, with two large families—one Italian and one Hispanic. The remaining units housed artists, dancers, and the owner of a comedy club, all of whom became our friends.

Each morning for two weeks, I arrived at the office of the city agency that was responsible for the fate of 280 Mott Street. I pleaded with the bureaucrat in charge to rent me the apartment. I think he took pity on me when I told him I was new to the city, expecting a baby, had limited resources, and was single. Technically, and legally, Jim and I had never wed, though we had declared ourselves *married in spirit* that one sunrise on Moonstone Beach when we had been very much in love. I didn't think I needed to share that information on the application form.

Eventually, I got the lease to apartment 2F, a 500-square foot dwelling at the corner of Mott and Houston, for $100 a month. The place was filled with old car parts, newspapers, plumbing pipes, and empty bottles. I later joked that we could not serve soup there because the floors were so slanted it would run out of the bowls. It wasn't Park Avenue, but we were finally living together, full time, as a family. John would have his father. I would have Jim. We would all have a new baby. With love, free paint from the city, and fresh pasta from Little Italy on Fridays, I made the dreary space as cozy as possible. At least I thought so. I later learned that Jim, unless he was stoned, resented our humble home. To him, being poor and surrounded by beauty in Rhode Island was quite different from being poor in Manhattan.

The Steiner School and the theater community proved a good match for Dr. Hauschka Skin Care products. Natural, organic, biodynamic, and holistic were new concepts at the time. I was awarded many opportunities to share my expertise and cosmetic treasures. Once, an actor friend of ours invited me to bring Dr. Hauschka to the Manhattan Squash Club where he worked. And the market kept expanding. It wasn't long before I was delivering products to the school, to theater dressing rooms, health clubs, fledgling yoga centers, and restaurants in the Village where actors and actresses found work between gigs. My confidence grew as I began to feel as if I had graduated from apprentice to journeyman in this new, sophisticated market. I referred to Dr. Hauschka as a garden in a bottle, and, when it was opened, one experienced the beauty and life force of a real garden.

Following leads to people interested in Dr. Hauschka Skin Care was like following breadcrumbs that were helping me find my way in my new world. They became the threads that held my life together. Although we were poor, I was consistently hopeful, never doubting that Jim would succeed. I longed for him to be happy with our small successes to stay afloat in the city while he pursued his career. He was seldom at the apartment; when he was, he mostly slept. During rehearsals, he was busy all day and would stay out with friends until after John and I were asleep. When performing, he would sleep most of the day, go to his performance, then go out with friends until the middle of the night. Sadly, he no longer laughed, played music, or told funny stories about the theater. Gone were the times when he would sit, watch while I made dinner, listen to Bob Dylan, and sing into my ear: "You gave me shelter from the storm."

"Why can't you come home when the play ends for the night?" I asked once when we did see him.

"I'm wired after performing. My day is just beginning. I can't sleep," was his reply.

"I could wait up for you, make chamomile tea. You could take a lavender bath like you did in Rhode Island. If you got to sleep earlier, had a more normal schedule, we could spend time together as a family."

He shrugged and sighed, "Lavender bath? Tea? This family thing wasn't planned, Susie. It just happened. Look, I told you it wasn't going to be easy."

I was really good at rationalizing that life with Jim was difficult because the life of an actor *is* difficult. I told myself if I just made everything a little easier for him, everything would be okay.

In the meantime, opening nights were exciting, and being with an actor had its perks. Occasionally, I attended theater events with Jim, sometimes at Sardi's Restaurant where, together with his friends, we waited for reviews.

In April 1980, we were invited to Al Pacino's birthday party at Café Un Deux Trois. Jim had been his understudy the year before in a production of *Richard III*. By then I was very big and pregnant. My friend Suzi surprised me with an off-white linen kaftan that she made for me to wear to the party. I felt like an earth goddess carrying a new life.

At some point during the evening, I was sitting next to Pacino when they brought out a cheesecake for his birthday. I asked him if he liked cheesecake, because it seemed kind of unusual for a birthday. He said he didn't, then asked if I'd like a piece. I told him I was trying to avoid sugar while I was pregnant. He looked at me and said in amazement, "Oh, you're pregnant." In that moment, I felt he must have thought that I was fat, not pregnant. I wanted to shrink into a corner.

When I'd let go of my life in Rhode Island, I'd thought that the new life coming toward John and me would have Jim at the center. But it turned out that I found the support to stay in New York through my connections to other parents at the Rudolf Steiner School and with my Dr. Hauschka clients. I began to realize I was as lonely living with Jim as I had been when we'd lived in Rhode Island. Life with him was like being in a maze: I continued to take care of everything. Each day brought little successes, and Jim always had an acting job, so between us, we made enough to pay John's tuition and our living expenses. We had lots of friends in the building and were invited to events through the Steiner School. But, through it all, Jim was emotionally unavailable. I knew nothing about what codependence, enabling, or caretaking meant, so I continued to forge ahead, relying on the kindness of strangers.

One of John's classmates was a boy from Holland. His mother, Willemijn, and I became friends. John went home with her son Marijn several days a week when I wasn't responsible for being a driver in the school carpool. Then I would meet them on Hudson Street in the large brownstone that had been provided for the family by the Dutch bank where Willemijn's husband worked. Willemijn had a small business of handmade dolls and wooden toys, which she ran out of the front room of her house. We drank tea in the garden, talked about holistic medicine, astrology, and the importance of play in a child's life while we watched our beautiful sons live out of their imaginations as they turned sticks into swords and became Knights of the Round Table in the churchyard next to the garden behind Willemijn's house.

As May approached, Willemijn and I made plans to stay in touch during the summer. She was going to take her son and her young daughter back to Holland for the summer holidays and to hike in the Alps. We were going to return to Rhode Island when John's school ended and when Jim's play was over so he could go with us. In the meantime, I had been travelling to Wakefield, Rhode Island, once a month to a women's health clinic where a friend was a nurse. The facility had a birthing center where I planned to have the baby at the end of May.

On April 30, 1979, a beautiful sunny day, Willemijn showed me how to make a small doll from raw wool. Hers looked like a pixie with a pointed red hat; mine looked like a gnome with a long brown beard. John and I walked slowly back to Mott Street after a lovely afternoon. We walked or took a bus on the days when the car was in a three-day parking space. I thought of all the new experiences that had come with our New York lifestyle, and I knew that moving to the city had been for the best. But I was grateful that we'd be returning to Rhode Island for the baby's birth and staying for John's summer vacation. September was a distant dream. Then, when we arrived at our apartment that afternoon, I saw a note pinned to our door. It instructed us to go to the Cavianos' apartment on the fifth floor. Upstairs, we found that the women of our building had prepared both a homemade Italian dinner and a baby shower for me. New York did have a very big soul, and I felt as if I truly had found home.

— 10 —

May Day

THE NEXT DAY, everything changed. I woke up with an odd sensation in my belly, a strong discomfort. But it was May 1, 1980, and it was going to be a busy, happy day. I had no way of knowing it would not go as planned.

John's school was going to have a May Day festival, centered on the maypole dance. I knew that the maypole symbolizes the tree of life, and that the children were going to take turns weaving long ribbons around the pole. The festivities were to take place in Central Park, followed by a picnic. Parents had been encouraged to attend. John was very excited when I said I would be with him. He told me proudly at breakfast that he had been chosen as the first one to start weaving a long yellow ribbon around the pole, alternating with the younger students. I quickly scribbled a note to Jim saying that John hoped he could meet us in the park. I left it beside him while he slept on the futon.

My friend Maureen — another parent at the Waldorf School — picked John and me up. With five noisy boys in the backseat, we headed from West Broadway up to the Steiner school on East 79th between Madison and Park Avenue. But while we traveled along FDR Drive, the odd sensation in my belly turned into sudden, sharp pains. By the time we arrived at the school, the pains had rapidly increased. I knew I needed to get to a hospital. The closest one was Lenox Hill Hospital on the Upper East Side. Luckily, I had received some free prenatal care there, so they had a record of me.

The night before, Jim had been out until after midnight, rehearsing for a play. I knew John would be terribly disappointed that I wouldn't be with him at the May Day celebration. I could have asked Jim to take my place, but I didn't have the strength to go into the school to call him. I hoped he'd see my note. If possible, I never asked anything of Jim these days. I had begun to understand how deeply he resented that I had moved into the city, and that I was pregnant again. One night recently, when he'd come home late—and high—he'd actually said that I kept getting pregnant to hold him back from his career.

Maureen dropped the boys off at the school. Then she drove me to Lenox Hill Hospital, stopping as close to the Emergency Room entrance as she could get. She had to get to work, and neither of us could afford the parking cost, anyway. She assured me that she would call my friend Willemijn and have her bring John home with her children.

I got out of Maureen's car and walked slowly toward the entrance on a path made out of chalky, white cement blocks. It reminded me of the sidewalk in front of the house where I grew up, where I'd spent countless hours chalking hopscotch squares. But ominously, this cement walkway was stained with blood.

Inside the emergency room, I described my pain. They performed the tests. And I waited.

Then, Jim showed up—Maureen had called him. By early afternoon the doctor told me all my vital signs were good, and I was not yet dilated. I was, however, still in a lot of pain. But the doctor released me. I was scared. But I didn't know what else to do.

Jim and I shared a cab downtown. He kissed me, then told me to call him if anything changed. He got out of the cab around midtown and headed to St. Clemens Theater. After all, he needed to rehearse Arthur Miller's *American Clock*. That night would be the critics' preview, an essential performance in the theater.

The cab drove me toward Mott Street. I hoped some rest would help.

The pain increased. By the time I got out of the cab at our apartment, it was difficult to walk. I inched my way across the sidewalk, bent over, feeling like one of the neighboring little old Italian widows dressed in black who shuffled halfway down the block to church each morning. Once inside the building, I leaned against the muddy brown wall and edged toward the stairs. I held onto the railing with both hands and pulled my very pregnant body up the gray concrete stairs, one step at a time. For the first time, I noticed how swollen my ankles looked. When I reached the top, I moved slowly to the dark brown metal door labeled 2F. I had trouble unlocking it because, by then, my pain was beyond any I had known. It felt like I was committing hara-kiri with a serrated red-hot sword. Tears flowed. I had been anxious when I'd seen the doctor—but now that anxiety had grown into raw fear.

Once through the door, I lay down on the kitchen floor, unable to move. I was grateful John was at school; I wouldn't have wanted him to see me this way. I felt as if I'd fallen outside of time. There was only space. Time was something that was outside my window, going on without me. The small, dark, noisy apartment with the sloping floors that I'd tried my best to transform into some kind of home had deserted me. Unlike Jim, I'd trusted that the place was a temporary solution, and that, with time, we would find a bigger place for our growing family. But now it felt lonely and lifeless, not like a home at all, as I cradled my pregnant body with tired, limp arms. I cried and moaned.

I stared at the kitchen table and at the clear glass canning jar that held four pale yellow daffodils slanted in different directions. Two felted garden fairies that I'd made the day before with Willemijn leaned against the jar. My gaze moved to the stack of gifts from the baby shower that were also on the table: red Chinese cloth slippers, blue-and-white quilted squares ready for assembling into a quilt, a yellow cotton baby snuggly, a wooden rattle, tubes and bottles of natural baby products, and a mobile of tufted white angels. It crossed my mind that these might be the last things I'd ever see.

Luckily, our dear friend Toby was passing by on the way to her apartment when she noticed my door was open. She came inside; she touched my cheek. I heard her gasp. She stepped back into the corridor and yelled, "Help! Is anyone home? Can you hear me? Help!" She stepped over me and went to the front room. She dialed 911 from the black rotary phone we kept next to the futon where we slept. Then she grabbed the large phone book and looked up the number at the theater where Jim was rehearsing.

The apartment went quiet again. Toby put a pillow under my head, held my hand, and waited for the ambulance—and Jim.

Jim arrived first. He sat down beside me, placed my head on his lap, and asked me to look at him or say something. I did neither. I heard Toby say she was going downstairs to wait for the ambulance.

They took me to Bellevue Hospital, which was the closest hospital to our apartment. Jim came, too. At the time, Bellevue was referred to as the hospital for the insane and the poor. A theater friend of Jim's had a friend named Dana who was a resident doctor there, so I was expected. But by the time I was admitted and examined, my unborn baby's heart was no longer beating.

They told me the baby had died.

My Lily had died, Lily Michaela. I had only picked out a girl's name.

I felt as if I'd stepped into a cyclone of pain, sorrow, and fear, and that my body was the epicenter of the storm.

The doctors didn't know what had caused Lily's death, but they said it would be best if the natural delivery process took place instead of having them induce the process too aggressively. They also did not want to perform a Caesarian section to remove her. So, Lily would stay in my womb until labor began. I cannot explain what that felt like—emotionally, physically, spiritually.

Jim held my hand, comforted me, and told me how sorry he was.

It was so hard to grasp what anyone said when I still had so much pain in my lower abdomen. Pain that no one understood or knew what was causing it.

"Your vital signs are all good," the doctors repeated over and over. But I had heard the same thing hours earlier at Lenox Hill.

I was more frightened now. And totally numb.

I remember giving up. Falling in and out of sleep, I felt misunderstood, but I was too weak to fight. The nurses encouraged Jim to go back to the theater. People always seemed impressed that Jim was an actor. I suppose his world appeared more important than theirs. Or mine. Whatever the reason, they assured him that I was in good hands. "It will take several hours for the delivery," a nurse said. "There is nothing to do but wait."

I remember watching the clock. Jim left at seven o'clock that evening. Eight o'clock came and went, then nine, then ten. I was in desperate pain, asking for more drugs.

"It's safer if you're not too drugged so you can assist in the delivery process," they assured me.

Just before eleven o'clock, my cervix dilated, and the birthing process began. There were bright lights, a few doctors, and nurses. Then Jim was back by my side. He wore scrubs and had a mask over his mouth. Their conversation was muddled. At one point, Jim dropped my hand, and I saw him follow the medical staff a short distance from the delivery table.

Then a nurse came back to me. "Do you want to see your baby?" she asked. Jim reappeared. I looked at him, and he said, "No, she doesn't. She's too weak."

I still regret that I never saw Lily. But at the time I was confused, vaguely aware of nurses moving around and of their quiet conversation. I faded in and out of consciousness.

Suddenly, a woman stood over me and shouted, "Susan's in trouble! Quick!" Immediately, I was surrounded. "We . . . operate . . . She's lost . . . blood . . . Call the surgeon. . . ." I heard slurred voices giving and responding to a flurry of commands.

The last thing I remember was looking at the surgeon by my side, holding a knife, poised to make an incision in my abdomen. I then looked up into the eyes of another doctor who began to place a mask over my mouth and nose. I said, "Please hurry, so it won't hurt."

He smiled. "Never tell an anesthesiologist to hurry. We can cause a lot of damage if we're not careful."

The next thing I knew, I was beyond the physical structure of the hospital room, beyond the walls that had become porous and easily penetrable by patterns of light. I was out of my body but still somehow connected to it. I could see my body in the hospital operating room: it was as though the walls were compacted patterns of light, and I was part of the source of light that permeated and held together what otherwise would have looked like a space constructed out of playing cards. A loving presence was at my side. Silence, stillness, and peace emanated from everything I saw as I watched the scene unfold. It felt mysterious, but at the same time familiar, the way I'd felt in church as a young child, as if I were in a garden of golden light and warmth.

From my vantage point, my body looked to be convulsing, struggling like a fish caught on a hook. I was born under the sign of Pisces, which is symbolized by two fish bound together, swimming in opposite directions. In my case, one now swam toward life, one toward death. Jim was on one side of me, and my best friend, Suzi, was on the other. I experienced their sorrow and fear: I knew they thought I was going to die.

The next thing I remember was being back in my swollen body, weary from pain, and very weak.

The days that followed were a blur. I was aware, however, of Jim leaning over my bed during his visits, running his hand through his hair, telling me bits of news, and pacing around the room. Once I thought I heard John telling me that he loved me. Everything I heard or saw seemed muffled, as if I were underwater, trying to hear and see life going on around me. Lying in the hospital, I couldn't keep it all together anymore. My uterus had ruptured, as had my dreams. Foolish me—I had fallen in love with an actor, someone who was in love with acting and only acting. Physically, I had come close to death. Emotionally, I knew that my relationship with Jim had also ruptured, and that my dreams of a happy family life were dying, too.

Jim charmed the staff with tales of a successful review in the *New York Times*. He had an uncanny ability to communicate with strangers as if he were their best friend. He and Suzi were allowed to come and go as they chose, regardless of visiting hours. Suzi was there whenever possible. She talked to the nurses who cared for me, and then sat in the corner of my room for long periods of time, praying, urging me back to life. Suzi had an identical twin who lived in Chicago; in her twin's absence, she and I had become like sisters.

While I was in intensive care, whenever nurses came to take samples of my blood or to check my charts, I could sense the difference between those who were really caring for me and those who were just doing their jobs. Their movements and sounds were very revealing. There was one special African American nurse who touched my forehead and stroked my face. She called me "Honey" as she ministered to me. Even if she thought I was sleeping or unconscious, she talked to me. I remember that she misted my face with some of my Dr. Hauschka products, including a toner with rose extracts. Jim must have brought them during one of his visits—he knew I thought that they helped with healing. I felt as though I had been lost in a desert, wandering for an endless time: the nurse's loving touch and the rose lotion were the first sensations that led me from the desert and slowly back to life.

After a week, when I finally was totally awake and conscious, I read her name tag: Nurse Grace. I thought she was the most beautiful woman I had ever seen, though the only glamour I detected on her was a floral perfume and a golden brooch of a swan. But she was like an angel; I felt love and gratitude for everything she did for me. On the day I was scheduled to be released, she came into my room. I looked at her kind face, the color of allspice, and her large, square body while she misted me with toner one last time, then gently applied cream to my face, helped me sit up, and brushed my hair.

"I wanted to say good-bye to you, honey," she said. "My shift is over, and I'm goin' home. You're young. You can have more children. You take care. Your family is coming to get you after lunch."

I thanked her for her kindness and longed to throw myself into her arms, beg her to take me home, keep brushing my hair, and mother me.

Later that morning, a nurse I didn't recognize came in to begin the discharge process. At that point I was in a room with several other women who had given birth. As I finished signing the release forms, she said, "So you're going home on Mothers' Day with a new baby, lucky you." She smiled and left the room. I was stunned by her lack of knowledge of my situation and thought to myself: *This could only happen in a movie—a bad one.*

Jim and John arrived to take me home, and we slowly made our way to the parking structure. John held my hand tightly. Jim walked ahead of us, smoking a cigarette, and carrying a bag of my belongings. Soon, I was back in the energy of New York City streets. Jim parked in front of a bodega on First Avenue and went in to shop for groceries before driving us back to Mott

Street. As I sat in the passenger side of our old Volvo waiting for him, I found myself unable to hold back my tears.

"Mommy," John said as he leaned over the front seat of the station wagon. "I learned to ride a bicycle with Marijn when you were in the hospital." He took a strand of my hair and wrapped it around his finger.

"That's wonderful, sweetheart," I said, but did not turn to look at him. I did not want him to see my tears. "So you and Marijn don't need training wheels anymore?"

"Yeah, and Sara said that I learned faster than Marijn, and he got mad." John had spent the last eleven days with my friend Willemijn and her family while I was in the hospital. Sara was the family's nanny. I was eternally grateful to Willemijn for being an oasis for John and making him feel like he had a second home while I was in the hospital. She felt like a spiritual sister to me.

I was thinking about that when I was startled by John suddenly screeching, "Look at the clowns, Mommy! They're so tall!"

A parade was passing by at the corner of First Avenue and 13th Street. Clowns on stilts surrounded our car, blowing whistles and honking their noses. One leaned down almost at eye level with us and, through the open window, handed John a balloon. It was May 11, Mothers' Day. The parade was celebrating Mother Mary and mothers everywhere. *This is unreal*, I thought to myself. Where else but in New York City could this scene have happened? I was a tragic, deflated woman, unable to comprehend how much I had lost, and I was in the middle of a clown parade.

We returned to my mother's house in Newport at the end of May when the production of *American Clock* closed. Jim stayed with us for two weeks before leaving for the summer to work at a theater festival in Ohio. He encouraged me to join him in the middle of August for the last week of the festival. "I thought you were going to die," he said, just before he left. "I don't know what I'd do without you. But I'll understand if you don't want to join me."

It didn't take much for me to tell myself the story that he needed me and to believe he really loved me.

John and I often went to the beach, either alone or with my mother and sister. We played in the sand and, as I got stronger, we bodysurfed and laughed, while we rode one salty wave after another onto the shore. At night we watched *Wheel of Fortune* and reruns of *The Lawrence Welk Show*, my mother's favorite programs. John was happy to watch anything because there was no television in our apartment, and the Steiner School frowned upon the "plug-in drug" for young children.

My mother made date nut bars and chocolate chip cookies, and always had boxed cereal on hand. I lowered my "whole food" standards during the summer because John was having such a good time. We spent time with Jim's family and our friends: they gave me enormous love and support, brought me flowers, books, and candy. Jim's mother came to visit with a gift of a beautiful pink terrycloth sundress. She told me how very sorry she was that I had lost the baby.

Although it was a healing time for me, I knew that I didn't belong in Rhode Island anymore. I was questioning who I was now, and what I was going to do. No one was talking about post-traumatic stress disorder at the time, but I think I was suffering from it. Instead of getting help, I dealt with my feelings very much alone, as I always had.

While going through some boxes left at my mother's house before we'd moved, I found a book about the root meaning of names, which I had used when choosing the name "Lily." I had learned that Lily was symbolic of purity, fertility, wealth, and also hope. I looked up the root meaning of the name "Susan" and was stunned. Susan originated from the Persian language word for lotus flower or lily. In Hebrew, the root of the name Susan is Lily. Susan means "to be joyful, bright, or cheerful," a name that embodies "joy of life." I wondered if I would ever be joyful again.

In September 1980, after I'd spent three months in Newport, John and I returned to Manhattan. Jim was back from Ohio: soon after our arrival, he and I were invited to the wedding of one of his theater friends, the one who had connected us to Bellevue Hospital. There I met the young resident doctor, Dana, who, it turned out, had been the one who'd saved my life at Bellevue Hospital.

Dana told me that on the night Lily died and I almost had, too, she'd been in the residency quarters. Our mutual friend told her I was there, but because she'd been on duty for eighteen hours, she knew she needed to rest. She left me with her colleagues. Then, around 11:30 p.m., she suddenly woke up when someone shook her and yelled: "Susan! Go help Susan!" Dana ran to the delivery room and saw the staff on the far side of the room looking at the tiny stillborn baby girl. She then saw me bleeding out on the table and screamed: "Susan's in trouble! Quick! We need to operate." I had lost five pints of blood because my uterus had ruptured, the placenta had blocked the rupture until the baby had been delivered, and that was when I had started to bleed. The staff went into a high state of alert to save me.

I told Dana how grateful I was that she'd saved my life. But, as she related the story from her point of view, she seemed unnerved by the incident, almost disturbed. She was especially uneasy when she told me the part about being awakened from a deep sleep by someone she couldn't see, someone who was calling my name. I sensed that she doubted her experience had been a spiritual intervention—she probably thought she'd been dreaming. I wanted to ask her if she knew what had happened to Lily's body, but I hesitated. Then she moved quickly away from me into the wedding celebration. I never saw her again.

I never found out what actually happened to Lily's little body. I thought maybe she was buried in a pauper's grave. Someone told me years later that there wouldn't have been a burial, but rather she would have been disposed of with other human tissue. I couldn't bear to think what that meant; the idea that she hadn't been buried was very painful for me. I suffered great shame about it for many years. At the time of her death, Jim seemed to think there was nothing to be done, or at least he led me to believe that when I finally was conscious. Since I had been in critical condition for over a week, and no one advised the hospital otherwise, they no doubt followed their protocol regarding the disposal of unclaimed bodies.

Jim moved through these events while drinking Irish whiskey and smoking grass.

I turned to the small church I attended called the Christian Community. It is part of a movement for religious renewal, sacred rituals, and freedom from dogma. Women are allowed to be ordained as priests. The church brings an esoteric understanding of Christianity to their teachings, teachings that are suppressed by the Catholic Church, such as the study of reincarnation and karma.

One Sunday, soon after our return, the congregation celebrated the Act of Consecration for Lily. The Act of Consecration looks similar to the Catholic Mass of my childhood but with a seriousness that is more meditative. In the service held for Lily, there was a special reading for the death of a child.

During a counseling session with a woman priest named Gisela, who was new to our small church, the idea of a near-birth experience manifested in our conversation. Although I had read much about near-death experiences and that many people have experienced crossing over to a spiritual world when they were close to death, the idea of a near-birth experience was new to me. Why would a baby need one? Why had Lily needed to come so close to the earth but not stay? And who had been the presence I'd sensed beside me as I hovered between life and death and looked at my body from outside it? Had Lily and I met in a spiritual space just beyond our daily physical perception for a reason?

Although I had no answers and couldn't speak to many people about it, the idea of a near-birth experience resonated with me. As I recovered my strength, I was sad, and I tried to understand why I had lost Lily. I came to believe that life is a mystery and a gift, and that both my near-death experience and Lily's near-birth one were equally important for me to hold in my heart, even though I did not understand them.

I believe that the many books on spirituality that I had read before moving to the city, coupled with my meditative practice, gave me the foundation to handle and maybe even transform my suffering and depression. They were books about the spiritual teachings of masters like Rudolf Steiner, who taught that the dead are always with us, and that they benefit from our loving thoughts about them; of Krishnamurti, who taught that self-knowledge isn't a conclusion or an achievement but an endless river; of Thomas Merton, who spoke of the need to find stillness and be contemplative in a world of action; and of Paramahansa Yogananda, who taught that, through meditation, one will develop spiritually and evolve to a higher consciousness.

They all spoke of a spiritual world beyond the senses, of reincarnation and karma, and of the importance of awakening love for the world in oneself. I felt that the loving presence that had been close to me during my near-death experience was somehow a manifestation or an example of those ideas. I wanted to learn more, so I continued to read sacred teachings.

And life went on.

Jim and I became more distant from each other. He was like a feral cat, coming and going without much commitment or communication, but always hungry for what I provided him; initially, wild sex, and then a cheap apartment, organic food, and invitations from the most cultured families at the Steiner School who seemed eager for me to share what I was learning about Anthroposophic Medicine and biodynamic agriculture. My relationship with Jim became like a loose tooth that I kept touching with my tongue, wondering if and how it would end. I realize now that our beautiful time on the mountain in Aspen just before we'd moved in together in the city had not been about our future but had been a final celebration of what had once been good between us.

I was happy, though, that John loved whatever free time Jim had for him. Jim took him to rehearsals when he could, and he let John stay backstage while he performed as he eventually moved from Off-Broadway and eventually to Broadway. I became immersed in parenting John, participating in his school community, and introducing people to Dr. Hauschka Skin Care and to the spiritual guidelines behind them. The loss of Lily and the dream to become a basket-carrying Waldorf parent with a growing family and a talented partner had ended. Selling Dr. Hauschka as a hobby that had helped pay the bills was quickly turning into an emerging, dynamic career.

11

In the Corner of the Woods

"LET'S TAKE GERMAN lessons," I said to Suzi. "Jim says most Germans speak some English, but let's take lessons anyway."

We walked up West End Avenue in Manhattan, through its canyon of shadows between large stone apartment buildings. The wind blasted us as it blew off the Hudson River and tunneled up the street between the city blocks. We each held one of John's hands, anchoring his slight, seven-year-old body to the ground.

Sometimes it was hard to believe that Suzi and I hadn't known each other our entire lives, that we'd only met when Jim and her husband, Doug, were in the Acting Company together. She worked at the Parks Department in Central Park, and, when one of her colleagues told her about an available rent-controlled apartment at Riverside Drive and West 98th Street, we were lucky to grab it. It was only six blocks from Suzi and Doug, which was an added perk.

Early in 1981, Jim, John, and I moved into our new place. It was a big step up from our splintered, slanting-floored, noisy, and cramped Mott Street digs. It was three times the size and had ten-foot ceilings, and a view of Riverside Park and the Hudson

River from the bedroom. It was also four times the rent but was nonetheless a good deal for $400 a month. Though Jim grumbled about the cost, I hoped that he would feel less stress living in an apartment that didn't scream poor and shabby and was close to a park. It seemed that we were moving in the right direction for Jim to balance an unpredictable career with being a family man and spending more time at home.

By then it had been five years since I had been introduced to Dr. Hauschka Skin Care, and I was planning a pilgrimage to Eckwälden, Germany, the village at the foot of the Schwäbische Alb, where WALA was located. It was going to be my first trip to Europe.

Heinz Grotzke had invited me to join him for a medical conference at WALA and to stay an extra week for extensive training in the skin care preparations. WALA had noticed that the sales of the products were steadily growing; when Heinz told them of my efforts in New York, they wanted to meet me. Beyond my work in the city, I had become the go-to-person for anyone in the United States who had questions about Dr. Hauschka. I convinced Heinz it would be helpful for me to bring Suzi along for the training, since she was good at graphics and helpful at securing locations like the Dairy Barn in Central Park to hold sales events.

By now I had repeatedly experienced that there was something "crazy/magical"—as one client had described it—about the products and their effect. "I'd rather give up my husband and shrink than give up Dr. Hauschka," she'd said with a laugh when I'd delivered another order to her high-rise apartment in midtown.

I was not surprised at her enthusiasm. The products had been a source of great healing to me as I'd rebuilt my shattered life and body after the devastating stillbirth of Lily. The fact that I'd come so close to death and Lily had come so close to life was difficult to rationalize. But, in my heart, I felt we were only separated by an invisible veil, that our souls had touched in the encounter, and that she was my spirit guide as I moved in this new direction.

As I used the herbal substances morning and evening, they nurtured me while I resumed life as John's mother, partner of the wildly talented but absentee J. T. Walsh, and seedling businesswoman. They'd also led me to a community of women who were emerging from a shifting paradigm of superficial beauty to one that included inner development. Many clients were women who seldom invested in what was considered conventional department store beauty products, but they seemed to recognize the living quality of Dr. Hauschka products and saw them as a staple of life, like wholesome food. Others were from the emerging healing arts world of macrobiotics, massage, reiki, homeopathy, yoga, and Pilates—all of which resonated with Dr. Hauschka's unique connection to skin care and good health.

Actors and actresses were also discovering the benefits of the product. Jim (he remained that to me, but he was J. T. to the world) had introduced the line to several makeup artist friends in the theater. Gradually, five-star celebrities enjoyed the healing benefits of using Dr. Hauschka products before applying the necessary evil of stage makeup, which had not yet been refined. They creatively incorporated our Silk Powder, Bronze Day Cream, and moisturizers into the harsh synthetic products that were needed under unforgiving camera lights. Jim called these clients my "More Prada than Prana women" after a phrase I'd playfully coined about the theater group. We still found moments of joy together.

From the beginning, the essence of the Hauschka philosophy had been for men and women to become who they are meant to be, not to cover up who they are, not to try to look like someone else, not to look like someone who's been airbrushed, as with products that are marketed through expensive ad campaigns that aim to suggest eternal beauty, love, and success. In the 1970s and early 1980s, the revolutionary idea of authentic beauty had begun to emerge; Dr. Hauschka's message that health and inner development were as important as beauty, love, and success resonated deeply in the niche market.

Conventional cosmetics focused solely on the "adorn" part of the original definition of cosmetics and in masking problems. But turning the focus of one's life to order and harmony opened the door to discussions about lifestyle, nutrition, meaningful careers, beautiful environments, and social justice—because who wants beauty at the expense of another woman's underpaid labor or at the expense of suffering animals used to test synthetic ingredients of the latest so-called "miracle cures" to prevent aging? I kept copious notes of the questions my Hauschka clients presented to me, and I assured them that I'd have much to share when I returned from Germany. In the meantime, I had been learning the language of Dr. Hauschka in the field.

Suzi and I took German lessons at Deutsches Haus at New York University every Saturday morning as we got ready for our trip. By our mid-May departure date, we felt empowered: we were ready to order cheese, bread, and wine and to instruct taxi drivers to drive *nicht so schnell* (not so fast) in reasonable German. Suzi convinced me that we should spend some time in Europe after we left WALA. We decided on a few days in Paris, followed by a week visiting my friend Willimijn who had moved permanently back to Amsterdam from New York. Willimijn and I continued to write to each other, determined to stay connected.

The trip would encompass almost three weeks, and I struggled with the idea of leaving John that long. He loved school, but he seemed frail; he was very sensitive, and I think he had internalized the impact of our struggles of the previous year. He wasn't gaining weight, and small patches of his golden hair were thinning. Though the doctor assured me that John had no major health issues that sleep, good food, and wholesome play would not remedy, I constantly worried about him. Our life in the country had been such a contrast to our city life, I'd begun to second-guess my choices.

Jim assured me that with the dozen frozen soups and casseroles that I'd prepared, and with the support of two families from the Steiner School willing to help out with childcare, all would be well. He even agreed to paint the drab grayish white walls of our new apartment while I was away. I prayed that he would use the colors that we'd chosen: golden fields for the living room, which also functioned as a sleeping area for John; pumpkin-orange for the kitchen; French lavender for our bedroom and the bathroom.

I hugged John before getting into the gold taxi and sniffed back my tears.

"I love you, Mom," he said. "Please make a picture of the airplane for me." He stood next to Jim and looked wistful at my leaving, yet excited to be with his father.

But as the cab pulled away, I shrieked to the driver to stop. I leaned out the window and called out, "Don't forget to read to him at night or about story hour at the Boat House in the park this Sunday!" I felt on shaky ground when I wasn't taking care of John or when he wasn't being cared for by one of his grandmothers.

While waiting in a long line to board the evening Lufthansa flight, I was happy and filled with eager anticipation. My professional world was expanding, and it felt great.

Then, in the middle of the clamor in Kennedy International Airport, in the middle of the bustling crowd, in the middle of the best thing that was happening to me in a long while, Suzi turned to me and said, "I found out this morning that I'm pregnant."

I hesitated only for a second, then I took a quick, deep breath. "Wow," I said, and hugged her. "That's amazing. I'm so happy for you guys." And though my heart constricted at the sad thought that we wouldn't have children close to the same age, and at the reminder that I probably wouldn't have another child, I was happy for her. And I knew I couldn't let my own drama get in the way of her happiness. I cleared my throat and added, "What a way to start your pregnancy by flying off to Europe. I bet the baby will be very cultured." We fell into our easy chatter, me asking about the baby's due date. Then, with our limited understanding of astrology, we discussed that it would be born under the sign of Aquarius so it would be forward-thinking and open to new ideas. Our happy babble followed us through the line and out to the gate at last.

But as we inched along to our seats in the last non-smoking row, I was relieved to be distracted by the buckling up and settling in. Soon, the magical Manhattan skyline disappeared behind us. I sipped the complimentary glass of champagne and stared out at the dark night, as I quietly practiced the German words I'd learned.

After experiencing the physical confusion of flying into tomorrow before yesterday ended, also known as jet lag, we were welcomed into the Geiger family's Haus in Eckwälden where Suzi and I were to share a large room and bath during our stay.

I think about that first trip to WALA as a significant chapter in the fairy tale development of my career. Eckwälden actually looked like a scene from a Grimm's Fairy Tale. The main street, Dorfstrasse, or village street, which leads to WALA, was lined with small stone houses that had window boxes of seasonal flowers that seemed to be competing with one another for "Best in Show." The statuary of goblins, pixies, mushrooms, and animals that I would find ridiculous in the United States looked wonderfully playful in the village. Most of the front yards had a fruit tree or two in full blossom.

Halfway up the street there was a farm. The barn served the family with elegant efficiency: It had been designed to shelter the farmer's herd of cows at one end and the farmer's family at the other end in a two-story apartment with a forest green front door that looked hundreds of years old. A large brass bell hung to the right of the door. As I peered through the barn to an opening at the back, I saw fields where I imagined that contented animals grazed every day before returning to their stalls at milking time. On the street side of the farm, a sturdy wooden case with glass windows displayed a variety of Schnapps for sale: they had been made from the fruits of the farmer's labor as well as from his fruit.

Close to the farm, a large stone building with wooden shutters served as a home for adults with special needs who took turns helping the farmer with simple daily tasks. It was very moving to see a large group of folks—who, at that time in the United States, were still referred to as crazy, retarded, or insane—so wonderfully integrated into the lovely village. One of them was a young man Suzi and I saw almost daily as we walked around. He stopped and asked us the same questions each time we met.

"*Wo wohnen sie?*" (Where do you live?)

One or both of us answered, "*Wir wohnen im New York.*"

He then asked, "*Wann hast Du Geburtstag?*"

I proudly told him my birthday: "*Februar neunzehn.*" (February nineteenth.)

Suzi followed with "*März, neun und zwanzig.*" (March twenty-ninth.)

He started to laugh and said, "*Fische und Widder.*" We understood that he meant the fish and the ram, the astrological symbols of our birth signs. He kept laughing and pointed to his head and feet. "*Kopf,*" he said. "*Und Fuss.*" The astrological signs, after all, correspond to the different parts of the human body: the fish to the feet, the ram to the head. We laughed, too, because it was apparent that he was having a good time and because he was so gentle and open.

As we said, "*Guten Tag,*" and tried to move on, he took our hands and lightly shook them up and down much like a child would. Then he said, "*Sehr schon,*" which means "very beautiful."

Suzi and I walked on to the *Badhaus*, or bathhouse (in German, "bad" rhymes with "odd") to partake of warm healing mineral waters that come from a natural spring. Everything seemed funny to us. We ordered robes, towels, and bathing caps in disjointed German, and we were loaned black swimsuits from the lost-and-found that were three sizes too big. Then we entered the locker room through the exit instead of the entrance and were quickly told of our transgressions by several other bathers, mostly retired elders, who, it turned out, were guests at the Kurhaus next to the Badhaus.

Later, we learned that the elders were taking a cure at the mineral bath and did not appreciate the young American women laughing and splashing during their quiet therapeutic routine. That's when it dawned on us that there was a protocol at the Bad. Along the circumference of the pool, spa-like jets were positioned at graduating heights. They started out at ankle level and moved upwards in a clockwise manner to target higher parts of the body as bathers moved around the pool; all the while the jets emitted powerful streams of warm mineral water that vigorously massaged each area of the body. The grand finale was at the noontime position of the pool where streams of cold water gushed out at neck level, thus completing the cycle. Throughout the process, a light and a gong sounded every two minutes, at which time each bather had to move to the next position. Suzi and I got hysterical when we saw old men linger for an extra turn at the water jet just below waist level.

Most bathers left the pool after one round and went to rest in the *Warm Zimmer* (warm room). But Suzi and I inched through the cycle five or six times until we felt as relaxed and limp as seaweed.

Soon everyone in town knew that we were *die Amerikaner* (the Americans). One day, as we walked along the street, an attractive man riding a bicycle and carrying a violin case over his shoulder rode up beside us and said, *"Ich bin Herr Koßmann von die WALA."* I recognized the name: he was the managing director of the company.

I liked to hear the rhythm to the word, *WALA*. It sounded like the name of a living being: *VaaaLaaa* — warmth, ash, light, and ash — all necessary for Dr. Hauschka products. By then I knew that at one point during the extraction process, the plant substance was dried and reduced to ash and later, near the end of the process, a small amount of ash was added back. Curiously, Wala is also the name of a Nordic goddess of dreams.

Herr Kossmann then told us a joke about Shakespeare, which he teased was pronounced *Shuttlespeare* in German. *Shuttle* is German for the verb "to shake." We laughed as we tried out our German, and he tried his English. I was happy that we'd taken German lessons and could communicate a little bit. The three of us then went to a food shop, where he introduced us to the lady who owned it and lived in the apartment above.

The name of the shop was *Frisch und Flink*, which means fresh and nimble. It was wonderfully stocked with displays of local seasonal vegetables; fresh bread, pretzels, and croissants — all of which were baked daily; cheeses, country patés, sausages, juice made from local cherries, apples, pears, and *johannisbeeren*, which I discovered are similar to currants. Handmade dolls and puppets sat happily among the displays of fine chocolate bars, cookies, and honey. Raw milk and fresh butter were delivered daily. The health food movement was still quite new in New York and focused predominately on vitamins and supplements, so this environment was particularly interesting to me. Herr Kossmann told us we should go to the shop whenever it was open, and that our groceries would be a gift from WALA.

"Please take whatever you like. We are so happy that you visit us from America, visit us here in Eckwälden." Then he smiled. "Do you know what *Eckwälden* means?"

We shook our heads. "It means 'at the corner of the woods.' That is where we say it is so quiet that the foxes say good night to the rabbits."

A small fountain stood at the cross paths of the village. After we said good-bye to Herr Kossmann, we sat under a Linden tree labeled "The Schiller Tree" in honor of the famous poet. Families strolled by holding baskets filled with vegetables and groceries from Frisch und Flink; young mothers ambled along with their beautiful, giggling children who were clothed in hand-knit sweaters, colorful cotton leggings, and sturdy leather boots. A young boy about John's age walked by with his pet goat on a leather lead; a donkey followed closely behind them. (We later learned that the goat and the donkey lived together, and, if the boy took the goat out for a walk without the donkey, the donkey made such a racket that the neighbors complained.) Of course, the young boy reminded me of John, and my heart ached because I missed him so much.

But Eckwälden was delightful, and I drank it deeply into my heart. It was filled with a sense that everyone was well cared for and content. I longed to be like one of the women carrying a beautiful basket filled with healthy choices, surrounded by friends and children, and loved by their husbands. The village represented the childhood I never had, the family I was not meant to grow, rather than the corner of my heart where I felt comfortable and where my career would be nourished in the years to come. My joy has always had a tone of melancholia wrapped around it, as though I only could have reached it by having gone through the pain I've felt.

Our greatest discovery in Eckwälden came on the next morning. It was a warm and sunny Sunday, the day before Heinz was to accompany us to the medical conference. While exploring the area, Suzi and I found a gate in the fenced-in garden behind the WALA building at the end of the road. We opened the gate, entered, and climbed several stone steps that led us to a corner of the garden above the windowed plant laboratory. The lab looked out over a verdant slope that was dense with medicinal plants. The garden was bordered on the far side by an outcrop of the

Schwäbische Alb, a small mountain thick with evergreens and ash. On the opposite side from where we entered, fields were lush with grasses, wildflowers, fruit trees, and horned cows that snorted their curiosity at us.

We walked slowly through the manicured paths, stopping to read the wooden signs that labeled the medicinal plants that went into the Dr. Hauschka Skin Care preparations and into the WALA remedies. Using our dictionary, I identified the plants less familiar to me, like St. John's wort, eyebright, marshmallow, quince, and anthyllis. As we strolled, birds sang hymns and dined on the bounty of insects and worms among the plantings; bees visited the eager new blossoms that were beginning their journey through the growing season.

I felt like Goldilocks as we explored the quaint garden buildings, where tools and baskets hung, awaiting the intensive harvesting labor that occurred throughout the week. One room in the building had a woodstove, a large table, and several chairs: it was where the head gardener, his crew, and the apprentices ate.

On a sunny, south-facing slope, twelve beehives were nestled within a small, protective enclosure of shrubs. We sat down on a well-seasoned teak bench that had been placed a comfortable distance from the hives and watched as the bees diligently foraged for their queen. I had never been so close to so many bees. Their humming and their graceful movement were captivating.

At the back boundary of the garden, more than a dozen compost piles meticulously formed long, narrow pyramid shapes. Between the bees and the compost piles, one area seemed to have been left alone: it was a little wild and uncultivated. A path had been worn down in the grass between a row of hawthorn trees and several long beds that looked newly planted. The beds led to a small pond carved between reeds and leafy watery plants. A large ceramic fountain (called a Flow Form) stood in the center of the pond; water sloshed from an elevated, cupped bowl down to other bowls, thus forming swirling vortexes that made their way back to the pond.

A bench close to the pond had been comfortably warmed by the sun. I sat, took off my Frye boots and tweed blazer, then pulled my long denim skirt above my knees and loosened the waistband so the sun touched the top of my scar. The care and love of the garden felt tangible. It was deeply moving for me to be there, to see where the plants used in the products were grown and harvested. I closed my eyes; I sensed Suzi stand up and walk away; I went deeper into a meditative state, feeling connected to the earth with my whole being.

And then, in the silence of my heart, I pictured John being protected by a cloak of warm light; I felt what I called the *Lily presence* in the space. Linear time seemed to stop; I was in creative time where everything felt connected. Later, when I recalled the moment, I wrote in my journal:

> *Virgin spring,*
> *wedded to winter's darkness*
> *and summer's light.*
> *Radiant beauty fair and bright,*
> *you weave with the air the water and fire*
> *transforming the earth*
> *into holy desire.*

Suzi returned to the bench and stood in front of me. I opened my eyes and watched her zip up her camera case.

"How is your scar doing?" she asked as she peeked at the top of the long scar just visible between my skirt and blouse.

I smiled up at her five-foot, strong dancer's stance. Her dark, wavy hair fell to her shoulders. She was eager for me to be okay again.

I slowly lifted my blouse farther up and pulled down the waistband of my skirt. We both looked at the stitching that stretched from below my navel to just above my pubic bone. The rays of springtime sun felt soothing on my skin. "It's fading a little," I said, then joked, "but it's not bikini time yet. *Das ist nicht so gut.*"

Inwardly, I knew that the scar on my soul would take longer to fade.

12

Inside the Castle

*D*RESSED IN A NEW, long, black linen skirt, white cotton blouse, turquoise sweater, and fuchsia strapped leather sandals, and with my new journal and Mont Blanc pen in hand, I felt like it was my first day of school. Suzi and I arrived early at the main building, where beds of flowing perennials lined both sides of the front steps: yellow rudbeckia, orange verbascum, delicate white fennel, giant grayish-blue thistles, grape hyacinths, forsythia, and lilacs.

We sat on the front steps and waited for Heinz to accompany us to the weekend medical conference on Anthroposophically extended medicine. The conference was designed for doctors, nurses, and massage therapists who worked from a holistic perspective of human beings and of healing.

My spiritual training came alive at the WALA building at the end of Dorfstrasse—a wide cobblestone path rather than a street. Although I had been meditating and reading spiritual teachings on my own for the previous seven years, at WALA I was introduced to a new way of thinking, one that could be applied in the practical world. The main tenet taught me the worldview that we are spiritual beings incarnated into human bodies in order to experience the material world and develop a higher level of consciousness. I learned that the earth is our classroom, teacher, and partner on this amazing journey through space and time. Quotes like "We are not human beings having a spiritual experience; we are spiritual beings having a human experience" by Pierre Teilhard de Chardin were no surprise to a growing community of globally minded citizens.

Inner geography, soul, spirit, interconnectedness, the Yoga mind, Buddha nature, Christ consciousness, and cosmic rhythms are only some of the concepts I had been studying in order to understand what it means to be fully human. But it was as if I'd been trying to learn a new language on my own, and I had finally traveled to a place where everyone spoke the same language. I thought of WALA as Camelot, and that I was now on a quest.

Directly across from where we sat, a small cemetery was enclosed by boxwood; a wrought iron gate served as the entrance. An old woman approached with a basket of flowers over her arm. She opened the gate, pushed it half closed with her elbow, and disappeared into the quiet space.

Then the gate mysteriously swung back open. I jumped up, crossed the road, and went inside. I closed the gate behind me.

"*Guten Morgen*," the old woman said as she smiled and looked my way.

I smiled back and watched as she created small bouquets from the flowers in her basket. When she finished, she turned to vases that were in the ground next to the dozen gravestones and replaced their faded blooms with the fresh, living color.

Then I saw a headstone that was engraved: Rudolf Hauschka. Below his name, the dates 1891–1969 had been engraved. I noted that he'd been born two years after my father.

As I stood by Dr. Hauschka's grave in the peaceful setting, I recalled reading stories about his early life in Vienna when he'd been a student of psychology and natural science, when he'd had to hide from the Nazis while he developed medicines for a New Age. I remembered his meeting with Rudolf Steiner in the Netherlands and his maritime adventures in Australia when he'd gone fishing for sharks and their valued therapeutic spermaceti.

Hauschka's goal in founding WALA had been to support the health of humanity and the health of the Earth through the development of medicines that were free of negative side effects and that cared for the Earth through regenerative farming practices.

It was Hauschka's belief that his business would be the change agent that could transform the world. It wasn't enough to produce healthy green products; it was also necessary to reshape the current global business model and find a new, healthier, paradigm. The more I learned about him, the more of a hero he became to me. In that moment, standing at his grave, I adopted him as my spiritual father—though I didn't really know then what that meant.

As cars arrived and voices emerged, I returned to where Suzi was taking photos. We watched as tiny, gas-efficient foreign cars (at that time not available in the United States) parked in postage-stamp-sized places along the narrow road. Then Heinz arrived in his brother's old Mercedes and walked over to greet us. A tall young woman about our age, who had dark brown curly hair and wore black framed glasses, unlocked the main door and welcomed the group of two dozen medical professionals and us into the lobby.

She spoke very slowly in near-perfect English.

"Hello, I am Karin Rotelli. I work in the WALA Export Department. I would like to help you enjoy your time here. Please let me know how I can be of assistance."

We were swept along with the group into the cafeteria, where tables for eight had been set with small plates, coffee cups, vases of flowers, platters of giant pretzels, and raspberry croissants. Bowls heaped with fresh butter and others filled to the brim with ripe strawberries and kiwis completed the luscious-looking feast.

Heinz spoke to one of his friends, whom he referred to as "the alchemist," who worked in the plant laboratory. Suzi and I enjoyed the strong coffee over animated discussions about holistic medicine.

"Are Americans really interested in Anthroposophic Medicine?" a young doctor asked us.

"The interest is mostly around Waldorf Schools and biodynamic farms," I replied, "but lots of people love Dr. Hauschka Skin Care."

"Yes, everyone loves Dr. Hauschka products, they are very fine. Everyone except our daughter, that is, who thinks they are for old people because her mother and grandmother like them."

We laughed. I told him that they were popular among young professionals, actors, healers, and trendsetters in New York City.

"Maybe you can help arrange a medical conference in your country so people will understand the background of the skin care products. They are of the same standard of quality as the medicines."

I jotted that in my journal as another important distinction to make when marketing Dr. Hauschka. The standards of quality needed for medicines are much higher than the quality of ingredients required to be used in skin care products, so it could be a significant selling point.

"It's very important that people learn how to support their health and not address only the symptoms of illness," the young doctor continued. "If we don't learn this, I'm afraid we will become dependent on synthetic drugs that have negative side effects. What we have now is more of what could be called illness care, not health care."

When I asked the doctor how he became interested in Anthroposophic Medicine, he said that as a medical doctor he studied pathogenesis or the development and treatment of illness. His interest as a doctor now had expanded to study salutogenesis—that which supports and promotes physical and emotional health. He found the medical conferences helpful because he was introduced to supporting therapies like rhythmic massage, curative movement, and painting therapy. (In addition to being the medical doctor in the early days of WALA, Dr. Margarete Hauschka, Dr. Rudolf Hauschka's wife, had also started a painting school in the neighboring village.) The young doctor now believed that all the modalities that were emerging needed to come under one umbrella, a "one health approach" that would not be considered alternative but, rather, more complementary to a healing process.

There were obvious lifestyle illnesses that he easily recognized, but he was grappling with the idea of deeper soul illnesses connected to one's karma. I understood the idea of lifestyle but felt unsure about what he meant about soul illnesses related to karma. It did flash through my mind that, although I ate organic food and used healthy products, I didn't think I was in a healthy relationship with Jim. I often felt insecure, and I still suffered from bouts of bronchitis.

The beauty of the WALA medicines, the young doctor further explained, was that they had no negative side effects and supported healthy processes in the body rather than attacking the symptoms of illness.

I wrote down almost everything he said. He was so earnest and handsome, he seemed like a knight on a crusade to champion a new model of health care.

As I listened, I began to realize that the idea of supporting health and healthy processes was really new and crucial for me to understand. As I looked around the room, I noticed it was filled with beautiful, wholesome people, not glamorous, but beautiful to me. I felt a sense of community, of purpose, and that I was coming home.

A bell sounded, and we rose and filed out, leaving our dishes in trays near the coffee urns and moving into the adjoining *Grand Salle* (large room). Heinz and Karin sat between us in order to translate the presentations that had been in German. The room became quiet. A young woman doctor who lived near WALA and was there to study the vast range of remedies sat at a piano and played a short piece by Mozart. Suzi and I glanced at each other, acknowledging that, so far, our experience was amazing.

For the next two days we heard lectures on diverse topics, such as how important rhythm is in one's life, and how we as humans have a fourfold quality by being related to nature through the elements of earth, air, water, and fire. It became obvious that everything is connected, and that these medical people were looking at the whole person when treating illness and not just looking at the illness. This was, indeed, a totally new healing paradigm. I recalled Dr. Laskey asking me years earlier if I wanted to heal or just get rid of the bronchitis.

The botanist spoke of healing plants, not just in terms of active ingredients, but also in regard to the plant's gesture or its body language, as I understood it. For instance, I knew that roses, with almost 250 active ingredients, were a very important ingredient in many of the remedies and in the skin care products. But we were now being asked to consider that the rose holds a great polarity—at one end the beauty and delicacy of the flower, at the other end one of great resilience as reflected by the thorns. I also learned that the rose, perhaps the only flower to do so, emits fragrance day and night, while most flowers emit fragrance only during the day while the sun shines. Those characteristics point to the unique healing potential of the rose. WALA was very interested in the qualities of plants as well as in their chemistry. The speakers explained that roses are considered to be a role model for the skin; they address the delicacy and sensitivity of skin function but also provide a protective resiliency captured in the rose wax.

I remembered Heinz telling me about the polarity of the rose and its thorns years before when Jim and I were living at Dr. Laskey's place; I now had an "aha" moment as I realized how resilient I had become during my life with Jim.

I couldn't get enough of what I was hearing. Recalling how I had sat through high school and college science classes staring out the window, almost comatose with boredom, I realized that I now wanted to learn. I wanted to know everything about the gestures of plants and how to understand this new approach to healing.

One idea really stuck with me: that illness is a healthy process but in the wrong place. For example, acne is an activity of digestion that occurs on the skin when it really belongs in the metabolism. The blemishes, oil, and eruptions visible on the skin are reflections of overactive metabolic activity in the wrong place. Those activities are healthy in the metabolism but turn into an illness when they occur on the surface of the skin. The treatment for acne is topical, but it also includes a dietary clay capsule with the healing herbs fennel and caraway, which stimulate digestion, along with a diet of wholesome foods that are—and this is crucial—free from synthetics.

The conference material was directed at the doctors, but it offered a great background for understanding why their skin care methods were so effective. They discussed that skin is a universal organ because it reflects and, to some degree, functions like all the other organs in the body. As I sat listening in the Grand Room of WALA, which was surrounded by gardens and farms, it started to make sense that the speakers took skin care products as seriously as medicines, precisely because skin is an organ. It also began to make sense that healthy products begin in a healthy garden. I jotted down a marketing bullet: Beauty Begins in the Compost Pile. Which made me laugh to myself.

Though Suzi and I tried furiously to take notes, at some point I sat back and let the knowledge flow into me. During one of the breaks, a doctor told me that I would understand what I was ready to know. I did continue to jot down marketing ideas in my journal as I listened to the lectures. One special favorite was: Skin care is not a luxury, it's a lifestyle choice to support health; Dr. Hauschka products, although luxurious to use, are pure and therapeutic. I also wrote: Purity/Therapy/Luxury.

"All we need are rhythm and roses," I joked to Suzi when the conference ended. We said our good-byes to Heinz, who would be flying home the next day. My training was to begin in the morning.

Upon returning to our room, Suzi read aloud the notes she had so expertly taken. Her handwriting is beautiful, and her notes looked like a work of art, with diagrams of plants, complete with highlights of the roots, stem, leaves or flower, and fruit and seeds, depending on where its medicinal punch was stored. She drew illustrations of a scientist holding a glass beaker with swirling vortexes spiraling within it. I realized how happy she was recording our stay through words, diagrams, and lots of photos.

"I'll copy them for you; it's a lot to take in," she said.

"Yeah, but it makes sense, doesn't it?"

"It does. Imagine living here!"

"What do you think about Jim and Doug breaking into German film or performing Shuttlespeare in Münchenland?" I asked, and we laughed ourselves to sleep.

The next morning, we met Karin in the cafeteria, which was buzzing with employees who were enjoying what they called their second breakfast—or what we call a coffee break but with nicer snacks. Robert, an American working on his doctorate and spending time at WALA for the practical part of his program, joined us. He was to be our translator and interpreter for the week. Our schedules included a full day in the Esthetics Department, as well as four afternoons where I was to experience and learn the Dr. Hauschka Classic Treatment. We would spend the remainder of the time in the plant laboratory and in production. Dr. Vogel, the head of the WALA medical section, was going to take us to lunch each day. It was the first time I'd heard of a Dr. Hauschka Treatment, and I was surprised and excited. I was also impressed that Dr. Vogel, who had been one of the main speakers at the conference, would spend time with us.

Robert escorted us along the first floor of the building toward the Esthetics Department on the second floor. We stopped momentarily at the end of the corridor to look at a large portrait of Dr. Hauschka. In the painting, he was wearing a white lab coat, holding a glass beaker, looking handsome and confident.

It seemed as if he was looking directly at me; his presence felt very alive.

We climbed a winding staircase of smooth white stone to the second floor and entered the esthetics studio. A lovely woman named Frau Hahn greeted us. She was in her early fifties and spoke no English, so Robert was to be our ears and voice for our time with her. The plan was that she would give me a complete Dr. Hauschka Classic Treatment, so I could experience what I would then be able to give clients and teach others how to give the treatment, too. It was an unexpected surprise.

The treatment room was lovely, in shades of soft white. Six reclining cosmetic chairs, made up with flannel sheets, a wool blanket, and a hot water bottle near the foot, faced windows that looked out at a sloping meadow filled with blossoming apple trees and woolly sheep. I realized that the studio stood between the garden in the back and the meadow in the front. I was having a treatment as close to the garden as possible, with products made from the plants grown in the garden.

We moved to the far end of the room; sunlight covered the lounge where I would sit. A cart was filled with Dr. Hauschka products, a vase that held a fresh, peach-colored rose, small brushes, and a white ceramic container with a candle under it for warming the oils that she'd use.

Frau Hahn motioned for me to go behind a screen and change into a spa robe, then return to the lounge chair. She was going to direct the demonstration to Robert and to Suzi, who would take notes while observing the atmosphere that Frau Hahn created. I was to relax and connect to the experience. She assured me that afterward I could ask questions and learn specifics of the techniques.

For the next two hours, I was transported to a deep state of relaxation and healing, thanks to fragrant aromas and the gentle, caring touch of this lovely therapist.

The treatment started with my feet, which were placed in a warm, almost hot, sage footbath. I began to breathe very deeply, and I relaxed as Frau Hahn moved me from one step to another in a flowing graceful rhythm. After drying my feet, she tucked me in snugly and placed a hot water bottle at the base of my spine. I didn't realize how tense I had been until my tension started to melt away, one layer after another. I could not remember ever being treated with so much care.

She then applied alternating hot and cold compresses: the hot one had lavender concentrate, the cold one, lemon. Both felt wonderful: as one expanded with warmth, the other contracted with cold. I recognized the scents of the familiar products and felt how they were penetrating into my skin, thanks to Frau Hahn's expert hands and her gentle rolling, lifting, cupping motions on my face and flowing movements with warmed oil on my décolleté, followed by a series of movements across my forehead and at pressure points beside my nose and around my mouth.

I felt pervious, as though the treatment were permeating completely through and around me, as my whole being was nurtured. Memories surfaced of lying in the hospital recovery room a year earlier as nurses cared for me. Some of the tears still in my heart from that welled up and were absorbed by the cotton compresses, moist with extracts of eyebright, firmly pressed on my lids. Frau Hahn was nursing me in a different way.

I dove into the experience, not quite asleep, not quite awake, but in a state of well-being where I was flowing yet felt fully connected to myself.

At the end of the treatment I responded with a deep breath and stretched my arms up over my head. I smiled as Frau

Hahn handed me a glass of rose petal elixir and water to drink. I remembered the night years before when Heinz's wife had served me rose petal elixir when I first heard of WALA. It was as though, since then, I'd been following a thread on a journey to find myself.

While I changed back into my clothes, Suzi and Robert had tea and cookies from a cart that had been wheeled into the room. When I joined them, they looked at me in my altered state. They smiled.

"You look great," Suzi finally said.

I yawned and said, "I feel great, but I'm not sure 'great' covers it. I feel filled with enough. It's as if I should feel this way all the time." My head swirled with thoughts of how fantastic the treatment had been, how fantastic I felt. I wanted to bring it all back home.

Frau Hahn joined us. She looked fresh and lovely, not as if she'd spent two hours working.

Robert translated as she spoke about the process. "The treatment has a rhythm to it, and one can't rush through it," she said with enthusiasm. "The healing substances in the skin care products are energizing for the esthetician, as well. We are breathing them in and applying them with our hands, so giving the treatment is a little therapeutic for us, too. I tell my students that they become more beautiful the more they give these treatments." She smiled with a gentle laugh.

"It is a healing treatment to bring balance to the skin and also harmony to the whole person," she continued. "Each of the elements is addressed in the process. First, cleansing the physical; the sage footbath cleanses the feet but also stimulates the kidneys to detoxify. Then the cleansing cream, facial steam, and clay mask remove the impurities from the skin—this is all very earthy and physical. The lymph and fluid body, or water element, are stimulated with the fine mink brushes. The aromatic oils used in the massage on the décolleté speak to the emotional body or to the element of air."

I thought she would explain that the fire or warmth element was the heated oil, but instead she said: "The fire element is the ego or individual spirit of the therapist. Her intention is to create a warm, beautiful, loving environment for the client, so the client can awaken and unfold her unique beauty and individuality. Each face is different and has a unique story behind it. When we work on the face, we are stimulating all systems in the body, because the face is like a map of the body. I think this is a good place to end for today don't you?"

Frau Hahn then left the studio, leaving me filled with gratitude for all I was experiencing. Even more incredible than sensing that I'd found my real home, I felt that I had been expected.

13

Lily as Medicine

*I*FELT NAKED, beautiful, and new. I wondered if everyone could see that I was inside out, that the beautiful me that I didn't know existed had escaped. As Suzi, Robert, and I left WALA to meet Dr. Vogel, I felt as if I had no boundaries, that the world was travelling through my whole body, and that all my senses were finally alive. The birdsong, flowers, spring aromas, and swaying tree branches flowed into me like dance music. My vitality emerged anew, throwing open the narrow door behind my eyes through which I had previously viewed the world. My uncontrollable response was to smile. I was high but not on drugs; the side effects were positive bliss.

The three of us chatted as we walked toward Dr. Vogel, who was leaning against an old gray Mercedes. I was learning that the perceived status of owning a Mercedes-Benz in the United States did not exist here: even the old farmer who moonlighted by driving WALA visitors to the *Flughafen* to catch a plane owned a vintage Benz.

During the medical conference, Dr. Vogel had been a fiery, dynamic, impassioned authority; now he looked as gentle as the straw man in *The Wizard of Oz*. He wore the same navy blue suit, beige V-neck sweater, white shirt (no tie), and slightly scuffed black shoes that he'd had on during the conference. The only thing new to his attire was a black beret worn at a slight angle over his white hair. I sensed he was wearing his only good clothes. He shook our hands, grasping them with both of his large, warm ones. Then he opened the passenger door, bowed slightly, and ushered me in. Robert and Suzi walked around the car, opened the back door, and settled onto the worn red leather seats. Dr. Vogel started to drive.

"We're going to the Badhotel Stauferland, which has a very nice restaurant," Robert said. "It's only a short distance."

"Another 'bad' experience!" I giggled softly to Suzi, thinking of the fun we'd had at the Badhaus, splashing around in the healing waters.

Suddenly, we stopped at a crossing. Slowly, and with precision, a shepherd with a flock of about twenty sheep and a German shepherd dog guided the animals across the road as if they were a group of well-behaved school children. It was a postcard moment for me.

Dr. Vogel turned and spoke to Robert, who translated: "The sheep are going to lunch, too, in the meadow over there. The farmer grazes them each day around this time."

The restaurant was near the top of a hill and was bordered on two sides by lush, sloping meadows. We were led to a reserved table on the outside terrace with a view of the meadows and blossoming fruit trees that resembled large umbrellas in an Impressionist painting.

The owner, his wife, and their son-in-law, who was the chef, came out to greet their first American guests. The owner's wife wore a frilly white blouse under a black, traditional-looking jumper with colorful embroidered flowers along the border. She held a lace handkerchief in her right hand and moved it lightly around as she recited the specials of the day in a high-pitched, almost musical voice. Apparently, though many young employees at WALA spoke English, Dr. Vogel and the local population did not. We relied on Robert for all communications.

"Why is the idea of integrating rhythm into the Classic Treatment so important?" I asked as we waited for our meals.

Dr. Vogel's reply took off like a racehorse, his answer lasting several minutes. Robert then translated by saying that every living thing has a rhythm, and nature unfolds through the rhythms of the seasons, which repeat themselves but are never exactly alike. He said that rhythm is a fluid balance between polarities: winter and summer are polarities; spring connects them through a rhythmic expanding and contracting activity as winter lets go and moves toward summer in a breathing kind of way. The skin is a perfect example of how rhythm manifests: healthy young skin renews itself every twenty-nine to thirty days like the cycle of the moon.

"Rhythm is very fluid: when you run quickly up a set of stairs, your breath and your heartbeats quicken in order to support the exertion. Then all is restored to a normal pace.

"The more we study rhythm, the more we see how we are connected to earthly and cosmic rhythms. When we create rhythm in our life we integrate with the earth and cosmic rhythms. Rhythm is the new hygiene. It will eventually transform medicine with the same immense impact as the discovery—150 years ago—of how critical it is for surgeons to wash their hands before surgery." I still was having difficulty grasping all he said, but I felt that it was true and very important.

My head was spinning as I watched Dr. Vogel try to summarize a lifetime of study and medical experience and convey it to me through Robert, who strove to find the English words that came close to his meaning.

Our discussions paused as each course of our meal arrived. The soup of the day, *Festtage-Suppe*, or festival soup, arrived in white bowls covered with metal hats or "huts," as they are called in German, to keep the food warm. It was one of the nicest restaurants I had ever been to.

I was suddenly reminded of my birthday celebration when Jim had taken Suzi, Doug, John, and me to brunch in the Rainbow Room at the top of Rockefeller Center. Our meals had also been served on large white plates, covered to keep the food warm until the last moment. Both Jim and the setting had been a big surprise. I remembered I'd been very happy as the five of us had sat together, enjoying one another and the stunning city view, with John at the center of our love and attention. Jim left early for a matinee—a lead role as the painter Manet—in a small theater production in the Village near Mott Street. As he leaned down and kissed my cheek, he told me that Peggy (one of our friends from 280 Mott) was going to the show, and that he'd probably grab a drink with her and the cast after the performance. He wasn't sure when he'd be home. At the time I wondered how he knew that Peggy would be at the performance: I dismissed it by reminding myself that he often got complimentary tickets for friends.

But as I sat now in a wonderful restaurant in the beautiful Schwäbische Alb, a shadow crept over me. I recalled how, at that birthday brunch, I'd felt a quick chill, then a hot flash of jealousy. And now, as the waiter removed the metal hat, I looked down at the young trout, caught earlier that day, cooked in wine smothered with thyme-seasoned local mushrooms, and I struggled to get back into the moment as Robert continued translating Dr. Vogel's words.

He talked about Rudolph Hauschka and how Hauschka's biography led him to discover how to extract healing plants with rhythm rather than by using alcohol, which traditionally had been used to extract substances from nature. When Rudolph Hauschka met Rudolf Steiner at a medical conference, he asked Steiner the very big question: "What is life?" Steiner had replied: "Study rhythm—rhythm carries life." Hauschka had held that thought for seven years before he discovered the seven-day rhythmical process.

I was surprised when Dr. Vogel then said that, as a very young man, Rudolph Hauschka had vehemently opposed the consumption of alcohol at social gatherings and thought that alcohol would have an unhealthy effect on society as a whole. Hauschka started the Templars Club at his university for students who didn't drink and wanted to explore poetry, philosophy, and the arts. He and other members of the club befriended alcoholics and took them out hiking and canoeing in nature, to art museums, to concerts, and to theater events as a kind of rehabilitation. This totally caught my attention. It felt as if my adopted father, Rudolph Hauschka, was speaking to me through Dr. Vogel.

It seems that, when Rudolph Hauschka and Rudolf Steiner had been discussing the idea of developing medicines to support health, Steiner said that it was necessary to be able to make medicines without the use of alcohol.

"You see, it was somehow part of Hauschka's life story that he resisted alcohol, and that his destiny was to develop our seven-day rhythmic process."

By the time our elderflower ice cream and cappuccinos arrived, the distracted heaviness I'd felt about Jim had passed. Once again, I became inspired by absorbing new ideas from Dr. Vogel, including about how minerals and precious stones are found in medicines and several skin care products, exemplifying that traditional Western medicine acknowledged a connection between minerals, certain precious stones, and the planets.

Dr. Vogel was so animated and excited that he seemed young and vibrant. As he finished his ice cream, he further explained that, in the fourteenth century, the word "hal" evolved into three words: health, whole, and holy. He said that only that one word—hal—expressed all three concepts almost synonymously and that, today, Anthroposophic doctors strive to reconnect wholeness with a sense of the sacredness of life to health.

I once had learned that healers have typically acknowledged a connection to something greater than we are, something spiritual—both Eastern and Western traditional healers studied the connections between the planets, plants, certain stones, minerals, and the human organism—and that Native Americans understood that nature was sacred. I now learned that the element of rhythm is the next step to this living history of healing.

Then Robert turned to Dr. Vogel and said he'd promised Frau Hahn that he'd have us back by three o'clock. We rode back to WALA, silent and content.

When we returned to the esthetic studio, my eyes fell on the lovely rose that lay next to the Dr. Hauschka products. I thought about the treatment and remembered that the meaning of the word *health* was once connected to *holy* and *whole*. While the treatment had touched me on a deep level, the conversation with Dr. Vogel seemed very connected, but in a way that I *felt* more than I *understood*. I knew that I had a long way to go to feel whole again: until then, my only conception of *holy* was when I'd received Holy Communion in Saint Paul's Church, when, with hands held closed like a spire on my heart, I had opened my mouth to receive the symbol of Christ's body in a small white wafer.

But now, though Frau Hahn, with her sunny smile, looked very conventional, she continued to teach us a more alternative approach to skin care than I'd ever imagined. She handed us several pages of diagrams and information, all of which were written in German. She apologized and said they would have all the esthetic training materials translated into English by my next visit. I reveled in the knowledge that I would return to WALA.

In the meantime, we concentrated on an illustration of a generic plant with arrows that pointed to the three layers of the skin: the roots pointed to the epidermis, the stem and leaves to the dermis, and the flowers and seeds to the subcutaneous tissue.

We learned through Robert's summations that healing plants have their active properties in different parts of the plant: for example, the flowers of calendula are most valued, whereas the leaves of rosemary are where the healing properties are concentrated; witch hazel has a root-like quality to the whole plant, and even the leaves are strong and resilient like a root; the rose is very special—the whole plant is often used—and it is a role model for the skin, offering protection for the skin's delicate nature, while promoting harmony and resilience as well.

I quickly saw that this was a science and that, though there have been guidelines for centuries about the connections of plants to the skin, it took many, many years to replicate these connections in a stable, effective, lovely-to-use product. I learned that the easiest way to describe Dr. Hauschka products was to explain that they are compositions that support skin functions rather than covering up symptoms.

As Robert translated Frau Hahn's closing words of the day, she smiled. "Perhaps you can visit the garden together tomorrow," she said, "and spend time drawing some of our plants so you get to know them better. They are healing beings, a therapist's friend, and they appreciate our attention." The thought of drawing the plants that I had seen in the garden sounded like a nice idea but brought up my insecurities about not being a good artist.

Then Karin Rotelli came to the studio and told me I was welcome to go to the plant laboratory each of the next four mornings to learn how the plants are prepared in a hands-on environment. The next morning at six o'clock I would be able to help process convallaria, more commonly known as lily of the valley.

As we left the building, I said to Robert, "Have you heard all this before?"

"Much of it is new to me, too. I think this training is a first. It's great to be around some Americans for a change."

Suzi would not be working in the plant lab, and, since one of the interns spoke English, neither would Robert. He told us that he'd get colored pencils and some drawing paper so we could meet in the garden after I finished in the plant lab and make botanical drawings. I remembered my father either painting or drawing each day when I came home from school as a young girl. It would have been wonderful if he had showed me how to draw as a child. I thought that maybe I could channel some of his talent.

As it turned out, it was very peaceful to sit on a bench in the garden and make simple drawings of calendula and other herbs. Even I had to admit that my drawings improved a little more each day.

When I arrived at the plant lab in the morning, a young intern greeted me and led me into a small room. I washed my hands and put on a white lab coat, a mask over my mouth and nose, a white cotton hair cap, and white paper booties over my shoes. Inside the lab we stood in a circle with seven older women. Years later, I would jokingly refer to them as the vestal virgins because they took their work so seriously and all happened to be single. One of them removed her mask and read a poem-like verse before we began our work.

The intern quietly whispered to me: "Reading a poem is a good way for us to focus and create an appropriate mood for our work together. Please feel free to ask me questions, but I think much will be learned by doing."

I was told then that the plant material I'd be given, lily of the valley, was used as a heart remedy. It had been harvested that morning at sunrise before the dew dried. The irony of the name alone was remedy for my heart. I felt that something beyond my understanding was happening and was essential for my healing.

The intern said, "The life force is most contained in the plant at sunrise. The plant is most still then and does not start to expand its essence into the environment until the sun calls it forth."

The plants arrived in several small woven baskets. They were thoroughly washed, then brought to us. We first tore the leaves and tiny flowers into small pieces. Then we placed a small amount of the bits into a mortar and began to pound, rub, and grind it with a pestle. The sound of our work was very musical.

"Lily of the valley is poisonous," the intern explained, "but when it is processed homeopathically and used in dilute amounts it becomes a medicine."

I knew enough about homeopathy to understand what she meant. My mind wandered back to losing Lily the year before. Her death had led me in a new direction. Inwardly, I knew that Jim did not want to help me raise a family, and that if I'd had a new baby, I would not be sitting here at WALA, learning all that I was learning, and receiving all the gifts I was receiving. Feelings somewhere between sadness and serenity moved through me. I felt deeply connected to Lily, though our lives were now in parallel universes. If she wasn't physically in my life, she could be with me in my heart.

The musical sounds of the pestles stopped. I stood and followed the others over to a cart where a large clay vessel had been placed. It was filled with water; a container with several large feathers was next to it. I followed the others and, using a large, grayish-brown feather, I gently swept the plant material into the water. When it all was processed, the container was placed into a box-like incubator that would keep out light and maintain a temperature of 98.6 degrees, the human body temperature. I was told that the incubator had been lined with peat moss to insulate it from cosmic influences.

The process would take seven days in the incubator. During that time, the watery plant mixture would be exposed to three polarities: warmth/coolness, stillness/movement, and darkness/light. An hour before sunrise and again an hour before sunset, the clay container would be removed from the incubator and brought outside the lab. At those times, it would be placed in an ice bucket and remain there, uncovered, exposed to early morning and, later, evening light. Each time, it would be gently stirred. The container would be returned to the incubator an hour after sunrise and sunset. Therefore, when outside, the plant mixture would be exposed to light, coldness, and movement—the polar opposite of the conditions within the incubator.

After three days of this procedure, the plant material was to be filtered out of the watery tea-like substance and dried. A small amount would be put into a white ceramic pot and placed over a flame, thereby reducing the matter to ash. A small amount of the ash would be added back to the watery substance in the container, where it would remain until the full seven days were up. Though

I would not get to see the results of the entire process, I learned that the substance would continue to be exposed to the various polarities throughout the remaining seven days, at which time the watery extract would be placed in a brown glass bottle and stored in a room below the laboratory for a year. This extract was referred to as the Mother Substance.

The intern told me that the different exposures were what the plant would have been exposed to in nature, and that it, too, would eventually return to an ash-like substance. The procedure stabilized the substance and released its potential into the water.

Now, on this learning journey, the name WALA really came alive for me—seven years after Heinz had tried to explain it when he'd asked me to represent the brand. Working in the plant laboratory, I experienced a sense of the sacred, and a feeling that we truly were doing something healing.

The lily of the valley would be transformed into a remedy for the heart. But first, the plant needed to be broken apart and subjected to life's rhythms of light and darkness, warmth and cold, stillness and movement before it became whole again as a medicine. My spirit had been broken, my baby lost, my uterus ruptured. My trust in life with Jim was breaking apart. Hopefully, I would find my whole healthy and sacred self someday amidst the ashes of my life after what felt like a very long trial by fire.

— 14 —

Deus Ex Machina

"I'M LEAVING YOU. I'm in love with another man. A doctor I met at the medical conference."

John turned nine years old on June 29, 1983. Jim was away, performing at the Berkshire Summer Theater Festival; John and I were staying at my mother's house in Newport. Jim called to wish our son a Happy Birthday. When they finished speaking, I got on the phone and told Jim my decision.

A long silence followed. Then he said, "Can we talk about this, Susie?"

"We can talk about it, but I'm not changing my mind." I hung up and buried my face in the dozen yellow roses that had greeted me when I'd returned from the annual Anthroposophic Medical Conference in Wilton, New Hampshire. I read the card again: *I can't wait to see you, Warren.*

Since my first trip to WALA two years earlier, I had been selling Dr. Hauschka Skin Care products to skin care therapists and individuals, and opening accounts at health food stores, yoga centers, bath and body boutiques. When we'd moved from 280 Mott Street to 260 Riverside Drive at the beginning of 1981, I'd kept the Mott Street flat for the sales and training parts of my business. The small apartment with the slanting floors where I had almost died had been resurrected as an office where I filled orders one day a week. Soon, it also was packed from floor to ceiling with cases of Dr. Hauschka products and training supplies.

In addition to sales, I was offering the Dr. Hauschka Classic Treatment to friends, actresses, and store owners in our apartment on Riverside Drive. After John left for school and Jim went to rehearsals, I transformed our pumpkin-colored kitchen into a mini salon and used our kitchen table as a treatment bed. It was a more appropriate environment for healing than the Mott Street office. In my naiveté, however, I actually charged more for my treatment than the famous salons behind posh red doors on Fifth and Madison Avenues. In addition, I held trainings for estheticians, makeup artists, and massage therapists at the Annemarie Colbin Natural Cooking School on the Upper West Side. Part of the Dr. Hauschka message was that healthy nutrition both inside and out is crucial for beautiful, healthy skin.

John loved school, I loved my Hauschka work, and Jim continued to get work in the theater. Life could have been good. But it wasn't. John and I were, as always, usually alone. Jim was often out late, and, when he was at home, he slept later and later. He was critical and restless in spite of my efforts to take care of John and all the parental responsibilities that came with keeping him in the Steiner School. If I tried to broach the topic of why he often seemed unhappy and was rarely home, he said something to the effect that I knew the life of an actor was difficult, and if I wanted a more rhythmic life then I should leave him.

Earlier that summer, a friend who was in medical school had invited me to give a presentation on WALA and Dr. Hauschka Skin Care at the Anthroposophic conference. The main presenter, Dr. Otto Wolfe, was a doctor from Germany where Anthroposophic medicine is known and practiced as a complement and extension of conventional medicine. Doctors, nurses, massage therapists, and homeopaths all attended the weeklong event, since there was so little training of its kind in the United States. Several medical practices that were represented already carried WALA skin care products and dietary supplements for their patients, so it was an opportunity for me to connect with them one-on-one. Also, the in-depth curriculum furthered my understanding of Anthroposophic Medicine and gave me ideas that could accompany my skin care activities.

One evening during the conference, I showed WALA's educational slide presentation. It featured the WALA gardens and medicinal plants used in the medicines and skin care preparations, depicted aspects of the seven-day rhythmic extraction process and several manufacturing processes, and provided a description of dietary supplements that were available in addition to the skin care products. I explained that WALA refers to skin care as the daughter of medicine and chooses to use medical-quality ingredients, resulting in higher standards than normally required for skin care and cosmetic products. I told the audience how the skin functions as a universal organ.

It was challenging for me to speak to such a professional group of people, even though they were very open and interested in learning about the small Anthroposophic pharmaceutical company. I forged ahead with great enthusiasm in spite of the fact the last ten slides of the show had been inserted upside down.

Several memories of the presentation are most vivid to me. One is that, after asking a question about a medicinal plant, a young doctor said he thought the products were expensive. I reacted quite strongly, saying that the preparations were not expensive but valuable, and that the cost was related to the labor-intensive rhythmical process and the biodynamic farming methods needed to create the medicines and skin care. "The value is contained in the product," I said. "There is no glamorous advertising or fancy packaging." I suggested that, of all people, he should understand, because he knew how much time he spent with each patient in order to have a complete picture of their symptoms. Feeling an empowering strength and clarity rise up in me, I asked, "Do you think your fees are expensive?"

After the presentation, a woman from Canada introduced herself and told me she was a nurse. She said she had studied at WALA in Germany a year before Dr. Hauschka had died in 1969, and that she had been a "house daughter" of the doctor and his wife. The nurse reported that they had treated her like a member of their family and added that Dr. Hauschka would be "very proud" of me for "championing his unique rhythmic production process and special remedies." I was very moved, with goose bumps rising on my arms; I recalled my first visit to WALA when, standing in the small cemetery, I had decided to adopt Dr. Hauschka as my spiritual father. It now felt as if he were sending me encouraging messages from another world.

When the nurse walked away, a tall, good-looking doctor dressed in shorts and a short-sleeved linen shirt with the top button missing, came over and stood close to me. He was a little thick around the middle but had an angelic face. I looked up into his green eyes; warmth radiated toward me.

He said, "Great presentation. You're a dynamic goddess. Wanna have dinner?" His name was Warren, and he told me he was a physician who practiced constitutional homeopathy.

We spent the rest of the conference sitting together at lectures and often found our way to the same communal table for meals. I told him about my diverse activity with Dr. Hauschka and that I wanted to open a holistic skin care and training center but didn't want to go into cosmetology because it sounded boring. He told me that, during his third year in medical school, it became obvious to him that orthodox medicine never reversed illness but merely slowed the degenerative process. He had searched for an alternative and found homeopathic medicine to be more effective in supporting health. He also said he was taking piano lessons, and that he wanted to play "Send in the Clowns" for me when I came to visit him at his new house.

During a free afternoon, we drove to Mount Monadnock in Warren's Saab with the moon roof open. He had invited me to hike the three-thousand-foot-high mountain. At the top, we stood together, resting quietly after the rigorous climb. I looked out at the beauty of the mountains and the distant lake. Reflecting on the fullness of the conference, I felt even greater enthusiasm for my future with Dr. Hauschka. My decision to move forward with my career had been confirmed.

Then I thought about the other decision that had been slowly forming in my mind. I suddenly remembered being in Aspen on a mountaintop several years earlier, when I'd been with Jim just before I'd moved to New York. My life with him had not turned out as I'd thought it would: instead, it had grown painful and lonely. In that moment, atop Mount Monadnock, I decided I was going to leave him.

As Warren and I returned to the trail and descended, I was surprised to discover that climbing down the mountain was harder for me than climbing up had been.

The rest of that summer was a tango of tangled emotions. While John and I were still in Newport, after the phone call on John's birthday when I made my announcement to Jim, I told friends and family that he and I were breaking up. It was important for me to tell people in order to make my decision real.

One of the toughest things I had to do was tell Jim's mother. I went for a short visit, and, after I explained how difficult everything had become, I somehow found the words. She said she understood. She also said that though she loved her son very much, she had wondered how I'd been able to stay with him for such a long time. She added that John and I would always be welcome in her home. I said good-bye, and my heart ached when I saw her standing in the window, watching me drive away. Jim's mother had been a dear friend and confidant to me. Over the years, whenever I had joked with her about Jim's eccentric behavior, she'd sympathized and offered only love and support. We had a little secret: she told me that, whenever she spoke about Jim and me to her sisters, she called us "Lady and the Tramp." I knew that the connection between Jim's family and me would never be the same.

Jim continued to call, urging me to visit him in the Berkshires. Warren called, too, urging me to come back to the city so we could go out. He lived just over the George Washington Bridge in New Jersey, where he practiced at his home office. I had wild fantasies of steamy lovemaking with Warren, maybe marriage, but definitely bringing homeopathy and holistic skin care to the world together. But mostly I wanted to regard him as a doctor. I was very interested in constitutional homeopathy and thought he was the doctor who would find the perfect remedy to cure my chronic cough, insecurities, and self-doubt. He would also take me away from my difficult relationship.

Jim and I decided to meet at our apartment in New York as soon as he was free. When the time arrived, I left John with my mother and went into the city.

Jim was waiting for me in the living room. Under a cloud of his ever-present cigarette smoke, he was crying. I stared at the walls that he had painted; they weren't the field of gold color that I had chosen but a harsh taxicab yellow. The paint mistake no longer seemed funny to me. He told me how sorry he was that that he hadn't been there for John and me in the way we both deserved. He looked terrible and said that the thought of losing us was devastating. He had seen a doctor who had prescribed medication for his anxiety. At the time, I felt no sympathy for him, but I reveled in the thought that he wanted me back. But an exciting, handsome doctor wanted me, too, and it was intoxicating to feel that I would finally be loved.

I spent several days with Jim, sharing with him everything I'd learned about homeopathy and Anthroposophic medicine, and telling him that I was going to start treatment with Warren. One of the things that had kept Jim and me together for twelve years had been our interest in Anthroposophy, so he was also interested in learning about homeopathy. Unfortunately, in addition to good conversation, we also spent a lot of time arguing, blaming each other, and crying together. He finally said he would move out of our apartment and crash on a friend's couch; we decided to tell John when he came back to the city to begin the third grade.

Life became very intense. I started dating Warren and also seeing him as a patient. As his patient, I shared not only my physical ailments but also emotional and mental sensations, what foods I ate, how I slept, my sexual patterns and menstruation cycles. I learned that in constitutional homeopathy the individual is considered as a whole and that symptoms from the body, mind, and spirit are taken into account when choosing a remedy.

Jim moved in with a "friend," who started seeing Warren as a patient, too. Jim's "friend" was a young actress with whom, it turned out, he'd already been having an affair back when he called on John's birthday and I told him I was leaving him. Learning that was a shock: the hurt was intense. I realized that, though he showed up occasionally in our lives, he had not been really present for years. I couldn't help but wonder how many other affairs he'd had while we'd been together.

Then, soon after I started seeing Warren as a patient, Warren stopped dating me. He said he could tell that I was still enmeshed with Jim, and that he couldn't risk becoming emotionally involved with me and getting hurt. I was devastated. I began to doubt my decision to leave Jim, but it was too late to change the sting of his infidelity or the fact that he was now living with "the other woman." Warren, too, was moving on with his life. It felt as if the universe had intervened, plucked me up out of one difficult situation and dropped me — heart first — into another.

The rest of the summer, I divided my time between Newport with John, our families, and New York, filling Hauschka orders and making business calls. It wasn't until August that I remembered the other decision I'd reached at the top of Mount Monadnock — the one about moving forward with my career. I found out that, in order to legally open a skin care studio and train licensed professionals in Anthroposophic skin care, I needed to go to cosmetology school and get a state license. The time had come for me to do that.

However, after learning esoteric skin physiology at WALA, which wove the human connection to the cosmos and harvested healing plants at sunrise in order to retain vital life forces, the thought of going to the Robert Fiance School of Beauty for 1600 hours felt like a prison sentence. I had to take an entrance test and apply for a Pell Loan for six thousand dollars to cover the tuition. The loan was approved, but I should not have been surprised that I failed the test, which consisted of questions like: How would you rather spend your evening? *A.* going to a concert; *B.* going to a gallery opening; *C.* going shopping; or *D.* blow-drying your best friend's hair. Honesty was apparently not the best policy in this situation. I didn't choose one *D*-like answer out of the dozens of multiple-choice questions.

Miss Gigi, the school's director, said she was willing to give me a second chance on the test since she thought I looked like a smart girl and that I'd look so pretty once I learned how to do my hair and throw on a little makeup. Miss Gigi was also very helpful to the 100 new students who enrolled every two months and were mostly from Harlem and Queens. She helped them secure the six-thousand-dollar loans so they could attend her very prestigious and lucrative institution.

Assuring me that, if I didn't miss more than ten hours of classes over the next ten months, Miss Gigi said that I, too, could open an establishment with my name above the door—maybe calling it *Miss Susan's Skin Care Salon.* "Most people come here to learn hair, but skin is the future. I think you will be very happy at our school," she added. I signed on the dotted line on a very hot, humid, August day when it seemed that no one but me needed to be in the city.

A friend offered to work for me, filling orders while I attended school. She lived in New Jersey with her husband and new baby; she said if I could arrange things so she could work from home, she'd be happy to have the small job of processing orders and making phone calls. Once we ironed out the details, I double-parked in front of 280 Mott Street and loaded the entire inventory, shelving, and training supplies from Apartment 2F into the back of my old blue Volvo station wagon. I waved to the men hanging out in front of the grocery store across the street. It was a bittersweet moment that I savored with salty tears. I had lost so much on Mott Street, but it was also where I'd become a New Yorker. The men waved back as I finally left the neighborhood where I had honed my skills of parallel parking in unforgiving spaces.

With the business end of Hauschka taken care of, I returned to Newport to be with John and my family. I rode my bike along Ocean Drive; I jogged past colonial houses to Easton's Point and went to Second Beach in Middletown with John, my mother, and my sister. John and I rode the waves in together while my sister and mother sat on the beach reading Maeve Binchley novels. I cried into the surf and rode wave after wave, hoping I would feel better, but I didn't. My heart ached; I feared I was making a mess of my life and of John's, too. I also faced my old fear of being alone and unloved. Though John had never wanted to leave Newport and his gramma's at the end of each summer, we'd previously had the happy promise that his daddy would be waiting for him in the city. But now John's young, protected world was going to change, too.

My mother and sister encouraged my decision to attend beauty school, which, I added every time I told someone my plans, was not beautiful. My sister, however, invented a new shopping mission to find fun tops for me to wear to school. My mother told us that she'd always wanted to be a cosmetologist and have a home business so she could be near her family. I knew that my father's business partner had ruined their aluminum siding endeavor, and that my mother had subsequently needed to work full time, so she hadn't had the luxury of staying home to care for her family. She repeated her mantras that it had nearly killed her each time she'd had a baby and needed to return to work after only two weeks.

"I would rather have gone on welfare than have left a child so soon after giving birth."

Yes, I'd heard it all before.

Instead of finally telling her that I'd been on welfare when John was born, I asked, "So why didn't you go to beauty school?"

"We didn't have the money. Your father asked Dori, that wealthy sister of his, for a loan, but she was insulted and refused. We couldn't get a loan because of the debt from Daddy's business. I would have loved to have been a hairdresser and been able to set my own hours so I could have been there when you kids came home from school."

I was surprised to hear this. My mother had once said that, when she'd been attending Pembroke College, she'd wanted to be a teacher so she could stay home with her future children during the summers and on school vacations. She'd said she'd always wanted to be married and have children. But when she had to drop out of college because her father could only afford room and board for her older brother, Bud, who was at Brown University, her guidance counselor advised her to enroll in a secretarial school. Apparently loans for a secretarial school were easy to get and easy to pay off. So my mother became a successful executive secretary and the main support of our family for over forty years.

As my mother reminisced, I thought to myself: *I already know everything I need to know about skin care. I'm only going to beauty school because I need a state license; you wanted to go, so it's not the same.* In short, I thought I was above going to beauty school. I didn't bother to tell her that I was interested in inner beauty and health, not in superficial appearances. I knew she wouldn't understand.

I was quite arrogant at the time. Life circumstances had taken my mother from Pembroke College to Katherine Gibbs Secretarial School early in her life; later, they had taken her from being a proud homemaker with three children (four when I arrived) and married to a successful "Tin Man," to becoming a full-time breadwinner. Although I was grateful for all she'd done for me, as always, I found ways to look for our differences, not our similarities. It was as if I was always trying to get away from being like my mother, though I always went back to her whenever I needed a place to call home.

John and I returned to our Riverside apartment after Labor Day weekend. Jim came to see us. We told John that Momma Bear and Dad were breaking up, but that we both loved him very much. Jim promised he'd visit John as often as possible, including on some school days when John would get home an hour before I did. When I told John that I'd arranged for both of us to ride with friends who dropped their sons off at the Steiner School every day, then went right past my new school on their way to work in lower Manhattan, he was excited. He was also excited to learn he'd get to come home on the city bus with several Steiner kids in our neighborhood and let himself into our apartment with his own key.

The logistics all seemed, well, logical. But my heart still felt vulnerable as I tried to navigate the unknown terrain without Jim. I knew what I had left, but not where I would land.

15

Unexpected Schooling

OHN AND I STARTED SCHOOL on the same day in September 1983. He was returning to the Rudolf Steiner School on East 79th Street between Fifth and Madison avenues, entering the fourth grade. I was starting at the "Not Beauty School" on East 38th St. and Fifth Ave. My curriculum was to prepare me for the state board exam by mastering finger waves, hair styling, manicures, and pedicures and how to apply a facial mask without it seeping into the hairline.

"Remember that some of our clientele like to run out for a facial during their lunch break, and they can't go back to the office with mud in their hair or on their scalp," Miss Gigi reminded us weekly during the esthetics part of the training.

A friend of mine from India once told me that in her country such a profession as esthetics and hair care would be considered for the "untouchables only," because one would be handling another's impurities. Untouchables are the lowest-cast Hindu group outside the caste system; my friend had almost been banned from her family when she became an esthetician.

I learned during one of my trainings at WALA that Elisabeth Sigmund—the esthetician who had helped Dr. Hauschka develop the therapeutic skin care line and who had developed the Dr. Hauschka Classic Treatment—was from a prominent family in Austria. Her father had been the Minister of Culture in Vienna before he died. When Elisabeth told her mother that she was going to become an esthetician rather than a doctor, her mother almost disowned her because her daughter was choosing such a common profession. My mother, on the other hand, was proud that I was going to beauty school. I, however, was apologetic and took every opportunity to tell my friends that I was only going in order to legally open a holistic skin care center.

John's school curriculum included a main lesson on Norse mythology and the tales of Loki, Thor, and Odin. The gods, goddesses, and giants in such myths embodied different personality characters and challenges they had to meet in order to gain wisdom. It was understood that children became so deeply immersed in the myths that it helped prepare them to meet their own demons and challenges in an authentic way.

As an earnest Waldorf parent, I knew that John was of the age when he needed a sense of security, unity, and a strong family to meet the feeling of separation that was naturally occurring between early childhood and the eventual transition into puberty. I was fearful that, by having left Jim, I had shattered all sense of security that John needed. I hoped that the richness of the Waldorf School community would help him meet his challenges the way that Loki, Odin, and Thor had met theirs, and that he would survive our unstable parenting dynamics.

For the first two weeks of school, I packed a lunch for each of us, and we walked four blocks up the hill to West 102nd Street where we piled into a Subaru station wagon that belonged to a Steiner School family who ferried several students, plus us. Before we rode through Central Park and arrived at the school, I had just enough time to review several vocabulary words with

John—words like valley, dragon, and battle. Once we arrived, the boys tumbled out of the car and merged with other students like a swarm of bees heading to a hive. I loved the carpool ride of the morning commute. But it quickly ended for me when a new student—a girl—arrived. The car was then filled with students; there was no room left for me. So then I had to take the subway from West 96th Street and Broadway to West 42nd Street, catch the shuttle crosstown to Grand Central, and walk four blocks to school.

On the first day of "Not Beauty School," I ran up the wide staircase as fast as I could, hoping it would make the transition easier. Several young women who were surrounded by a cloud of smoke were slowly climbing the gray-treaded stairs.

"God, I hope we can smoke in the lunchroom during breaks," I heard one of them say as I bolted past their platinum heads and strong perfume.

Miss Gigi stood inside the glass doors at the top of the mountain of stairs and greeted us every morning of the first week. Her lipstick and nail polish, which always matched perfectly, were to change daily to various shades of red.

I found a seat at the end of a long, gray metal table where a few people in their twenties—two women and a man—sat talking and laughing. When I caught my breath and looked more closely at them, I noticed that they all were incredibly beautiful. *Thank God not everyone here teases their hair*, I thought.

Eddy, the young man (friends called him "Ed"), said he'd recently moved to the city from Norwalk, Connecticut, the day after his twenty first birthday. He wanted to be a model. His sandy-blonde hair fanned across half of his forehead; his green eyes had gold flecks and darted nervously from one of us to the other as he crossed one tight-black-jeaned leg over the other and told us his story.

"I love to cut hair and do makeup. I've practiced on my mom for years, getting her ready for church every Sunday and the Polish American Club every Saturday. I thought that between modeling jobs, I could cut hair for extra money. I figured that in order to do that, I'd need a license. My boyfriend works on Wall Street and has a beautiful apartment on the Upper East Side and is paying for me to come to school."

Yvonne had freckled, pale Irish skin, light blue eyes, and long red hair. When she'd turned twenty-eight, she'd decided it was time to get out of Washington State so she could become a singer. She'd met Mo, short for Mohammed, while they were working at a custom meat facility there. She married him so he could become a U.S. citizen. She was from an Irish family of eleven siblings and usually smiled and spoke very slowly.

"Yeah, my father is a butcher," she said, "and three of my brothers and I are licensed meat cutters, too. The pay is good, but I don't really want to spend my life in a meat factory, you know?"

Mo had wanted to move to New York, which made it ideal for Yvonne to follow her dream. Her large family assured her that she had a real gift for singing. They threw her a big party, at which she sang *New York, New York* before she and Mo boarded a cross-country bus. Once in the city, they stayed with a cousin, who was a friend of someone that Mo's sister knew back home in Iran.

"I thought since I'm good with a knife, maybe I'll be good with scissors, too," Yvonne explained. "I want to sing in clubs and join a tennis club. I was the best tennis player in my high school. I love tennis like I love singing. So, I want to get a license and support myself cutting hair till I make it as a singer."

Wendy, with chin-length black hair, eyes the color of blueberries, and snowdrop-white skin, had a husky laugh and not a hint of vanity. She moved to New York from Texas soon after she, like Ed, turned twenty-one. She planned to attend art school. She lived in the Village with Eduardo, a musician from Portugal. Wendy had a job on weekends sweeping the floor and sterilizing supplies at *La Boîte A Coupe*, a fashionable men's salon on West 57th Street. She was learning to cut hair from someone named Laurent, a master cutter who owned the salon.

"He's brilliant. He uses these huge scissors like for cutting fabric, and he lets me cut some of his friends' hair after the salon closes when everyone is drinking French wine and having a good time."

When she'd still been living at home, Wendy had also cut her mother's hair. After her parents got divorced, she went to boarding school in New Hampshire, a Waldorf School, called High Mowing, where she cut all of her classmates' hair and even some of the faculty members'.

When I told Wendy that my son attended the Steiner School, we bonded and shared common Waldorf-world experiences, especially how great it was that all the children played an instrument, that no television was allowed except the smallest amount on the weekends, that the class plays were terrific, and that there was an abundance of high-quality, natural-fiber clothing worn by students and teachers alike. At thirty-four, I was only seven years younger than Wendy's mother, and she said I reminded her of her.

When I learned that Wendy knew about Anthroposophy and had attended a Waldorf School, I felt better about being in beauty school, less isolated. It felt like a sign from the spiritual world that I was in the right place, and that there was something karmic about this small group of new friends.

I told the group all about John and his talented father, about my goal to open a holistic skin care center, about Dr. Hauschka Skin Care and my training in Germany, and about how Jim and I had started out on Mott Street but then moved to the Upper West Side. I even shared with them my anxiety about having left him.

"I don't know whether or not I did the right thing, or if we'll get back together."

Ed decided to call us the "Uptown, Downtown" group, and soon that's how everyone in the class referred to us. We quickly fell into a daily rhythm, which included a run to the café across the street for coffee and a scone, a call on the pay phone to hear our daily astrology forecast, and Ed washing and blow-drying our hair while he admonished the three of us for not taking better care of our grooming.

"You guys are beautiful! You'd be so hot if you even tried a little," he said as he perfected his styling techniques on the sisters that he'd never had. I felt happy that Ed thought of me as even remotely as pretty as Wendy and Yvonne. As depressed as I was about my relationships with Jim and Warren both ending, I was glad to have friends and a place to go every day, even if the school culture took me outside of my comfort zone.

Our instructor, Mr. Ralph, sensed that we were not his usual students. He told us that he would pretty much leave us alone as long as we punched in and out on time five days a week and completed our 1600 hours. Each day we spent time doing whatever we wanted to learn the most, or whatever we knew we needed to practice. Wendy and Ed were as talented as the instructors and spent their time giving haircuts to anyone in the class who wanted one. When they finished the haircuts, they highlighted everyone's hair.

Yvonne and I stayed with the class during the hair-cutting sessions because she was serious about working in a salon. As long as I had to be there, I wanted to at least be able to cut John and my mother's hair by the time I graduated. I also had to make sure I knew how to accomplish the famous finger wave that was necessary to pass the state board exam. It took me many months to prefect making the S-shaped waves with goopy wave lotion, drying them, and having the hair fall successfully into a lovely shape that Bette Davis would be proud of.

My favorite quote to share with Jim and my friends outside the school was one from Miss Gigi: "Look at the gift we released in your hands. With just a jar of wave lotion and what you learned here, you can bring beauty anywhere you go. That alone is worth the six-thousand-dollar tuition!"

While Yvonne and I were learning alongside the other students, we heard about their personal lives. Miss Mercy and Miss Darleen, who were both from Queens, discovered that both their boyfriends were doing time in the same prison upstate. They became best friends but were kind enough to invite Yvonne and me to go to a club with them in Queens "any Thursday night you wanna come. Thursday is topless night." My excuse for not going was that I needed to get home to my young son. Yvonne said she didn't feel comfortable about being out on the subways alone late at night. And that her Muslim husband wouldn't appreciate her being in the club's environment.

"I get it," Miss Mercy eventually said to me. "You're one of them, you know, natural ones? Is that it? That's why you never wear makeup?"

I finally gave up trying to explain that whatever you put on your skin goes into your system so it can either be a support or be unhealthy. But when I brought my Dr. Hauschka supplies in, created a pop-up garden salon, and started doing mini treatments on my classmates, I became as popular as Ed and Wendy. Soon the fragrances of lavender, rosemary, and lemon bath concentrates permeated the school, bringing aromatherapy to the community before they even knew what it meant.

Due to the ethnic diversity of the school, which included Hispanic, African American, and Asian students as well as Caucasians like me, it was a great opportunity for me to examine many different skin types. My classmates loved the warm, scented compresses that I used before I cleansed their skin and applied herbal lotions and creams. I offered nutritional advice to those who were open to it. Upon my recommendation, Miss Mercy even cut back from six daily cans of Coke to two when she saw improvement in her complexion. One woman from Spanish Harlem told me that I reminded her of her grandmother, who had a large garden in the Dominican Republic and kept the family healthy with good food and herbal concoctions that she made from fresh plants.

My new world continued to surprise me.

Jim came to visit John and me several times a week and remained unclear about where he was living, except to say he was crashing on couches again with friends. "No," he said, "I am not serious with the actress I was having an affair with when you left me."

I wasn't sure how I felt about that.

He loved hearing about my school friends and the funny things that happened daily with Miss Gigi and Miss Mercy. John told him about Loki fighting with Thor and how scary it was.

In those moments in our kitchen when we sat around the table having dinner and visiting, I found myself crazily imagining that we would eventually become the kind of family I had longed for.

Starting in early December, the school opened its doors to the public for inexpensive beauty services provided by the students. By then our Uptown, Downtown group knew each other's backstories pretty well. Wendy didn't love Eduardo, but the sex and his drugs were "fabulous." "And who," she asked, "could resist a lover who signs his Valentines and poetry to me with his own blood to prove his love?"

Yvonne didn't really want to be married to Mo, but they were good friends, and, for now, "It works."

Ed told us that Robert got so jealous when they were out that he couldn't help it if he hit Ed once in a while because he loved him so much. "When you're fucked up on booze and drugs," he added, "it really doesn't hurt." We urged him to get out of that relationship, but he told us that he wasn't strong like the rest of us; he needed someone to take care of him.

They knew that I wanted to get Jim back, and that there was no hot sex for me with anyone.

Every Friday, clients could receive cuts, coloring and styling, manicures and pedicures, and mini facials—all for less than five dollars. I told Jim, my friends from the Steiner School, and my Hauschka clients to come in and ask for me, or for Yvonne, Ed, or Wendy. Jim arrived on the first day, thrilled to get a bargain and to meet the friends I had been telling him about for months. I let the three of them take care of him. Yvonne placed hot lemon compresses on his face, Wendy cut his hair with her giant fabric-size scissors, and Ed gave him a manicure. I stayed at a distance and watched them all laughing. I was eager to hear what they thought of him.

When he left they said that yes, he was really attractive, in an unusual sort of way, not typical-handsome but very charismatic, smart, and funny. Their consensus was that I needed to start dating other men, smoke some grass, maybe even do a little cocaine, have some fun, you know, but don't wait around for Jim. I nixed the suggestion of taking drugs but agreed to go to a jazz club with Yvonne, where I met a stockbroker who did art in his spare time and lived close to my apartment.

When Fridays arrived, I counted on friends to come and get services at the school so I wouldn't have to wait on anyone that I didn't already know. Wendy and Yvonne also mostly took care of their friends or friends of friends. But Ed took care of the old ladies who came off the street looking poor, bedraggled, and almost dirty, and as if they had nowhere else to go. He danced around them, washing their hair with an added scalp massage, cutting and neatly rolling their locks before putting them under the dryer, and then handing them a magazine along with his big handsome smile. He joked with them. They left looking at themselves in his mirror, smiling as though they were headed to the Birdcage tearoom at Lord & Taylor to meet friends for lunch—not back outside to the lonely streets.

We teased him one day about all his admirers who returned weekly requesting, "Ed, the handsome young man who's so talented and nice."

One day over lunch he said to us, "You know, I never told you, but my father's an alcoholic. When he's drunk he slaps my mother around. He thinks it's her fault that I'm gay. She always let me help her cook and practice cutting her hair and applying her makeup. 'A real momma's boy,' that's what he called me."

When his mother was on the floor crying after his father had slapped her around, then slammed out of the house, Ed used to help her get up. He would then wash and set her hair and apply some makeup.

"She always felt better. She stopped crying, reached up to hold my hand, and told me she loved me. You know, a little makeup can make the world look better. It can bring harmony back into your world."

Ed thought if he moved away from home his father wouldn't treat his mother so badly. When he took care of the women who came to the school, it made him happy to make them happy. He thought of his mother and prayed that she was finally happy now that he was gone. "She sounds okay when I call, but I'm afraid she just doesn't want me to worry. When I make it as a model, I'm going to get her out of Norwalk and bring her to live with me"

Wendy, Yvonne, and I were afraid that Ed's boyfriend, Robert, would hurt him. We kept urging him to leave him, but Ed laughed us off. He rationalized his father's and Robert's behaviors by believing that, somehow, both were his fault. If he only had done something differently, his father would not have been upset; it stood to reason that now, if he did something differently, Robert would surely change. It flashed through my mind that I was always trying to make Jim happy, and that I thought that, if only I tried harder, he would love me. Jim never hit me, but I felt bruised inside.

But nothing changed for any of us in the Uptown, Downtown group, and life continued at the "Not Beauty School."

The school year moved quickly from winter into spring. My Uptown, Downtown friends came over for dinner most Friday nights before they went out partying. They hung out with John, trimming his hair, playing music on the turntable that Jim left behind along with his collection of records, and building Lego projects while I prepared the food. We talked about next steps: I was looking at professional spaces to rent and had one in mind on West 44th Street between Ninth and Tenth Avenues.

"Can you believe it's on the same street as Jim's agent?"

"I know. I bet it's a sign," Ed said, and we all laughed.

Wendy was hoping to go to a summer class at the School of Visual Arts and to keep working at La Boîte.

Yvonne was singing with two other women most weekends, and they were hoping to audition at some clubs in the Village.

Ed was going to spend the summer on Fire Island, and, "you know, get serious about modeling in the fall."

On the last day of school—after reviewing what to expect on the written and practical parts of the state board exam that we'd take the following Monday—we were dismissed early. I went to meet John at school, and we took the bus home together. We hadn't seen Jim in several weeks: he'd told us he was going to California for the month to check out acting options. As John and I were getting on the elevator in our apartment building, our neighbor— whose daughter Leah babysat for us sometimes—joined us. He was also an actor.

"I saw Jim at an audition downtown last week," he said. "Sorry to hear you guys are splitting up. Leah is around if you need help."

I hesitated a couple of seconds, more than a little surprised that Jim had been in the city only the week before. "Thanks," I finally said, "but I think we're good. My mother is coming for a while." My mother was going to be my client at the state board exam, and then I planned that John and I would show her around New York and visit John's school.

John didn't say anything until he and I were in our apartment, the door closed behind us. "Why did Dad say he was going away and then stopped coming to see me?" he asked.

"I don't know, sweetheart. You'll have to ask him the next time you see him." Quite unexpectedly, I started to cry. I felt as if I had been beaten, as if those inside bruises were now raw and swollen.

We sat on the couch. John put his arm around me and said, "Mom, don't cry. Everything will be okay. You've got me, and Gramma's coming."

We got through the first half of the weekend, and I was glad when my mother arrived on Sunday.

On Monday, Yvonne, Wendy, and I met at the examination location along with our brave volunteers. As a surprise for Ed, the three of us had decided to dress in stylish clothes, wash and blow-dry our hair, and wear makeup. We looked around, but couldn't find him, so we found three stations together. I was still uneasy about the finger wave, but I followed Ed's advice and put lots of wave lotion on my mother's thick, tawny hair before sculpting the S-wave. The instructors wandered around the room, stopping frequently to watch each of us execute one of the required techniques. Except for giving my mother a small burn on her forehead with my curling iron when I rolled a section of hair away from her hairline, it seemed as if I did well. Thankfully, my mother didn't complain. In fact, she was wonderful throughout the whole process, no doubt being thrilled to be a small part of the kind of the school of her dreams.

When we had finished, Yvonne, Wendy, and I laughed and joked about making it through the school year together while we packed up our professional cases with the tools of our trade.

That's when Mr. Bruno, a friend of Ed's from school whose last name I never remembered, came over to us.

"Did you hear about Ed? He died on Saturday. Sounds like an overdose. He and his partner were fighting. That's all I know."

I was stunned, the noise in the exam room faded into the background. Sorrow enveloped me.

Bruno said that he and some friends were going to organize a service for Ed, and that he'd let us know when it was happening.

Then Yvonne, Wendy, and I held each other, crying, while we said our good-byes and agreed to stay in touch.

My mother and I took an uptown bus to the Steiner School to surprise John. I leaned my face against the bus window, quietly crying as I thought about how much I had learned at the Robert Fiance School of Beauty and how unexpected my lessons really had been.

Then I remembered Ed reminding us to never cry if we were wearing mascara.

"It isn't pretty," he'd said. "Really! So just don't do it."

16

Calendula

*M*Y NEW YORK STATE cosmetology license arrived on Friday, June 29, 1984, John's tenth birthday, and a year after I'd told Jim that I was leaving him. After sixteen hundred hours of attending the "not beauty school" and passing both the written and practical examinations, I was legally able to operate a business in New York State.

Wendy, Yvonne, and I went to a memorial service for Ed at a Catholic church in Greenwich Village the same day my license arrived. They had just received theirs, too. Ed's body had been returned to his family in Norwalk for the funeral. His friend Bruno from the Robert Fiance School had attended the services at the church in Connecticut and had organized the memorial service for his friends in New York. We cried and laughed as his motley group of friends shared stories about beautiful "Ed not Eddy." The three of us glared at his boyfriend, Robert, as we walked past him, confident that Robert could have prevented Ed's untimely death.

We stopped at a café for lunch and toasted our handsome spirit brother one last time over a glass of chilled white wine. I realized how much of a family the group had become for me during the last ten months; hopefully, we would remain friends. I told them of my summer plan to visit my friend Willemijn from the Steiner School. Though Willemijn and I had continued to stay in touch, I had seen her only twice since she had moved — once when Suzi and I had visited after my first trip to WALA, the second time the previous summer when Willemijn stayed with me at my mother's house in Newport when she'd come to the United States to hear a friend play in a jazz concert at one of the Newport mansions. When I told her I'd be going to WALA for another training, she invited me to visit with John, and then leave him with her and her children while I was in Germany. They would drive to Switzerland to her family cottage in the mountains and return to Amsterdam when I was finished at WALA. It seemed like a terrific plan; in fact, we would leave on Monday, right after the weekend.

John was excited to be flying to see his friend, and I was happy that he'd visit Willemijn's family, see a little of Amsterdam, and hike in the Swiss Alps. Jim had reemerged in mid-June with apologies and excuses for why he hadn't contacted us for several weeks. As always, I was very forgiving. Slowly I was realizing that leaving him was not an event but a long, painful process. He was encouraging about our upcoming trip and offered to drive us to JFK. When the time arrived, he picked up my new-old 1979 Honda Civic from the garage in Spanish Harlem and met us outside our apartment.

John looked very grown up in his new jeans, a black baseball cap with a bright red B on the front (even as a New Yorker, he remained a Red Sox fan), the new, still-stiff hiking boots that I'd given him for his birthday, and his backpack secure over his shoulders. He was definitely ready for our big adventure. When Jim picked him up and swung him around, John laughed and looked like a happy, carefree little boy again. Then Jim surprised him with a brand-new yellow Walkman and a cassette of Bruce Springsteen's *Born in the U.S.A.* Jim's joy was contagious, and I was grateful that he was back in John's life. However, my heart ached as I wondered why it couldn't always be like that, the three of us together, ready for the journey ahead.

Willemijn, Marijn, and Linde were waiting for us after we exited the plane, weary but happy, and made our way through customs and baggage claim amidst the sounds of several different languages at Schiphol Airport. The boys quickly fell in together and took turns listening to John's Walkman and climbing trees in the garden behind the house. They lived very close to a park where we walked several times a day while the children rode bikes alongside us. Willemijn made waffles topped with whipped cream and prepared new curry recipes; she and I drank cup after cup of tea and caught up on our lives. She assured me that John would be loved and well cared for while I was at WALA for the next two weeks. John also told me not to worry, that he would be careful hiking in the mountains. Finally, I said good-bye and was able to relax and enjoy the almost seven-hour train ride, while gazing out the window at the unfamiliar landscape, reviewing my notes, and drinking strong coffee served with a *Banketstaaf*—a sweet Dutch pastry filled with almond paste.

When an associate from the export department at WALA picked me up at the train station in Stuttgart, the weather was warm and sunny. I was very excited about the upcoming training and eager to meet the international community of esthetic trainers and sales associates from around the world. On the drive to the Hotel Panorama, which was about a one-mile walk to WALA, I learned that, although I would be in an intensive training with the international trainers, I would also have the opportunity to harvest calendula during the week if I didn't mind getting up very early. I was thrilled to learn that my request had been heard. Another American was also staying at the hotel—a man named Charles from Houston, Texas, where his family owned an apothecary called the Chemist Shoppe that carried the full range of Dr. Hauschka Skin Care. Charles was scheduled to join me in the garden to harvest alongside the gardeners and the head of the plant laboratory.

There was a welcoming dinner at WALA soon after I checked into the hotel. I met all the esthetic trainers and sales associates who would be part of several or all of the workshops and lectures that I'd attend. Five of the trainers were also staying at the Panorama, and I was grateful to discover that they all spoke English. I was eager to train and become an authorized trainer for WALA , but I was also very pleased that, during the next several mornings, Charles and I would have the opportunity to harvest calendula at sunrise before the dew dried. I had requested to spend time in the garden as well as learn to be a trainer during the on that trip. I had no idea that I would never forget my morning harvesting calendula with Charles.

"Let's jump from the balcony in your room," Charles said to me as we stood alone at 4:40 a.m. in the lobby of the Panorama Hotel. It already felt hot even though it was still dark. We were due at the WALA garden between 5:15 and 5:30 a.m., and I didn't want to be late. After all, the company took its flowers seriously.

Of the twenty-five participants who had come from all over Europe, the USA, Australia, and New Zealand for the two-week training, only Charles and I were going to the morning harvest. But the front door of our hotel was locked; we couldn't get out. We tiptoed around the entire first floor through the dining room, conference rooms, and reception office, but there was no one to help us, and all the doors were locked.

I was excited to join the others and eager to learn as much as possible about how the products were made, which included understanding the plants, their properties, and the growing methods employed. It was also fun to be with Charles. He was about my age, mid-thirties, and single. He looked like a cross between Richard Burton and Rudolf Nureyev, with dark brown, wavy hair, and Alpine-pool green eyes. My excitement, however, was quickly turning to anxiety as I thought of being the American who didn't make it to the garden on time.

Charles looked at me, looked at his watch, and said, "I don't think it's that far to jump."

We climbed the stairs to the first floor, which Americans consider the second floor. In Germany the ground floor is what Americans call the first floor. I unlocked my door with the enormous brass key the size of a small sparrow, which in German is called *der Schlüssel*. Charles followed me into my room. We stood quietly in an awkward moment of silence, looking around the space. My white silk nightgown was thrown on the floor on top of the clothes I'd worn the day before—a three-tiered denim skirt and sheer pink peasant blouse that I'd taken off very late and dropped unconsciously beside my bed. There were books, a candle, bottles of essential oils on the bedside table, and a picture of John that I carried wherever I went.

Charles took me by the shoulders and headed me toward the balcony door. He pulled aside the natural linen curtain panel and stepped out onto the small wood structure that big enough for a small table and two tiny chairs. Below us was a well-constructed compost pile, a beautifully maintained tomato patch, and a row of brussels sprouts. There were small heads of lettuce growing in the shade of the tomatoes and arugula, the same leafy greens that I'd recently discovered for soups and salads. They were quite exotic compared with the iceberg lettuce of my childhood.

From the balcony, we could see lights aglow in the adjoining building where the chef and his wife lived and cooked for the hotel. Across the garden, several chickens and a rooster pecked at the rich brown loam, catching the early worms.

"See? It's not that far to jump. Here, I'll go first," Charles said as he swung one leg then the other over the railing onto the thin ledge, and then jumped down to the ground. "Come on I'll catch you!"

I followed his lead and held onto the rungs of the balcony, and then, when I felt his arms encircle my thighs, I let go. It happened so quickly that my only thought was relief that my legs were still tanned from a recent weekend at Second Beach in Newport, and that my white linen cargo shorts were clean.

By the time we were both safely on the ground, we realized that we still had to climb over the garden fence. We started to laugh, and the chickens started clucking, the rooster started crowing louder than I've ever heard one crow. Then a dog started barking as he ran around the small yard that surrounded the garden. Then, as Charles helped me climb over the fence, the door to the kitchen flew open; we started running toward the road. The chef was waving a knife and yelling at us. Then he abruptly stopped. I heard him say to the woman who had followed him out into the yard, *"Die Amerikaner, verrückten Amerikaner."* Apparently, he'd recognized us.

"I think *verrückten* means crazy," I said to Charles as we hurried, laughing, along the road past the hotel and toward Eckwälden, the adjoining village where WALA and the gardens waited.

The narrow road was wide enough for a tractor but barely for a car, even a small European model. It stretched between lush meadows, apple orchards, grazing sheep, and a quaint shuttered cottage that reminded me of the home where Snow White lived with the Seven Drafts. We ran most of the way but still arrived thirty minutes late. About eight people were already spread out among rows of golden calendula plants; they wore straw hats and had baskets attached to their waists by leather straps. It looked like a mix between a photo shoot for Smith and Hawken garden tools and a painting by Turner. I was deeply moved by the beauty of the moment and was determined to catch up with the others, who had been harvesting since sunrise.

Charles and I found the belted baskets and hand shears on a large wooden table in the garden shed where the tools were stored and the workers shared meals. I headed toward a row of calendula—the orange-gold flowers that were still shaded by a stand of hawthorn trees—and started to cut the blossoms as quickly as possible. The others in the garden moved slowly, exchanging occasional words that blended with the sounds of birds chirping as they darted among the trees and landed in the tall grasses around the small pond. As I became lost in my task, I thought about the story of calendulas and how the botanist said they're often called the "pharmacy of Europe" due to their extensive use in skin care products and as topical treatments. At WALA, active ingredients are only one piece of a plant's profile. The story of the plant is also considered important.

Calendulas are sun-like marigolds whose blossoms follow the course of the sun: they open at daybreak and close as soon as the sun goes down. It's believed that this calendar-like movement in time with the sun is what led botanists to give the plant its scientific name from the Latin *calendae*—the first of the month. Because of its odor, which is both aromatic and reminiscent of decay, it became a symbol of redemption after death in Christian mythology. Its inexhaustible vegetative growth also caused it to become a symbol of eternal life, and people often planted it on graves as funeral flowers. In Mexico, it is also considered a flower of death, believed to have originated from the blood of the Indians slain by the Spanish conquerors. In the Middle Ages the flower was called *Solis Sponsa*—bride of the sun—and was dedicated to the Germanic goddess Freya, later to the Christian Mary, hence the name Marigold, Mary's Gold.

I loved hearing the stories; the history of the flowers made me feel more connected than ever to the earth and the garden. Among the most fascinating tales was that plants that flower at the most important points in the course of the sun, and whose shapes resemble the sun, have always been considered sacred. Included in that group are the daisy, St. John's wort, and chicory. As a magical plant, marigold was an essential part of any love charm. The legend was that, if a girl planted or sowed the *"Nie-welk-blume"* in the footprints of her loved one, he would have to—whether he wanted to or not—come to her forever. I smiled to myself and stuffed a calendula flower into my pocket in case I ever needed a love charm. In Spain, sorcerers were convinced of its magical powers and carried it with them as a talisman. I thought about the death and loss in my life during the last several years and was definitely ready for some healing, magic, and new starts.

Suddenly, Mr. Salinger, the head of the plant laboratory, quietly appeared at my side. Inwardly I was thinking, "I bet he's going to compliment me because I'm going so fast and filling my basket with beautiful flowers." Instead he held one of the flowers from his basket in his hand and pointed to the blossom whose petals were unfurling as we watched. "This is good to harvest; they are opening, waking up." He then picked a flower from my basket and showed it to me. "This is still closed. Better to wait until it begins to open." I could see exactly what he meant. The flowers I was harvesting were tightly closed around the calyx. He smiled and added, "Sometimes bees that can't get back to their hive land on calendula flowers and spend the night protected as the flowers close them in safely for the night." I thanked him and took my wounded pride farther down the row where the sun was warming the flowers awake.

At 8:30 a bell sounded. I followed the others to the garden shed for a "second breakfast"—strong coffee, enormous freshly baked pretzels, and fresh butter from the local WALA farm. The coworkers who had been so quiet in the garden were eager to practice their English with us and learn more about us and the American market. They were surprised and pleased that we had risen so early to help harvest the plants "before the dew dries." Between answering questions, I sipped coffee sweetened with honey from the WALA bees and lightened with fresh cream. During a lull in the conversation, I related the adventure of Charles and me jumping from the balcony, upsetting the chef, and running the distance to the garden.

"Don't you have *einen Schlüssel*, ah, you say *key*, to the hotel?" a young woman asked.

"Yes, we have room keys, but the outside door was locked."

One of the gardeners laughed a little and said, "The key is for your room and also for the front door."

I started to laugh, too, and the whole group joined in. I glanced over at Charles, who was scanning the landscape of young women, and I realized then that he reminded me of someone. He reminded me of Jim. Not his looks, but his charm. He was also a little dangerous like Jim, and not someone that I would be jumping from any balconies with again.

I still thought of Jim often, how much he'd appreciate hearing about this training, and how I would appreciate telling him about my adventure with Charles. Even after a year since our break the summer before, I still held hope that he would change his lifestyle, and we would be together but better than before.

After the second breakfast, the morning harvest ended for the day, I went to the training for international educators, and Charles joined the one for sales and production. He and I were together when both groups met to hear speakers, but we were never alone together again. Later in the week, I was told that he'd left early, having been inspired to go on a spontaneous adventure with a new friend he'd met while he'd been en route to Germany. I appreciated our spontaneous morning adventure and was grateful we'd arrived at the garden in time to harvest calendula. But I'd had too many responsibilities most of my life to be spontaneous; I'd tried living spontaneously with Jim, and ultimately it had only led to more responsibility.

This trip was another turning point for me in a spiral between WALA, my work in New York, my life with John, and being less enmeshed with Jim. My star continued to rise at the company, and since I'd become licensed in New York to practice skin care, I was now officially acknowledged as an authorized trainer for the United States. This training with the international community of esthetic trainers was an amazing experience. There were ten of us in the group, plus the new trainer, who had replaced Frau Hahn when she retired, and two assistants. We gave and received a treatment each day from a different participant, thus giving us the opportunity to experience different skin conditions and feel different healing hands. We focused on how to use the products for different skin conditions such as acne, rosacea, and menopausal skin. We also learned how to use color light therapy during a treatment: we practiced shining blue light on someone with rosacea to calm the redness during the mask application, and shining red light over the abdomen of someone who had acne while applying a clay mask—the concept was that red stimulated the metabolism, which was sluggish in an acne condition. We laughed when the trainer innocently used the "red-light district" as an example of how stimulating red is for the metabolism.

In addition to learning more procedures to use in my soon-to-be studio and to teach them to estheticians in the United States, I enjoyed getting to know the International trainers. It was inspiring and comforting to be part of this community. When not in class, we took walks together or, with one or two others, sketched plants in the garden, and shared our biographies over dinner. We exchanged addresses and phone numbers and open invitations to visit if any of us were in a country where a trainer lived. We hugged teary-eyed on the last day and were consoled by the knowledge that we'd be together again the following summer at the annual Training for Trainers.

The train ride from Stuttgart to Amsterdam helped me transition from the sadness of leaving new friends at WALA to my happy reunion with John.

Willemijn and the children met me at the train station. John was glowing with health and could hardly contain his excitement

about hiking in the Alps. I felt so grateful that he'd had such a
rich opportunity. It saddened me that he was an only child; having
him spend time with Marijn and his sister doing wholesome, fun
activities was comforting to both of us. John didn't like the fact,
though, that the he'd had to wrap a long cord around his waist
that Willemijn held tightly on narrow paths because he knew he
"wouldn't slip"—he was "such a good hiker." He happily related
how each morning he and Marijn went to the local farmer where
the farmer's mother filled their pail with fresh milk for the day;
he proudly added that the farmer guided his herd to the high
meadows in the summer to graze, and then down to lower fields in
the autumn: "That way the cows don't overgraze the meadows."

We had a great weekend together before John and I flew
back to New York. We agreed that if possible we would return
the following summer when I returned to WALA for continuing
education. When we said good-bye, I couldn't help crying. I
missed Willemijn. It went without saying that she'd been an angel
of light for us during our early days in New York.

When John and I arrived home, Jim was waiting for
us outside the baggage area. John raced into his arms; Jim
picked him up and twirled him around. On the ride back to the
apartment, John shared his hiking stories—making each trail
higher, narrower, and more dangerous—and his adventures
riding around Amsterdam on a tram. Then he fell asleep in the
back seat. I told Jim about the wonderful training, the calendula
adventure, and how great my time with Willemijn had been. He
said that nothing much was new in his life—"The theater is pretty
quiet in the summer." He unloaded our bags in the lobby of 260
Riverside Drive and said good-bye. I never asked anymore when
we'd see him again.

As John and I took the elevator up to the eighth floor to
unpack and settle in, I remembered the story about calendula.

It has robust and prolific growth, and at the same time it has a slightly decaying aroma. Symbolically, it is connected to life but also to death. I felt the paradox of parts of my life dying as new parts were becoming. I also thought of the lore of calendula being the love charm, and I was glad I had known not to toss calendula petals on Jim's path as he'd walked away.

— 17 —

My Refrigerator Isn't Sexy Anymore

HE PROFESSIONAL SPACE that I rented on West 44th Street between Ninth and Tenth Avenues in September 1984 was ideal—it even had a garden. Coincidentally, as I'd told my beauty school pals, it was on the same block as Jim's theatrical agents, Hogan and Hogan. I kept holding on to these sprinklings of connections to Jim. Leaving had been a long, painful process and not one that could be accomplished in a single phone call when I'd been emboldened by a romance with someone else.

The rental was a ground level walk-through of a three-story brownstone owned by a woman named Sue. She told me she'd lived there her whole life with her parents, both of whom had died—her father more recently. He had been a doctor and had used the space for his practice, while the family had lived upstairs.

The front room was filled with sunlight that streamed through barred windows. Sue said she'd just completed renovations.

I quickly determined that the room would be a perfect location for Warren to see patients two days a week. Because I had continued to see him as a doctor after our personal relationship had ended, and I'd mentioned that I'd been looking at spaces to rent, he'd suggested that we share an office where he could see clients on a part-time basis while continuing with his practice in New Jersey. After two months of screening possible rentals, I knew this was it.

"I need to find the right tenants," Sue added. "I'm a librarian, and I work all day. It would be good to have someone here when I'm away. You know, to keep it safe."

I assured her that someone would be there every day. "I'll also hold trainings on some weekends, but we'll be very quiet when you're home."

Then she showed me a translucent door that optimized a sense of light in the windowless room. "I had the contractor install this retractable screen door between this room and the ones in the back to make the space versatile," she said.

We moved to a third room that looked out on a rather large garden: it was perfect. I would be able to close it off to use as a treatment room, then open the screen divider when I needed my large packing table to double as a surface for a classroom.

We continued walking through a corridor that connected the three rooms and led to a bathroom, which had a second door leading to a small hallway and out to the garden.

My excitement escalated as we stepped outside. "Would it be okay if we sat in the garden during nice weather?" I asked. "After clients have a treatment, it would be wonderful if they could spend a few minutes in nature before having to reenter the city."

Sue shuffled around the unkempt garden beds in old slippers and a faded cotton dress that tented her large body.

"I could clean up the garden and plant herbs and annuals," I quickly added. "It would be so amazing to have access to a garden in the city." The space and my enthusiasm grew as we paced the area. I imagined lavender and thyme spilling over the paths. Maybe even rosemary could winter over if I planted it in the sunniest corner at the north end of the garden, close enough to the foundation so the building could protect the tender perennial from harsh winds. I could have a parade of annuals: beginning with pansies in early spring; then petunias, portulaca, and geraniums celebrating summer; and end in the fall with chrysanthemums.

"You can do whatever you want," Sue said. "I don't have the time or energy for gardens; I hardly ever come out here. We stopped planting anything after Mother died."

"Oh, I can make this really beautiful. I used to work at an herb garden. And you'll have a window view." I pointed up at the windows.

Sue was a little bewildered about natural skin care, esthetic trainings, and treatments, but she seemed pleased that the products I used were named after a doctor. She was especially happy that a "real doctor"—Warren—would be signing the lease with me.

Warren came to see the space and agreed it was great, so we signed the lease. I moved the shipping and training supplies back into the city from New Jersey. It was the first Dr. Hauschka center in the country.

I hung a brass plaque at the entrance that read: Dr. Hauschka Skin Care Center; I naively adopted the brand name as my business name, and my identity gradually merged with Dr. Hauschka's. Some people actually thought I *was* Dr. Hauschka. The importer and WALA applauded my accomplishment, and my bond to the company continued to grow.

I also promoted Warren's classes on homeopathic first aid to my clients and friends. Several times a year, he offered a series for ten consecutive Wednesday evenings: as a result, many of my clients and friends ended up seeing him as a doctor; several of them also dated him for brief, intensive times, until he decided they weren't a good match for him. It seemed strange to me that he dated so many of his patients, but it made for colorful gossip for my close friends who were seeing him only as a doctor.

I was convinced that, between homeopathy and Anthroposophic homecare such as Dr. Hauschka treatments, elixirs, skin care, and a diet of organic and biodynamically grown food, people could take their health into their own hands. When I asked Warren to tell his patients about the open houses I held on natural skin care and the importance of nutrition, he told me that people only needed constitutional homeopathy—that everything else was superfluous. "When people learn to follow their intuition after being treated homeopathically, they will make healthy decisions about their needs," he said with his usual pompous majesty.

The irony of my situation wasn't lost on me. But, as with Jim's talent as an actor, Warren's gift as a physician trumped my confidence for a while.

Still, it was a dynamic time in my life. Sales steadily grew, word was out about the "Hauschka Treatment," and clients arrived on foot, by taxi, and several in limousines. I loved giving the treatment that I had experienced at WALA, and I strived to make it as healing for my clients as it was for me. The center soon became a unique oasis in the city. People expressed that they felt renewed. They became committed to bringing rhythm into their lives with meditation, therapeutic bathes, and essential oils. All was well in my world.

My education continued as I studied homeopathic first aid with Warren and holistic dermatology with another doctor in the city. I also continued to attend all Anthroposophic medical conferences and training at WALA every summer. Estheticians, massage therapists, managers from health stores in New York, as well as other Dr. Hauschka distributors and sales representatives, reached out to me for trainings. I was stretched into many roles and juggled my professional life with trying to be a good parent.

Karen (a friend of my best friend, Suzi), who was married to an actor friend of Jim's, started to work for me. She filled orders and organized trainings, scheduled my appointments, helped with in-store demos, and entered the *Hauschka Vortex*, as I called it. She began seeing Warren as a doctor.

Linda, a client who came for regular treatments and to purchase products, was deeply touched by the principles, products, and philosophy of the company that manufactured the brand. She offered to assist in the esthetic trainings and workshops that I offered the public. She also succumbed to Warren's charm and started treatment with him.

Karen, Linda, and I became fast friends as we spent most weekdays together at the center.

In November of that year, soon after I opened the center, Suzi and Doug—John's and my second family—moved to Northampton, Massachusetts, with their daughter, my goddaughter, Deirdre. They had been a big reason that I had felt confident about moving to the city in the first place. After they were gone, John and I felt like orphans. We missed sharing dinners together several times a week, visiting Suzi at her office in Central Park, watching films with them on my new VCR, and going to the park together on the weekends. Whenever I had a date, John had spent the night with them. And Doug always made pancakes for Sunday breakfast.

Now we spent nights and weekends alone, except for Jim's occasional drop-in and the Saturday sports programs that I enrolled John in. Although John loved school and I loved my business, there was a big emptiness in my heart and soul. I felt as if I was always running to keep up: to get home by 4:00 p.m. so John wouldn't be alone after school; to park our car in a garage on 109th Street so it wouldn't get vandalized, and then jog home a mile to try and escape getting mugged; to drive John to Newport for school holidays and to camps and back to my mother's house after camp during the summer. I desperately wanted to find someone to love who wanted to be in a lasting relationship and who would be comfortable with the fact that I had a son. On several long weekends, John and I went to visit Suzi, Doug, and Deirdre at the farmhouse they were renting in Northampton. Life outside the city looked peaceful: I felt lucky to have a getaway where we had close friends. Suzi and I even talked about John and me maybe moving there someday. But the reality was that our lives were solidly in New York.

In the summer of 1986, Karen, Linda, and I decided to have an open house celebration at the Hauschka center on the Fourth of July weekend. Warren was on board with the idea and agreed to pay 40 percent of the expenses if we did all the work. We invited all our clients, Warren's patients, my friends from the Steiner School and some from the Robert Fiance School of Beauty, and any single men we could think of. Linda was eager to meet someone, and, though I was dating a very nice man, he just wasn't "the one."

Soon after we'd moved into the office, our landlady, Sue, had retired. She seemed to now live a little vicariously through our goings-on at the center, and she quickly gave us her approval for the event. As a special touch to the invitations, we had a picture of the Statue of Liberty on the cover and added some gold-glitter bling to the patina of Lady Liberty's stately robe.

My single, handsome next-door neighbor at 260 Riverside Drive played the accordion in a Klezmer band with his childhood friend, a clarinetist from Israel. They agreed to provide live background music. I bought all the current Madonna, Paul Simon, and Steve Winwood CDs to play before and after the Klezmer music. As Karen, Linda, and I arranged organic food platters and wine and hung strings of lights around the garden, we loudly sang *Higher Love*, filling the air with what we hoped were good vibes.

The party was a great success: over sixty people dropped in to celebrate with us before they slipped into the New York night for a late dinner or another party. I went home alone.

That year, John was away for most of the summer at a camp in the Adirondacks and also spending time with his best friend at his friend's grandparents' house close to the camp. Except for one parents' weekend when I saw him for an afternoon, we were apart for eight weeks. After the party, which I'd planned as a celebration of things to come, the thought of moving out of the city began to surface more frequently.

Though Jim and I had been separated for three years, he still came and went in and out of my life. Because he sometimes spent time with John after school when I was at work, he'd kept his key to the apartment. Since he still didn't have his own place, I often prepared meals for him and John. I left them alone, hoping it would prevent John from feeling he had lost his father.

Interestingly, Jim tried to remain connected to me even when John was away. He was, as it turned out, still living with the wannabe-actress with whom he'd been having an affair when our relationship imploded. Yet he had continued to deny any serious commitment to her and maintained that he was staying with different friends on different couches. I eventually found out he had been lying and that he had not been sleeping on anyone's couch but hers for the last three years.

Although our twelve-year kind-of-marriage had been tumultuous, it was almost impossible for me to leave Jim once and for all. He was like a drug to me. My identity was so bound up with him that, even after three years of separation, I still second-guessed myself, thinking maybe I could have tried harder. I still secretly hoped that a miracle would happen, that Jim would become a responsible, committed partner, and we could be a happy family.

He gave me just enough attention for me to think my fantasy might be possible. He often appeared at my door with gifts—tickets to the theater or a book he knew I would appreciate. He frequently stopped by my office for products or just to visit. The most telling gift was the book he gave me titled *The Green Snake and the Beautiful Lily*, by Goethe. It is a tale of magical transformation about crossing a river and building a bridge from one's inner soul life to the outer world—a challenging task, though the book claims that everyone can experience it when the time is right for them.

In this situation, however, the book was merely a prop for J. T., the actor, a prop that sent a subliminal message to me that said: "See, we're bound by something deep and profound. We have a spiritual connection." Jim had led me to my spiritual path, Anthroposophy, but then dropped me off at the door and encouraged me from the sidelines. I dove completely into the study and practice of it, believing that he would take the journey with me. I wanted both the gift of Anthroposophy and the giver. But *that* Jim existed only in my own fairy tale, the one I was still enmeshed in.

(My near-death experience in 1980 during the unsuccessful delivery of Lily had left no doubt in my mind about the reality of a spiritual world. Thirty-seven years later, I can still recall the experience of being out of my physical body and connected to a world of warmth, light, and a familiar, invisible presence beside me.)

Students of Anthroposophy know well the fairy tale of the Green Snake; I knew Jim had used it to keep me emotionally hooked into him. He was, after all, a brilliant actor both on and off stage. But because I was finally dating again and slowly (albeit painfully) working on accepting that there would be life after him, I felt less vulnerable around him. Still, I had to establish internal boundaries.

Whenever Jim dropped by unexpectedly, even when John wasn't home, he had a habit of prowling through the refrigerator, eating leftovers, and examining the contents as though they would resolve some mystery of life.

During that summer of 1986, I had cleaned out the refrigerator and bought only what I most wanted to eat. When I opened the door, the cool, white, uncluttered space reminded me of the numerous sparse art galleries in SoHo that I'd explored. The groceries I bought included a cobalt blue glass bottle of water, a heritage tomato, two slightly bruised but unsprayed peaches, and farm-fresh eggs from the Farmers Market on Amsterdam Avenue. In addition, a twenty-dollar bottle of Pouilly Fuissé created a dialogue with expensive French cheese from Fairway Market, smoked salmon, 88 percent dark chocolate from Zabar's on Broadway, and leftover cold sesame noodles from the Hunan Balcony. I'd arranged and rearranged the contents as if it were a still life, a painting of a life I was struggling to create.

Living alone that summer was especially difficult, but, when not at my center, I filled the days: I sent care packages and letters to John at camp; I rebounded on a small trampoline to Madonna CDs that I'd kept after the party; I jogged in Riverside Park. One of the men I was seeing wanted to get married, but I wasn't ready. We did spend a lot of time together, and he eventually felt comfortable enough to open my refrigerator and serve himself.

"You know, your refrigerator is kind of sexy," he told me one day. "I've never met anyone like you. Who buys water because they like the color blue of the bottle, or cares about eggs and how the chickens that lay them are treated? Yeah, it's kind of sexy." It made me smile and helped me forget some of my sadness to think of my refrigerator as a sexy still life.

Soon after I'd purged my temperature-controlled masterpiece, Jim stopped by. It was a hot August afternoon; I ushered him into the apartment, and as we walked through the taxi-cab yellow living room, he threw his baseball cap onto the sofa, slid his Danish School Bag from his shoulder, and dropped it next to his hat. I often wondered but never asked what had happened to the leather backpack that I had given him for Christmas the year I discovered I was pregnant with John. He headed to the kitchen. There was a letter on the table from John, which I had left out to read to Jim.

Dear Mom,

Please send me some real candy and soda, not the stuff from The Good Earth. *It's fun here. Eli knows lots of kids because he's been coming for a long time. Sometimes I'm lonely. The silk powder and rosemary ointment you sent healed the cracks between my toes, and everybody in my cabin uses it now. Can you send more? I missed you after parents weekend. Will Dad come visit me? I hope you aren't mad at each other anymore. Do you think*

*he'll take me to a baseball game when I get home? We're playing
basketball this week and it's fun. Wish we played it at Steiner and
not just soccer in the park. Please write to me. I get more letters
than anyone in my group—and send more treats.*

Love,

John West

"I think it's so funny he signs his letters John West, not just
John," I said to Jim. "I'm so glad he's out of the city for eight
weeks, playing with lots of kids. Thanks for helping me pay
for camp."

"Why doesn't he write to me?" Jim asked. He opened the
refrigerator, stooped down and gazed into it.

"Probably because I packed ten self-addressed, stamped
envelopes with notepaper to make it easy for him. If you have an
address, I'll tell him to write to you there if you want." I knew he
didn't want to admit that he was living with his girlfriend, and I
wanted to make him squirm.

I lingered near the sink, standing behind him, watching as he
peered into the refrigerator, silently getting his bearings in the
new terrain. He turned back and looked at me as he ran his left
hand through his long, sandy blond hair. He lit a Marlboro and
took a slow drag, as though the cigarette provided fresh country
air. Then he looked back into the cool interior.

"Hmm, there's no marmalade!" he said. His shoulders
slumped as he closed the door.

After his last visit, I had consciously forced myself not
to replace the classic white jar with black lettering of Dundee
Orange Marmalade, Jim's favorite. He had finished the last jar
by dipping his fingers into the sticky sweetness and spreading it

onto a piece of bread that he'd ripped from a loaf of artisan bread lying on the counter. He hadn't bothered to clean up his crumbs.

Now empty-handed, he turned and stood beside me near the sink. He abruptly jerked on the cold spigot, doused his cigarette butt, and leaned down to drink from the cold water, letting it run long after he was finished. (People who knew him accepted this habit as one of his eccentricities.) The room had grown silent, except for the trickle of the running water and the ever-present sound of sirens on the street below. I turned off the faucet.

Close to tears, feeling guilty, petty, and smug all at the same time, I doubted myself again. I had a momentary mental battle about whether to buy or not to buy marmalade in the future. But deep in my gut, I knew it was too late. It had taken courage on my part not to buy any. He and I both knew it was a significant gesture.

I turned away and stepped toward the window to look at the pie-sliver glimpse of the Hudson River, fearful that I would get angry or sad if I spoke.

He moved beside me, our shoulders barely touching. Then he lit another cigarette and sighed. "Suze," he said, "you didn't make a mistake leaving me. It was the best thing."

I was unsure where this was going. He stood, staring out the window toward the brick wall of the adjoining wing of the building. I could hear him take deep breaths as he inhaled cigarette smoke.

"I'm an alcoholic," he said, barely audibly.

I felt dizzy, stunned, unsure that I had heard him correctly. I stepped back, feeling like he was conning me.

"What do you mean, an alcoholic?" I asked, almost laughing.

"It means I can't stop drinking. I can't stop anything—the drugs, the sex, all of it. All those nights when I didn't come home, I drank, got stoned, and went home with whoever was left drinking with me."

It seemed unreal to me. How could I not have known this? At the time, I'd thought: *He's just irresponsible. He just doesn't want to be with us.* But now I didn't know what to do, so I sat down at the table. I was tired of fighting with him, tired of trying to figure him out, and too tired to speak.

"You should get help, join a support group," he added. "There's one for the family of alcoholics."

"*I* should get help?" I asked in a defensive and agitated tone, as I slapped my hand against my heart.

"Yeah, at least think about it. I'm going to check into a clinic in Minnesota, so I won't be seeing you and John for a while. It might be for a couple of months, and then I might move to L.A."

I sat perfectly still at the large butcher-block table that we'd found on the street, but I was reeling on the inside, crumbling, really. He walked over to me and put his hand on my head. I remained still and took deep breaths. Then he left the room quickly and walked out of the apartment. I heard the elevator clang its way up to get him.

I remained seated, quietly crying at the table, in timeless suspension. It felt as if my tears ran down the eight floors of the apartment building and continued down Riverside Drive, where they flowed under the West Side Highway into the Hudson, restoring it to its normal level after a dry spring had left it lower than usual. When I stopped crying, I lit a cigarette from the pack Jim had left behind. The light in the kitchen was fading as the sun moved closer to the horizon. I opened the refrigerator and looked inside. It didn't seem sexy anymore. It just looked empty and sad. As a surge of the unending problems of my life with Jim flooded my heart, I felt like I'd opened Pandora's box.

I took out the container of cold sesame noodles and the bottle of wine. Then I returned to the table. As I sat there smoking, eating the leftovers, and drinking from the bottle, I remembered a story that Jim used to tell me about when he was a child in the 1950s, when he and his family had lived on a military base in Schwäbisch Gmünd, Germany. (Later, we had discovered the interesting fact that Heinz Grotzke, the man who owned Meadowbrook Herb Garden and had asked me to represent Dr. Hauschka Skin Care, had actually lived with his family across the street from the same military base where Jim's family was. It was another of those details we'd thought of as karmic.)

Jim's father was one of the non-military personnel working for the U.S. government to organize the city after the war. The story Jim often told me that bothered him about his father was this: When Jim and his three siblings would leave the house to play on the base, his father waited until they were halfway down the street, then whistled for them to come back. When they did, their father said he'd just wanted to see how far they had gone. He did this several times a day whenever they left the house. His siblings thought it was funny and laughed about it later in life at holiday gatherings when recalling their life in Germany. But Jim harbored anger at his father for this so-called game, and he never really forgave him.

As I sat and reflected on my relationship with Jim, I realized that he always called me back when I was breaking free of him. I was sure it wasn't conscious—but it was definitely the same behavior his father had employed on Jim and his siblings. It was a wound that nagged at him and had made it difficult for him to ever trust anyone. He didn't want to be with me, but he didn't want to completely let me go. He wanted to know how far I had gotten after our relationship ended. That afternoon when he saw there was no marmalade, it was as though I had said to him, "I'm not running back to you just so you can see how far I've gone." I think it freed him to finally tell me the truth that he was an addict. I had yet to learn that alcoholism is a family disease, and that I also was ill.

Although he didn't want to be in a committed relationship with me, Jim was proud of my growing success with Dr. Hauschka. Our mutual friends repeatedly told me that he loved me in his own way, and that he was proud of John and me.

Jim never married again.

Soon after his confession, I heard from a friend that he did go to a clinic for six weeks, and that he'd invited his girlfriend to attend "family week" as his guest. I felt confused, angry, and betrayed all over again. Weren't John and I his family?

I finally realized that I needed to get away from Jim completely, that he really had become my drug of choice.

It was time for me to get out of the city that I had come to love, the city where I had resurrected my life and found material success. It was time to build a new life that was healthy not only for my body but for the rest of me that was dying to emerge. Within weeks I found a house to rent in Amherst, which was just a short drive from Doug and Suzi. I made arrangements with Karen and Linda to take care of my business while I moved and figured out whether I would commute several times a month from Amherst or decide to move my business completely out of Manhattan. I watched VAN GO movers pack up what was left of the past. Then I drove over the George Washington Bridge and headed to pick John up from camp so we could begin our new life. It reminded me of when I'd moved into the city on the day that Pope John II had been visiting and had spoken about finding the soul of New York. This time, though, I was leaving, my soul somewhat black and blue. Maybe I would find hope again at the bottom of my Pandora's box.

18

Moving Into the Unknown

JOHN AND I OFTEN PRETENDED what life would be like if I married someone who didn't make me cry, if we had a house with a yard for a garden, a house where he could have a bike that wouldn't get stolen if he forgot to lock it, where our latest Siamese cat, Sweet Pea, whom we got from a shelter when Miss Dummy died, could go outside, climb trees, and catch mice. Those are the things I talked about when I picked him up from camp and headed north to Amherst. I had found a new yellow ranch house for rent at the top of a small hill in a nice neighborhood where I had already seen several boys his age playing in the street. John would have his own room, not half the living room blocked off by a Japanese screen with a large dirty window that faced a brick wall.

He sat in the front seat holding Sweet Pea, listening to me. Then he told me what was awful about camp and what was pretty good and asked if he could go again next year. We talked and talked about other things. When it seemed that we finally ran out of words, he said: "You mean I'm not going to see my class anymore or get to say good-bye?"

I kept my eyes on the road, not wanting to glance over at him because I feared I would see his disappointment. I took some deep breaths, trying to ease the constricting anxious feeling in my stomach that I felt more and more these days. "We'll go back and stay with Sherri and Eli for a weekend after school starts again," I said. "I talked to Mr. Trostli. He said you could go to school with Eli and spend the day. He also said you could visit the class anytime we're in the city. He's eager to know how you like your new school."

What concerned me most about leaving the city was taking John, now twelve, out of the Rudolf Steiner School at the end of sixth grade and not letting him finish lower school with his class. It had always been a safe haven for him, and I felt it was the best education he could receive. But the Amherst public schools were rated quite high in the country, so that was great. I also hoped he would like to be in a larger class and have more sports opportunities and many clubs and after-school activities available.

But the new house and our adventure apparently didn't disguise John's sense that he'd been abandoned. Or mine.

As we tried to settle into our new environment, we became the odd couple and did everything together. Jim used to call us "Susie and Little Man" when we "went on a new adventure" as I used to tell John when we were trekking off to meet Jim wherever he was. The CB radio Jim had installed in our old Volkswagen had meant we could always find our way back to him. Without Jim as our North Star, I felt that the two of us were lost, rather than on a new adventure. I had to keep reminding myself that this was our new life, and it was filled with new possibilities.

Every weekday morning, I walked John to the school bus stop until he was teased about needing his mother to walk him to school. Most nights either we went to Doug and Suzi's for dinner or they came to our house. I bought a new Honda Prelude with a sunroof and picked out a new bicycle that John could ride on the street or off-road. I took him to the school pool and watched him swim laps during family swim time. My mother came to stay with us and made curtains. The man who thought my refrigerator was sexy when I'd left the city came to visit for the weekend and brought John the latest *Sports Illustrated*.

In a few weeks, we went back to New York so John could visit his class and say good-bye. He missed his school, he missed our funky apartment with the river view, and he missed seeing Jim. I left messages for Jim on his girlfriend's answering machine; I mentioned the move, and I shared our new phone number. We didn't hear from him for six months. By then, I had decided I was not going to be the one who always organized plans so Jim could spend time with his son. If he wanted a relationship with him, he would have to work for it.

John was a very good student and did well scholastically. He played the violin and joined the orchestra. Each day when he came home from school I asked him how it was going. He told me he missed the Steiner culture. He especially didn't like the bells ringing and having to run to another floor to his next class. I continued to check with him every day; eventually he said, "They're not really human beings, Mom. Everyone runs around like robots when the bell rings, and there's lots of pushing."

Luckily, however, he made friends with a boy named Justin who lived on our street. Justin had two brothers, and soon John was spending all his free time at their house. I was grateful because it was a nice family, and John was very welcome in their home. The boys all had dirt bikes and roamed the woods and the open field behind the neighborhood. John was finally having fun playing outside until it was time for dinner and homework.

I continued to ask him about school, hoping he'd begin to like it. One day after my daily inquiry, he said, "Everyone in class laughed at me because I decorated my paper with scrolls and beautiful color around my essays like we did at Steiner, so I just stopped doing that. It isn't so hard anymore."

My heart ached when he told me that. I began to doubt my decision to move. *We can always move back if it doesn't work,* I thought. But what I said to John was, "Let's just give it a year here, and see how it goes."

At the end of September 1986, I left John with Doug, Suzi, and their four-year-old daughter, Deirdre, to go to the Natural Products Exposition in Washington, D.C. Six months before I had decided to leave the city, I'd made plans to attend the Expo. It was a first big step for me to appear at the trade show as a Dr. Hauschka distributor. The goal was to open new accounts in my territory, which included New England and other states not represented by another distributor.

Before heading to D.C., I went to the Dr. Hauschka center in New York and met my colleague Linda, who was helping Karen run the office while I was away. Linda was in Beauty School and practicing the Dr. Hauschka treatment in my treatment room on several of our friends. We loaded the car with products and marketing materials and began our drive south for the four-day event. We caught up on the office gossip about Warren and compared our blank notes about having no men in our lives. Both Linda and I still longed to meet someone, preferably someone who wanted to be in a long-term relationship. In my case, I also wanted someone who would welcome John into his life. I told

Linda that I had recently found an old journal titled *Life after Jim*. In one entry I had written that, in addition to commitment and welcoming John, a man on a spiritual path would be welcome. We laughed hysterically as I recalled the friend of hers whom I dated for a short while who insisted that John and I watch nine hours of *The History of the Jews*. Most recently, in addition to the attributes of commitment and welcoming John, I had added "a God-loving man" to my list. More than once, Linda and I sang *Higher Love* (which had become our unofficial theme song) on the four-hour drive from New York to D.C. in my new Honda Prelude with the sunroof open. It was a relief to be focused on business again and not second-guessing myself about having moved.

After a few hours, we arrived at the venue. We set up the booth with products, posters, a big vase of roses, and pots of fresh herbs; we looked like the sophisticated professionals we wanted to become. Then we walked the floor with trial sizes of Dr. Hauschka's newest cream, called "Rejuvenating Mask," and scoped out our competition, interesting exhibitors—and men.

The Expo was like a small city—a portable city encased in a cavernous convention center, with the promise of being filled with 30,000 people from all over the country and around the world.

"I wish all the men at these things didn't look 'macropsychotic,'" I said to Linda as we floated back to our booth, biting back laughter. We were revved up after having consumed diverse free samples: wheat grass juice, strong coffee, kava extract, and organic chocolate. Dr. Hauschka trial-size products provided great bargaining power for free samples.

"I know what you mean," she said. "They look like they've eaten a little too much brown rice."

But my impression of Expo men was about to change. So was my life.

Back at our booth we found Denise, the Dr. Hauschka distributor from the Southeast, who was helping two men arrange a bale of straw, sunflowers, posters showing small farms, and colorful brochures in the booth adjacent to ours. The booth belonged to the Biodynamic Association, a group committed to creating a stronger presence for the relatively new sustainable agricultural movement. Although biodynamic agriculture predates the organic movement, it was not well known in the United States. Europe has recognized biodynamic agriculture as the benchmark of regenerative farming that went far beyond organic. My apprenticeship at Meadowbrook Herb Garden and the several trainings at WALA had helped me become comfortable with some of the big ideas of biodynamics, including preparations made from healing herbal plants — silica and cow manure stuffed into cow horns and other sheaths, then buried during the winter where they age into a sweet-smelling substance. When applied to the compost pile, soil, and plants, the mixture acts as a kind of living technology to receive the organizing wisdom of cosmic forces.

Denise had smartly arranged for them to be next to us, thus underscoring that the foundation of our products was Mother Nature. Our packing actually said: *Nature's Treasures transformed for Man.* Early on, I had registered my concern with the manufacturer that in our market end users wouldn't realize that "Man" meant humankind. It was a marketing challenge that took me several years to resolve.

We passed around introductions; I learned that the more handsome one, a tall, dark-haired, blue-eyed man, was Clifford Kurz. He shook my hand, smiled, and said, "Kurz means 'short' in German, but as you can see, I'm not."

I felt a seismic shift inside me. From that moment on, I had to force myself to try and focus on the small talk — the run-on chatter about the Expo attendance, farm certification, and how the ingredients in our products were grown and extracted at sunrise before the dew dries. Was it obvious to everyone that I could not take my eyes off this stranger? Or that I was trembling in his presence?

I moved closer to our display and started to rearrange the products I had already arranged. Clifford moved closer to me and started to fumble with the boxes I had stacked in pyramids according to their colors: apricot bands around white boxes for face care, blue for bath concentrates, red for body care, green for hair care. Then, as if Clifford, too, had been trembling, one pyramid after another collapsed. We both laughed, until Clifford's friend Caleb said it was time for them to go to a pre-conference workshop.

Once they left, Linda rushed over to me, "Wow!" she exclaimed. "He's not only handsome; he could not keep his eyes off of you."

"He also couldn't keep his hands off our boxes." I said with another laugh.

We grilled Denise about the men. She said that Caleb had a small sheep farm in Pennsylvania, and a wife and two children. Clifford was married, but Denise thought she had heard him tell Caleb that he was getting divorced.

The anxiety unfurled into excitement. I thought Clifford was too handsome to be single; I also knew that conventionally "handsome" wasn't usually my type. I was more drawn to interesting men, attractive maybe, but not handsome. I remembered when my mother told me that, when my father had first walked into the mortgage company where she was a secretary, she immediately knew that she loved him. *Oh no,* I'd thought then and now again, as I stood on the floor of the bustling convention hall. *Love at first sight doesn't really happen ... does it?*

The next day, an acquaintance from one of my accounts stopped by our booth before the show opened. He asked if I knew Clifford Kurz. He had several pounds of cheese from certified farms that he needed to get to Clifford, who wasn't in sight. I figured he must be on another level where the workshops were taking place. But the man was late for a panel discussion and said he needed someone to find Clifford. I was quite happy to have a good reason to do that.

"It's like the universe is setting this up. Must be karma," I told Linda after I'd succeeded in my happy mission. Clifford was easy to find outside the lecture hall. I handed him the cheese and said something like, "This cheese stands alone, it's biodynamic." He laughed, thanked me, and said he'd see me back at the booth. He also said something about lunch.

Meeting Clifford was the central focus of the Expo for me. Everything else was a blur. Through it all, he and I had frequent, intense eye contact while we tended our booths, and we spent coffee breaks, lunches, and every dinner together. The first night we went to a Chinese restaurant in the District. Clifford's fortune read: "Love will be." Mine said: "Your life is about to change." The evening before the Expo ended, we had dinner together and walked in and out of noisy bars to catch glimpses of the World Series. By the time we got back to my hotel, I knew that Clifford had grown up in John Steinbeck country—Salinas, California; he bragged that he and the author had attended the same high school. Which, he added, was where the similarity ended. Clifford said he must have been a slow learner, though, because it had taken him many years and many attempts to get his college degree. He'd majored in the sciences at UC Berkley and UC San Diego, and then taken a detour to Emerson College in Forest Row, England, to study biodynamic agriculture. While there, he apprenticed at a biodynamic farm in Germany before returning to the United States to finish his degree in agriculture at Cornell. I also noted that he was the only person I know who said "golly," but I think it was his love of horses and hearing about the rodeo (which he pronounced like the famous street to shop in L.A.) in his hometown that closed the deal with my heart. We moved close together on a couch in the lobby and talked till after midnight. We sat so close that we still argue to this day about who kissed whom first. I was relieved to learn that he'd been separated from his wife for two years, and that the divorce was all but final. My relationship with Jim had ended three years earlier; I was definitely ready to move on.

On the last day of the Expo, while we were all disassembling our booths, Linda and I decided to follow Clifford and Caleb out of the city and stop for lunch en route back to New York. Clifford had to catch a late flight to Switzerland out of Kennedy airport; Caleb had to get back to his farm. They planned to go to JFK first; then Caleb would then take Clifford's car to Pennsylvania.

Because both vehicles needed fuel, we pulled into a gas station, Clifford driving his red Nissan, and me following in my new car with Linda. While stopped at the gas pumps waiting our turns, our cars tapped each another. I pushed hard on the brakes. "Did I just bump into him?" I screeched. But it kept happening, until Linda and I realized that Clifford kept rolling back, lightly hitting my front bumper. We laughed hysterically. Then Linda said, "This is ridiculous. You should ride with Clifford. Caleb can come with me till we stop for lunch."

During lunch, I volunteered to bring Clifford to the airport and save Caleb the trip. "It's on my way home," I said. Caleb said he'd be happy to drop Linda off at her apartment in Hoboken. I was more than pleased and eager to spend more time alone with Clifford.

By the time we reached the airport, it was clear that something special was happening between Clifford and me. I stayed with him as long as possible. Before going through security, he needed to use a pay phone to call the Biodynamic Association. I stood behind him as he dialed; he turned, pulled me closer, and then wrapped me near his heart while he left a message at the office. It felt like the most intimate act I had ever experienced. We kissed good-bye and exchanged numbers: I gave him both mine and Suzi's because I was usually at one house or the other. We made promises: he said he'd call from Switzerland; I said I'd meet him in New York when he returned in two weeks. And then he left.

Several hours later, when I arrived at Suzi's to pick up John, she asked, "So who's Clifford? He called to say he'll call again once he's landed."

He did. In fact, he called every night for the next two weeks and sent me five letters in which he wrote how strong his feelings were when we first met, and how they were growing stronger every day he was away. To say the least, I was in an emotionally charged state, blissful and yet afraid to trust that this man who had entered my life so quickly really wanted to be part of my small family of two. I had told him about John, about John leaving the Steiner School, and about how difficult life had been with Jim. I let him know that my son was the center of my world, and that any man that I was with would need to be on board with my being a mother. Although Clifford had no children, he assured me wasn't hesitant about having a young boy in his life. I wanted that to be true, just as I wanted John to have a sense of being part of a whole family.

Clifford was due to return on a Friday. The night before, John and I went to New York. We stayed with Sherry and her sons, Eli and Daniel: the plan was for John to hang out there for the weekend while I hung out with Clifford. On Friday, John went with Eli to spend the day with his old class, and I went to the airport.

As Clifford walked through the concourse toward me, I noticed his confident, happy stride. I smiled. He reached me, and we kissed. He held me for a moment and kissed me again. Then he said he wanted to meet John. And I knew I had been silly to be afraid.

Back at Sherry's, the introductions were swift. Clifford gave John chocolate bars and a beautiful calendar with photos of the Swiss Alps. Sherry looked at me, smiled and mouthed the words: "He's handsome."

Eli opened the calendar and put it on John's head like a hat. They ripped into the chocolate bars and raced, laughing, into Eli's room, closing the doors behind them. I knew that Eli had made plans for them to spend all day Saturday without parents or his little brother. It was clear he was happy that John was there, and I could tell that John was thrilled to be back in the city.

It was a spectacular, warm fall weekend. Clifford and I drove to my office; I showed him the Dr. Hauschka center, taking pride in sharing with him what I had accomplished. When we wandered into the garden, I told him about the party and how it had been an ending for me; we walked around the corner and ate dinner in a romantic outdoor restaurant. We talked for hours. There's nothing like a beautiful night in New York when you're falling in love.

Conveniently, Linda was away for the weekend and had offered to let us to stay at her apartment. So after dinner, Clifford and I drove to Hoboken. I knew I was moving into unknown emotional territory. But apparently I was ready. And I knew Clifford was right for me. I savored every minute of that weekend as though I were famished from having been deprived of love and was finally being nourished—a flower that had been without sunlight and water for too long. A flower ready to step off the wall.

Clifford invited John and me to visit his cousin in South Carolina for Thanksgiving. John didn't really want to go, so I didn't push him; he opted, instead, for my mother's house in Newport. Although I hated to be apart from him over the holiday, I also knew he'd be more comfortable in familiar territory.

Early on Thanksgiving morning, as Clifford and I were having coffee in our room, he started talking about marriage. He said he hadn't thought he'd get married again, but now he didn't know. He wondered if I'd ever thought of marriage because he knew I hadn't been married but was in many ways more married than he was because of John, and that, though he had been married, maybe he hadn't been ready then, but maybe he was now, and he wondered how I felt about marriage in general. He sounded very confused, so I finally asked, "Are you proposing to me?"

"Yes, I guess I am," he said.

"What took you so long?" I said.

It was two months after we had met.

And, for me, moving into the unknown with Clifford was where I wanted to sow my future.

19

Bittersweet

WHEN THE ROTARY PHONE beside my bed rang, I grabbed the receiver before I could wonder who was calling in the middle of the night.

"The kids are heading for Versailles! I'll get a flashlight and meet you," the caller said before I had opened my eyes. I knew it was our neighbor, Jo, short for Josephine, who owned Third Hand Farm with her husband, Larry. I also knew what she meant, so I jumped quickly from my empty bed. Clifford was away at a farming conference and John was spending the night at his friend Justin's house. I pulled my red denim skirt on over my night gown, ran downstairs, stepped barefoot into my Wellies, and headed to the shed to get a bucket of rich grain, or dessert, as I called our herd's favored food. Our dog, Jamocha, was at my heels as I crossed the small incline that divided our twelve-acre farm from Jo and Larry's four-acre meadow of hay. I spotted Jo waving her flashlight as she stood near the row of bushes that separated her property from our "kids'" forbidden temptation — a vast vegetable garden and pool owned by the neighbor to her north. The week before, when the herd had escaped while Clifford was home, we'd joked that, compared to Third Hand Farm, the neighbor's well-groomed garden estate looked like Versailles.

I arrived as the large, dark shadows of the cattle formed an unruly cluster. Jo shone the light on their lowered heads, and I shook the pail in front of them. I tossed grain into their circle and dangled the pail close to them. Surprisingly, they followed me back toward our meadow behind the house, the night silent except for their snorting and heavy breathing and an occasional bark from Jamocha, who ran just ahead of me.

Clifford and I had purchased a small farm soon after we'd met and just before we married. He convinced me that the versatile Dexter breed of cattle would be a necessity to enhance soil fertility and would provide compost for my gardens. He never told me that I would have to coax their collective five thousand pounds back to their fenced-in home at midnight and repair the fence before returning to bed. As I slowed my running to a power walk, while trying to calm the adrenaline pounding through my heart, I softly recited their names: the cows, Lilac, Laryssa, and Lucy; the bulls, Rambo, and Rambini. Their warm breath followed the scent of the grain. Luckily, I'd had a trial run steering them home with Clifford the week before.

Falling in love with Clifford was a spectacularly sweet moment for me. He was almost too good to be true. We had the same interests, and he was happy to be in a family.

John, however, was not as open to having Clifford be part of our lives. He was mildly curious when Clifford came to Amherst for a week at a time. He tolerated a weekend trip to visit Clifford on the farm where he lived outside of Ithaca, New York. But, when Clifford moved in with us in February 1987, and we started to plan our wedding and look for a small farm to purchase, John went on strike. He barely spoke to me. He wouldn't look at Clifford. Every night after dinner, my son retreated to his room, locked the door, and played music on the bright yellow Walkman that his father had given him.

Soon after Clifford moved in, I got upset with John for misplacing his house keys for the second time. But I quickly apologized for losing my temper when I noticed how down he seemed.

He said, "Oh it doesn't matter. I'm just sad because you stopped loving me."

John felt that, because I loved Clifford, I had stopped loving him. No matter how often I told him I loved him, he felt abandoned. I felt a throbbing, swollen ache between my heart and my throat as I realized that all the pretending that John and I had done about me finding a husband and having a house and a bike hadn't really meant much to him. It had only been a pretense. John was not able to think of Clifford—or anyone that John had pretended he wanted in our lives—as a father figure. When Clifford and I bought the small farm in nearby Hatfield, John was convinced that his life was totally ruined.

Fortunately, Jim made contact with him during all the transitions. Jim had returned to New York after his month at the treatment center. He even invited John to the city for a visit. We made plans for John to take the bus to the city once or twice a month and during his spring vacation. John was thrilled to spend time with Jim, and he liked Jim's new girlfriend. I was very grateful that she was kind to John. They made spaghetti sauce and worked on jewelry projects together.

In the summer of 1987, just months before Clifford and I were married, we slowly began the move from Amherst to Hatfield—and I began to move the Hauschka business up from New York. It was a big transition and especially difficult for John when we left the neighborhood where his friend Justin lived. We made sure, however, that their friendship stayed intact. Justin thought our farm was kind of cool, and he and John were soon riding their dirt bikes around the fields. John, however, assured me that Justin was only being kind about liking where we lived, and he reminded me that we now lived in "the epicenter of nowhere."

There was another change for John. Because we had moved out of the Amherst school district, we had to enroll him in a new school. A friend had told me about the Bement School in South Deerfield—a small, K–9 private school that offered promises of integrity, joy, and significance for their students. I took out a significant education loan, and, in September, John—who had turned thirteen in June—entered eighth grade in non-denim pants and a shirt "only with a collar" as required by the dress code. The eleven-mile drive back and forth to Bement gave John and me quiet time together to try to heal from the whiplash of our recent moves and lifestyle changes. My bitter angst about ruining his life sweetened a little each day as I saw his happiness return through his new school.

"It's kind of like the Steiner School," he told me. "The teachers are really nice, and they hang out with us during outside time and lunch. We do art and can play soccer." John was an outstanding student and wanted to excel. Having him talk so freely to me again and knowing he was enjoying school was sweet honey to my soul.

The farm we'd bought had a small Sears, Roebuck kit bungalow called "The Sheridan" built on it, a rundown tobacco barn, and ten acres of what used to be very fertile soil. The Connecticut River Valley was once considered to have the most fertile soil in the country until tobacco farmers started to grow wrapper tobacco for cigars.

Clifford immediately got to work putting up an electric fence for the small herd that we'd bought from a local organic farmer. Our neighbors, Jo and Larry, had never sprayed their field with pesticides or spread chemical fertilizers, so they were happy to let us use it in exchange for mowing it, which Clifford was very willing to do. It was a great way to feed our "kids." Clifford also enclosed their field with an electric fence. Within a short time, we had animals on the land—which was most important for Clifford. In order to advise other farmers, he felt he needed to be connected to a farm.

Then he insisted on getting the outside of the barn in some kind of shape before our wedding. He and John started tearing down vines that appeared to be dead and had grown up around the barn doors, making it almost impossible to open them. I pruned old dogwoods and weeded around well-established hosta (also called plantain lilies) and iris beds. When I came upon vines of bittersweet that were strangling Concord grapevines, I pulled them down, remembering the crowns I'd woven as a child when I'd been so lonely staying at my aunt's house. But now I wasn't alone, and I was happy to know that soon I would be wearing a crown of flowers at my wedding. I threw the bittersweet into the compost pile, not realizing how invasive it is, and how difficult it is to permanently purge it from the landscape.

One day a week in late summer and early fall, Clifford and I drove to Boston to meet with a priest from the Christian Community Church to prepare for our marriage. It's recommended that people who wish to marry in the Christian Community become conscious of the importance of marriage. The priest interviewed us, and we shared with him the history of our relationships with others, and how strongly we both felt ready to commit to each other for a lifetime. He said that a marriage was as significant as one's own incarnation, that it is an opportunity to grow and learn to love another in a way not usually possible. He told us we would experience the wonderful sides of each other, but that we would eventually see the other's shadow and have our own shadow side reflected back to us. We were positive that we were up for a lifetime commitment.

In the midst of our move to the farm, relocating my Hauschka business from New York to Hatfield, planning a wedding for eighty guests, getting John settled at Bement, starting a vegetable garden, caring for our small herd of cattle, building fences, pruning unwanted shrubs, and painting walls, I discovered that I was pregnant. Although I was surprised because we weren't planning to have a child so quickly, I was happy to know that I still could get pregnant after the traumatic result of my pregnancy with Lily. Unfortunately, almost immediately after learning I was pregnant, I miscarried. It was just weeks before our wedding; I buried my grief amidst many to-do lists and greeted the world with my shield of confidence.

Instead of an engagement ring, Clifford had given me a golden locket in the shape of a heart. The week before the wedding, on the day of my final fitting for my wedding dress, I lost the locket. I searched for it desperately. But, as guests and family began to arrive from out of town for the wedding, I had to put thoughts of it aside. Then John sprained his ankle playing soccer, and the vines that he and Clifford had been cutting down finally rebelled. Clifford had been correct in thinking that they weren't poison oak, which, because he was from California where poison oak was abundant, he knew well. But it turned out they were poison ivy. Both John and Clifford had the beginning of what would become a nasty rash.

Somehow, we managed to persevere, and we were married at the Porter Huntington Phelps Museum in Hadley, Massachusetts, on October 3, 1987. The ceremony took place in a restored corn barn on the site. A golden hue radiated from the walls; a string quartet played music before and after the service; the air was filled with soft scents from lovely rose gardens.

There were two witnesses for the marriage: my best friend, Suzi, and Clifford's good friend Rod. Clifford, I, Suzi, and Rod walked down the aisle in a single file to the front of the barn where the priest waited for us. The quartet played a piece that one of them had composed for the event. As I walked toward the front, I felt very exposed and vulnerable at the seriousness of the ritual being presented in front of my family who didn't really understand this alternative path to Christianity. Then I saw John in the front row; he smiled at me and softly said, "Mom," as I walked by. Reassured, I smiled back, touched by his love, and held back a tear as he stood there on his crutches with an angry red rash creeping over his shirt collar. I think having me for his mother must have been — and sometimes still can be — bittersweet.

There are some similarities between traditional wedding rituals and the Christian Community ritual, such as taking "each other to be man and wife." In addition, the priest shared a little of each of our biographies, noting that we had a strong bond because of our professions. He said that I was a healing artist because of my work with medicinal plants contained in the Dr. Hauschka preparations, and that Clifford was a biodynamic farmer and therefore also was a healing artist, but his path was healing for the earth. Toward the end of the ceremony, the priest took two small wooden sticks cut from branches and tied them together with a red ribbon as a symbol of the two of us joined together in marriage.

It was a beautiful wedding. Many friends from the Steiner School came with their children. The family we had carpooled with for years brought their two sons. John's best friend from the city, Eli, came with his mother. My Hauschka family of business associates and clients and even Warren made the trip to help us celebrate.

After the ceremony, a reception followed in a tent in the rose garden. A lively contra dance band arrived as friends mingled with all the new families we had met in our short time living in Amherst and Hatfield. Wherever I looked, friends were smiling. Their children ran and tumbled on the rich green lawn. Warren was smiling at a single woman friend of mine. I noticed John leaning on his crutches, laughing with both his new friends and his city friends gathered around him as he proudly bragged about riding his dirt bike very fast through the fields along the Connecticut River.

Western Massachusetts can be at the peak of Indian summer in early October, with very warm days and cool nights. As it happened, the skies were cloudy when the day had started, but as we'd walked out of the barn to the rose garden the sun began to shine brightly. The temperature had been in the low seventies but slowly dropped to the high sixties as the afternoon unfolded. Friends who had driven over Walker Mountain from Lenox even reported driving through snow flurries. A friend of mine said that, in Japan, having both sunshine and snow or rain on one's wedding day was a good sign. "It's a metaphor for a marriage," she proclaimed, "which will have both wonderful moments as well as difficult times."

Bittersweet, I thought.

And yet my wedding day was magical.

The day after the wedding John's rash seemed to be starting to heal, and he looked forward to going to school, where his new schoolmates applauded his valiant effort at soccer, despite the sprained ankle. Several of the girls offered to open doors for him and carry his backpack around campus. Clifford, however, had woken up with an angry poison ivy rash on his arms and face. John and I agreed that he looked like the Hulk. We ate leftover wedding cake for breakfast as John chided us for choosing carrot cake instead of one of "those," he said, "you know, normal fluffy white ones. You guys are weird." But for the moment, we were a small, happy family.

It was an enormous lifestyle change and only the start of many changes to come. Soon after our wedding, Jim left his girlfriend and New York and moved to Los Angeles. He was getting work in the film industry; he quickly put down roots by buying a house in Studio City. Now, instead of short weekend trips to New York to visit Jim, John would be flying to California for Christmas and much of his summer vacation.

I was grateful that Jim was committed to having a relationship with John, but it meant that John grew less connected to Clifford and me, especially on holidays. It also meant that John was seeing Jim through unfiltered eyes, which included getting to witness Jim's never-ending string of girlfriends—one of whom had multiple personalities and was a former stripper, as he confessed to me years later. John couldn't help but be impressed with his father's new life of hanging out with famous movie stars in Hollywood mansions and riding in expensive sports cars that belonged to Jim's friends. John also took trips to movie sets where his father was becoming recognized as a talented character actor. I had to admit I felt rather proud and hopeful when John reported that Mel Gibson's wife prepared the same kind of food for her family that I did. Maybe it would help John see that we weren't so much in "the epicenter of nowhere." Still, I knew that the contrast between our life in Hatfield, where we were trying to heal the soil with cover crops and cows, and Jim's new life in the fast lane would be a difficult polarity for John to integrate.

It was, naturally, bittersweet. And ironic that John had felt deserted when I'd met Clifford, and now I felt like I was losing John to Jim. In my head I knew it was important for John to be with his father, but in my heart I felt less important to my son.

Jim's magic and charisma were hard to compete with, and John was eager to be bicoastal. Part of me missed the odd couple status that John and I once had.

As a newly married woman, I felt in the middle of a vortex of change. I had learned about vortexes from my study of Biodynamic agriculture. We started using the BD preps on our farm. To prepare the horn manure prep for spraying on the soil you need to mix it with water. First, you fill a bucket with tepid water and add the prep, which looks like a soft, fine portion of compost. Then, using your hand, you stir the prep into the water until you create a vortex going into one direction. When the water begins spinning, you aggressively reverse the direction of your hand and create chaos, thus dissolving the vortex. Once chaos is in the mixture, you start to stir in the opposite direction until you create another vortex. You repeat this process for an hour. By the time it is ready to spread on the soil, the water feels like silk. Clifford showed me how to take a small straw broom-like tool, dip it into the silky prep, and then broadcast or scatter it onto the soil and garden.

I realized that John and I had been living in a certain circular movement like a vortex for twelve years, our lives spinning in both Carolina and Newport, Rhode Island, and in New York with Jim sometimes at the center, sometimes at the periphery. I had created chaos when I'd taken John out of the Waldorf School and moved to Massachusetts, leaving behind the rhythm we'd been used to. We were thrown into a void, a state in which chance is supreme. When I met Clifford only a month after the move and soon began planning a wedding, starting a farm, and establishing a new home for Dr. Hauschka, we had quickly created another vortex. It had been hard for John to move in a new direction because he was lonely. But he slowly began to create a new vortex with Jim, with L.A. as another home, as well as with new friends from his new school. He'd even agreed to feed a new calf from a bottle for us when we were away at feeding time.

The difference between the chaos created in the BD prep and the chaos I'd created with the abrupt move out of Manhattan is consciousness. While making the prep, one consciously creates the vortex-chaos-vortex, with the goal to open the soil treatment to cosmic forces. But, when I'd left the city so spontaneously, not knowing what the heavens had in store for us, I'd created a different kind of chaos by acting from my gut with no definitive goal beyond moving.

Over the next several years, our lives were in a big mixing bowl. Clifford's position with the Biodynamic Association ended. He went from being a weekend farmer making hay to planting vegetables on two acres of land and becoming a market gardener. I continued to "run with the bulls" when they occasionally headed to Versailles, but I also learned how to drive a tractor pulling a baler when making hay. I rented a commercial space in downtown Hatfield where I hired a friend to help with distribution of Dr. Hauschka, and I was able to hold trainings for estheticians and massage therapists on a larger scale than I was able to in New York.

During the trainings, Clifford joined the Dr. Hauschka vortex and spoke about the importance of growing healing plants and how important compost was to healthy soil. "Healthy skin care begins in the compost pile," he half-joked, but he also knew it was true. I recalled how I had joked that beauty begins in the compost on my first trip to WALA; I felt blessed to have found a life with Clifford. He described the comparison between human skin and the soil as the skin of the earth. One of the points I made in the trainings was that Dr. Hauschka products were to the human being what biodynamic agriculture is to the earth.

John continued to head west to California during holidays and school breaks. He began to dream about someday working in films as a producer and director. Both John and his father became valued ambassadors for Dr. Hauschka to the film community, where its popularity was quickly reaching A-List actors and actresses.

And we all were walking on new fertile ground.

20

Cosmetics and the
Harmony of the Cosmos

I FELT LIKE THE PROM QUEEN when both the U.S. importer and WALA agreed that Clifford and I should become the next U.S. importers. It was like putting on a fine coat that fit well and looked great. When I had adopted Rudolph Hauschka as my spiritual father years earlier in that small cemetery across from the main building, I had imagined that the whole company belonged to me in some unexplainable way. As a spiritual daughter, I was responsible for bringing his global mission to heal the earth and humanity through honest marketing and education about the methods of skin care.

We had begun to attend the company's international importers' meetings in 1990—two years before we took over the importation business. It was a dynamic time. We spent an extra week after the biannual meetings at WALA to learn as much as possible. We were grateful that our farm apprentice (who wanted to become a sustainable former) was happy to farm-sit for us and care for our animals. As Clifford spent more time helping me in the business, he had less time for the farm, so our apprentice had become essential. Also, after graduating valedictorian from his ninth-grade class at Bement, John entered the tenth grade as a boarding student at Northfield Mount Hermon School, which was about half an hour north of us. The idea that he would be immersed in student life and be surrounded by friends seemed like a good one. He came home most weekends but was able to stay at school whenever we travelled on business. Still, John and I both suffered "homesickness for each other." I felt it was healthy that we both had a new direction in life, even though it was painful.

My focus at WALA expanded to include understanding how they marketed to various segments: pharmacies, health shops, and estheticians. I developed friendships in many different departments: export, education, esthetic, and marketing.

Clifford concentrated on logistics, which included ordering enough products in advance to meet a growing market. WALA needed to know our projected growth so they could grow enough plants to keep up with the demand. If we sold too much Rose Cream and they hadn't planned for it, they wouldn't have enough rose plant material to make the product for when the market wanted it. I often encouraged our retail customers to pass along that information.

Because Clifford was fluent in German, he translated all printed materials we thought would assist us in our training and marketing efforts. He was also helpful at business meetings and medical lectures, which were still being held in German in the early 1990s. Sometimes there were simultaneous translations into English, French, and Italian, but Clifford could direct our questions to meet the needs of our specific market. My world quickly expanded to an international community.

Because of my enthusiasm to learn everything possible about the brand, I was getting a reputation as a rising star among the international community. Apparently, the company hadn't experienced anyone as eager as I was to know all things WALA in order to tell the story in the United States. My background in Anthroposophy, homeopathy, and biodynamics, as well as being an esthetician and an authorized WALA educator— combined with my marketing acumen—apparently gave them confidence that we would represent their ideas honestly and without distortion to the American consumer and retailer. Only Germany and Switzerland were selling more products than the U.S. market, and before we became importers my territory had represented 85 percent of total national sales. It was the beginning of a golden age for Clifford and me in a new level of international business. I was in my early forties (which, in Anthroposophical human development, was referred to as the Mars years), and I was about to learn that I needed to become a spiritual warrior to accomplish our goals.

After long days of meetings, WALA *schnapped* and dined our group of more than two dozen attendees. We laughed together over *spätzle mit käse*, a kind of mac and cheese; schnitzel that was courtesy of the local cows and sheep; *Hefeweizen*, a local wheat beer; and, yes, schnapps that was made from local fruits and served with or over elderflower ice cream. I felt as if I was married to WALA as well as to Clifford, and that the whole community was my family. It was my Camelot.

To accommodate the importation business, we rented an additional old tobacco barn in Hatfield; we figured it would meet our needs for at least ten years. We filled it with pallets of products, packing supplies, new staff, and two cats named Tigger and Cleo who kept the small critters away at night. The next task was to develop a brochure. National sales had also been flat when we'd taken over from the former importer; it was crucial for us to get the Dr. Hauschka WALA story directly into the end-users' hands. We decided on a printed piece that would also serve as a consumer guide to the correct protocol for the right products for their skin condition. We began a search for our "Marlboro man"—an American icon that had been a hugely successful marketing image for Marlboro tobacco products. But who or what would be the face or image for our brand? Would we be able to find a perfect Dr. Hauschka image?

We met Paul Margulies, a top-notch Madison Avenue advertising executive, at an Anthroposophic workshop in the Berkshires. Although retired, he agreed to work with us on developing the brochure. He thought it would be interesting and maybe even fun to help brand a company of such high quality and standards that it was working within the guidelines of Anthroposophy. I felt it was a sign of great things to come for the much-needed brochure.

And when Paul added, "My wife and daughter love Rose Cream," that bolstered my optimism, too. His daughter was becoming a well-known actress.

He told us that it often had been a stretch to find something interesting or wonderful about the more commercial brands he'd worked with during his long career, so he'd used his creativity to liven things up. One of his classics that I recognized was the ad campaign he'd developed for Alka-Seltzer's "Plop, Plop, Fizz, Fizz, Oh What a Relief It Is!"

Paul reviewed the brochures we'd received with the import business—we called them the "German-English brochures," which meant that they'd been produced in Germany, translated into English, and printed by the former U.S. importer without any rendering of the content or sensitivity for an American consciousness. They were off-white with a maroon band and had lots of copy, but no pictures of people or plants.

"I can't tell by looking at them if they're for auto parts or hemorrhoid medication," Paul said.

Being able to work with Paul was an extraordinary opportunity. He also brought in a close friend, Jeffrey Metzner, a talented designer also from the "Madmen" heyday of Madison Avenue ad firms. Both Paul and Jeffrey had the Waldorf parent experience in common with each other and with me. Jeffrey's wife, Sheila, whom I remembered from the Rudolf Steiner School, loved Hauschka products, too.

Clifford and I spent several days educating Paul and Jeffrey on all aspects of the company philosophy, biodynamic gardening methods, and unique composition of the products. Paul admitted that it wasn't as easy as he'd thought it would be because WALA had such a big story to tell. But it was all there. He said he didn't need to invent something catchy like "The city that never sleeps" or another classic of his: "I can't believe I ate the whole thing." Instead, he needed to focus on clean, concise, lovely copy that would make complex concepts accessible for our market. His goal was to set us apart from conventional companies that promoted enhancing exterior "looks" and only addressed symptoms of skin conditions rather than healthy skin functions. For Dr. Hauschka, the task of cosmetics was to restore the harmony, reveal the transparency of skin that had become opaque, and let the beauty shine forth in a star-like quality from within.

Jeffrey wanted to work with an artist friend of his to create a collage that would be photographed to use on the cover. If we liked the collage, he would commission smaller ones to use as a thread throughout the brochure to support Paul's poetic copy.

Two weeks later, we returned to the Berkshires, excited to see the first draft of the layout. The copy Paul wrote was elegant, powerful, and easy to follow. On the cover a headline appeared in simple lower-case letters in the lower left-hand corner and read: "cosmetics and the harmony of the cosmos." The overall text design was laid out in a way that strongly connected the words "cosmos" and "cosmetics." Along the edge of the right side of the page falling vertically below the gold embossed logo the copy continued:

The
word
cosmetic
comes
from the
Greek,
kosmos,
meaning
harmony,
order,
cosmos.

It was understated, sophisticated. I was thrilled to see how our message looked thanks to Paul's ability to distill hours of information in such a tight and clear way.

Then Jeffrey set a mock-up of the cover artwork in front of us. It included the copy and the collage that his colleague had created. Clifford was speechless. I burst into tears. The image was interesting and layered, much like the avant-garde art I had seen in SoHo galleries. But my intuition told me that it wasn't right for our precious Dr. Hauschka brand. My confidence in the project shattered momentarily. My reaction had spoken volumes, but Paul quickly calmed my fears.

"We'll figure something out," he assured us.

The next day Sheila, a well-known contemporary photographer in New York, offered us a selection of her museum-quality photographs to use in the brochure—at no charge. The photos that Paul and Jeffrey recommended were mostly sepia tones: for the cover shot, we liked a profile of a strong, beautiful woman looking into the distance. Though the image was a woman, it wasn't so feminine that it would exclude the male market. As I had learned from WALA, Dr. Hauschka is a brand that meets the needs of all human skin condition for all ages from the cradle to the rocking chair.

I went to sleep each evening thinking about the quality of the artist's work; the array of photos we had to pick from, which were mostly desert landscapes, naked bodies, and flowers not found in our products; the brochure and what it would mean for our customers. I awoke each morning, sat straight up in bed while Clifford was still yawning and stretching, and talked about how excited I was to be able to introduce the brochure later that summer at a workshop for distributors and estheticians in Vail, Colorado. Several weeks after that, in October, we were going to take copies to distribute at the large, all-encompassing international importers' meeting in Germany.

"Can you at least wait until breakfast to start talking about the brochure? It's not even printed yet!" He wasn't as excited about the photographs as I was because the selection of flowers only included images of a wilted tulip and a Calla lily, neither of which were signature plants for us—the rose was. However, since the flower images would be inside the catalogue and connected to a skin condition. I thought they could work. Clifford continually reminded me that the tulip and lily were monocots; the rose, a dicot. Although I also knew the significance of the rose in our products, I thought the lily was a sign from my Lily, a thread leading us through the process.

Finally, we went to the summer workshop at Vail. The head of the plant laboratory at WALA, a chemist (whom we good-naturedly referred to as "the alchemist," as Heinz had called him several years ago), was the main presenter at the training. During his keynote speech, and at our request, he talked about how three of our top-selling products were composed to support the functions of the skin. He described the manufacturing standards and techniques that were held to the same exacting levels as the medicinal remedies they produced, a quality that was self-imposed. At that time, cosmetic manufacturers were not required by law to have such high standards as those for remedies. (This holds true today.) He further explained that WALA considered cosmetics to be the daughter of medicine, and therefore they manufactured the skin care products with the same dedication that they did for their medicinal products.

Everyone loved "the alchemist" because he had a spiritual aura about him when he spoke about plants and their being. They also were impressed to hear from a scientist who was so sensitive to the spiritual healing potential of plants and precious minerals. In addition, Clifford and I had become quite friendly with him during our biannual trips to WALA, and we'd even been invited to his home for dinner. I was eager to show him the new brochure, certain that he'd appreciate the effort and the resources that had gone into the project.

We waited until the last day of the workshop, which was devoted to marketing, to unveil the brochure and the story behind it. The response was varied. The estheticians and spa owners were thrilled. But the distributors had mixed feelings because they thought that, while it would work for the esthetic market that would appreciate naked bodies and barren landscapes to depict dry skin, it was too edgy for the natural products market. But I wasn't daunted by their reaction — I was used to the distributors challenging every decision that Clifford and I made to improve the business structure. Our friend the alchemist waited until we were alone with him to say that he found the brochure shocking.

"It does not represent WALA," he said.

He then recommended that we take the eighty-thousand-dollar project to the dump.

I had trouble sleeping between the August workshop in the Rockies and the October meeting at the foot of the Schwäbische Alb; I was concerned that WALA would regret their decision to give us the importation rights. In my usual style, I joked to my friends that WALA would probably sew a scarlet A on my chest for adulterating the purity of the company. But in my heart I knew that my initial excitement about the international meeting and presenting the brochure had turned to anxiety. I was frantic with worry, as I knew that the entire WALA board would be there, as well as all department heads and worldwide importers. The latest CEO had been hired from outside the company and had spent almost a year getting to know the brand and all aspects of the company, so his reaction would be critical. When he'd first arrived at WALA, he'd been very encouraging to us; he acknowledged that the United States was potentially WALA's largest market. In preparation for the meeting, he sent a copy of *Total Quality Management: The Key to Business Improvement* to all the global partners, asking them to read it in order to be better prepared to work together during the gathering. He said he wanted to make "the best-kept secret in the world at the edge of the woods" (as many referred to WALA and their products) an international brand.

He also said he planned to focus on more transparent management within the company and to offer more marketing support for the international community. At the time, everyone acknowledged that WALA was brilliant when it came to development and manufacturing of products, but that it had been quite casual about marketing.

"Our customers find us because of our quality. Word of mouth has always worked well for us," was what I'd often heard. But the new CEO—along with Clifford and I—wanted to bring the company into the twenty-first century with marketing efforts that matched the quality of the brand.

Although my confidence in the brochure to meet our market needs remained strong, I'd been unnerved by the alchemist's reaction to it. He was, after all, a highly respected director in the company. The cartons of newly printed brochures were still sitting in our warehouse waiting to be distributed. I'd told our German colleague at the Vail workshop that they had already been shipped to the largest outlets. Instead, I'd thought to myself: *There's no way they're going to the dump.*

I was scheduled to present the brochure on the morning of the second day, the day allotted to international marketing needs. There was lots of talk about the "American brochure." Other importers also had only taken WALA brochures and translated them into their country's language. No one, not even WALA, had produced comprehensive literature to meet the needs of the now global market. The lack of focus on marketing was taking its toll; sales had become flat worldwide as holistic, all-natural competitive brands were beginning to appear on retail shelves seemingly everywhere. We'd invested resources that were considered large for the WALA culture in order to get our story, products, and information on how to use them directly into the hands of new customers. Now it was my challenge to tell the story of the Cosmos brochure to WALA.

I carefully planned what to wear the day I was to address the group: I kept in mind that I'd once overheard a WALA director comment that a young secretary who wore Manolo Blahnik stilettos to work "doesn't have her feet on the ground." I also remembered that a friend of mine, a vice president at Citibank and a Waldorf parent, had told me that bankers didn't trust women with long hair.

"Cut your hair if you want a business loan," he'd said, only half in jest.

Unwilling to cut my hair, I wrapped my chest-length, caramel-highlighted locks into a French twist that morning. Black trousers, a white tuxedo-styled blouse, a simple string of pearls, a golden yellow blazer, and low black leather pumps that protected my peek-a-boo red, freshly pedicured toes from being stepped on, would be my armor for the day.

I skipped breakfast and left Clifford in the dining room of the Seminaris Hotel with the loud, laughing group of WALA partners. The garden was calling me. Seeking solace to calm my anxiety, I quickly walked through the quaint village to the garden gate behind the main building. Once inside, I found the head gardener giving an apprentice instruction for the end-of-season tasks; they nodded in my direction, comfortable with the many visitors to their domain. I slowly walked up and down the garden beds, past drooping stalks of sunflowers that had been left standing long after feathered friends had sought their seeds.

Recalling the meeting the previous day when the CEO had talked about a lifeboat as a metaphor for prioritizing marketing needs, I decided to link the brochure to what he'd said and position the brochure as our lifeboat. As I strolled past the many compost piles at the eastern boundary of the garden, my head filled with the growing story I would share. The beehives and their diligent tenants all around me captured my attention; I sat down on a bench that provided a comfortable distance for both the observed and the observer. The humming of the bees and their light, steady movement brought me inner stillness. Once again, I thought of being in my aunt's garden as a lonely little girl finding peace while eating warm fresh vegetables and blueberries and dancing with my life-size Pinocchio doll while waiting for my aunt to come home; then I recalled walking in Dr. Laskey's garden that opened a lifetime interest in food as medicine for me. I reminisced about my days apprenticing at Meadowbrook Herb Garden and being in the greenhouse the morning my water broke, then driving myself to the hospital to give birth to John. I also thought of our small farm in Hatfield where our Dexter cows now grazed contentedly, and our large garden that offered Clifford and me abundance. Gardens were where I connected to the harmony of the cosmos, and here, watching the bees in the WALA garden, I felt the richness of how far I'd journeyed. Slowly, a lovely, peaceful feeling enveloped me. I felt as if I were in a space outside of time and was being embraced by invisible hands of love. Tears spilled down my cheeks, but I wasn't sad, and, finally, I wasn't scared. Instead, I knew I was ready.

I promptly left the garden, eager to find Clifford and rejoin the group.

The foyer outside the great hall in the main building also sounded like a beehive as a crowd of people laughed and conversed in several languages over small white cups of very strong coffee or herbal tea. Every person I greeted smiled and said they were eager to see what we had done. Judith, the export manager, told me that she had inserted a copy of the brochure for each member of the group in a company folder along with other information sheets and a schedule for the day. The CEO greeted me warmly in his South African accent and said he wanted me to go first because the day was going to be devoted to marketing topics. I found Clifford merrily joking with friends. He put his arms around me and assured me that I would be great.

After the meeting was called to order, Judith welcomed everyone and invited me to the front of the room. The attendees were seated at long tables arranged in a U-shape around the room; a folder had been placed at every seat. One by one, the group opened their folders, and the Cosmos brochure appeared. Then, behind me, a door opened, and a number of giggling young women from various departments filed in and stood in the back; another door—that one leading to the breakfast room—opened, and several young men I recognized from the manufacturing department walked in and filled what little space was left. Judith smiled and said everyone was excited to hear about the brochure. I briefly remembered the first meeting I attended in this Grand Hall, fifteen years earlier, when I'd savored every word that Dr. Vogel had shared about healing. And now I was the one standing where he'd stood then. I took a deep breath; the room quieted.

I began by explaining the process we'd gone through, how we'd focused on our need to tell the American market about how special WALA and Dr. Hauschka really were. I told the audience how we'd met Paul and Jeffrey, and about the collage and Sheila's photographs. It was easy for me to share the process because it was so alive for me. I noticed that everyone was listening. There wasn't a single cough, a chair scraping, or a dropped pen. A few people were even smiling. Forty minutes passed in a flash. I ended with quotes from Bob Dylan and Mick Jagger, which startled me since I hadn't planned to say them. But happily, there they were.

"The times they are a-changin,'" I pronounced with honest enthusiasm. "And WALA needs to meet these changes proactively." Then I added, "You can't always get what you want, but you might find you get what you need." Our brochure wasn't exactly what we'd wanted, but it was what we needed. And I knew it.

I thanked everyone for their attention and walked toward my seat. The room erupted with applause. People jumped up from their chairs. Several young employees sang "The Times They Are a-Changin.'" The president of the WALA board, who was at the end of the table closest to where I'd stood, jumped up and hugged me. "That was great," he said. "*You* are what we need here in quiet Eckwälden."

Something new inside of me emerged then, a feeling I'd never experienced before. I felt comfortable being *me*. But it had been a painful process; it was like giving birth, albeit a self-birth. Now I no longer felt like a prom queen; I felt that I was learning to become the queen of my own soul. Inwardly, I glowed like a star. Outwardly, I felt myself at last becoming visible.

21

The Jupiter Years

*B*Y THE MID 1990s, the business had become a robust, dynamic entity with colorful characters, growing resources, and unsolicited mentions of Dr. Hauschka by celebrities. When the importers from English-speaking countries wanted to purchase the Cosmos brochure from us, WALA recognized that they needed to take the lead on marketing materials for the international community. Peter Kreft said that, if unchecked, the U.S. market would become the tail that wagged the dog. He initiated the IMSCG—the International Marketing Strategy and Consulting Group—to include Germany, the UK, Holland, France, and the United States. We then met twice a year: once in one of the focus countries, and once at WALA. The meetings in the focus countries were arranged around visiting the various market segments of that country. For example, when in the UK, we met the beauty department sales staff at Harvey Nichols department store, which carried the full Dr. Hauschka line; at a health shop in Notting Hill; and at the training center for estheticians in Worcestershire. The goal was to find a common thread for the brand but also to be sensitive to cultural differences and to find images and copy that positioned us as an international brand.

Being part of this group was a rich experience for Clifford and me. I remember standing in our local bank at one point while purchasing traveler's checks in preparation for an IMSCG meeting in Paris. I became filled with a tremendous feeling of warmth. I knew I was now on a team of caring, creative people who'd been given an important task that was helping make important changes in the world through the ways in which we did business. We all felt a strong love and commitment to WALA and the ideals of a company. With its commitment to manufacture only products that were needed, and to do no harm to animals, people, or the earth in the manufacturing process — including the use of environmentally friendly packing material — WALA was years ahead of the later trend toward sustainable business. When Dr. Hauschka started the company early in the 1950s after he discovered how to extract substances using rhythm instead of alcohol, he said it was important not only to develop healthy products but also to conduct business in a new way. He believed that his discovery of working with rhythm was a gift from the spiritual world, and that he didn't own it but was more of a steward of new methods for preparing remedies and skin care. (As a result of that thinking, WALA is now held in a trust. There are no individual owners — instead, there are stakeholders: the environment, the product, the employees, and the customers. The company is protected from being inherited by family members and from the potential to be sold to persons or companies that might have a conflicting mission. Even today, I love to say, "WALA is not for sale.")

Being grounded in WALA's ideals made me increasingly proud that I had adopted Dr. Rudolph Hauschka as my spiritual father. That feeling became even stronger as I witnessed one small, holistic, organic company after another be bought up by large corporations that needed "greening," in order to appear idealistic, socially responsible, and committed to biodynamic and organic farming even though the bottom line was still their driving force.

On the personal front, my relationships were shifting, too. When John graduated from college, he'd moved to L.A. to live with Jim. We didn't speak very often. On John's occasional visits back east, I noticed that my formerly sunny child now wore only black, drank espresso martinis, and chattered enthusiastically about his experiences working on the set of *Dark Skies*—a sci-fi television series in which Jim had a role as a member of "Majestic 12." Between those visits, Jim called several times. He praised John's work ethic but shared his concern over John's latest girlfriend (who also wore only black) and the couple's drinking habits.

"He has the Irish virus," Jim said with a cynical snort.

I dismissed his concerns. Since admitting years earlier that he was an alcoholic, Jim claimed that almost everyone we knew was either an alcoholic or a drug addict. I was also very arrogant and thought John couldn't possibly be an alcoholic because I was such a good mother. Little did I know then that addiction is an illness, not a character defect. Still, it was great to be on good terms with Jim and co-parenting—even if it was a little late. He was doing well. He had risen to notable fame as one of the most talented character actors in the business. He had sold his small house in Studio City and bought a larger one in Encino when John went to live with him. In spite of his success he was thrilled to have a wholesale account with Dr. Hauschka. He told me that he continued to use the products daily, and, while on TV and film sets, he insisted that only Hauschka was to be used for his sensitive Irish skin. He also gave the products to "some actresses I know." And though I knew it was important for Jim and John to finally spend "normal" time together, I missed John. And I retreated more and more into my work.

Around that same time, my sister moved to Florida. I felt more responsible for my mother, who was living alone in Newport. Whenever possible, I invited her to stay with us on our little farm in Hatfield. She loved coming to the Hauschka offices, filing paid invoices and doing odd jobs for the shipping department.

Overall, things were good. Actually, they were great.

(Years later, around the time that I felt called to write a memoir, I began to take a three-year program at the Center for Biography and Social Art. An important element of the training was to look at one's seven-year life phases, each of which embodies a quality of the planetary spheres. I learned that the Jupiter cycle is the life phase from forty-nine to fifty-six years old—in my case 1998 to 2005—and that the essential gesture of Jupiter is: wait a minute, step back, take it in, sort it out. Jupiter phase reflects abundance, wisdom, and a mature perspective gained during life. I realized then that, back when I'd felt that life had been "going great," I had been gaining wisdom from my work with Dr. Hauschka and the growing relationship to WALA and its international partners. There had been a fulfilling sense of abundance as sales initially doubled, and then eventually settled into a strong 25 percent annual growth.)

By 1998—the first year of what I would come to learn had been the Jupiter cycle—our staff had grown from a handful of employees who answered the phones and helped us process orders to fifty in-house coworkers, plus ten independent sales representatives, twenty-five demo givers across the country, and three esthetician educators. I also had coined the phrase "Purity, Therapy, and Luxury" to distinguish our market segments, and I'd helped develop training protocols specific to each segment. My perspective regarding all things Hauschka had expanded as I moved from one activity to another: sales to training to marketing to PR. As the company had grown, I continually relinquished one duty after another to staff members who took what I had learned and compiled the information into appropriate formats. I was becoming more of a mentor to our staff than a leader. The handwoven basket I'd once used to deliver Hauschka products to friends and family while I was living on Black Acre Farm in Rhode Island had been replaced by hundreds of orders stacked high each day awaiting a UPS pickup.

In February 1998, Clifford and I celebrated my forty-ninth birthday in Frankfurt at the annual WALA IMSCG meeting. We'd been invited to join the team as their guests at Biofach, the world's leading trade fair for organic food and natural products. It was an especially important show that year because WALA was launching its newest line of products—a complete range of makeup, which, despite our protests, WALA was determined to call "decorative cosmetics." Our end users were happy, and it was a great opportunity to offer our products to the professional makeup artists who worked in film and theater.

On February 27, during the trade show, I received a message to call our newest sales manager, Holly, at the home office in Hatfield. I remember only three things about Holly: she was an ice-skating champion in Western Massachusetts, she had experience working for a large cosmetics company before we hired her, and she is the woman who told me that Jim—J. T. Walsh to the world—was dead. He had suffered a heart attack while detoxing at a health clinic in San Diego.

I stood in stunned silence at the bank of phones near the edge of the convention hall. It didn't seem possible that the person I had loved, hated, and finally found peace with was gone. He was fifty-four years old, younger than his father had been when he'd died when Jim was eighteen.

After I hung up, I did not move. I just stared at the phone. My legs had begun to ache; the sounds that drifted from the convention floor had become muted. I knew I must be in some kind of shock, yet I didn't know why. I remembered one of the many conversations I'd had with Jim—with the help of Clifford acting as a mediator—after we had become friends. Jim had confided in me that he was afraid that he was going to die. He was concerned that his heart was weak. I'd urged him to meet with a friend of mine—a Dr. Hauschka esthetician who was also a nutritionist—and to follow a healthy diet to gradually detoxify and lose weight. He opted for a radical detox spa where he could lose weight quickly while eliminating unhealthy substances from his diet. I believe it was too drastic a cleanse, but apparently he'd been determined. But while he was detoxifying, plaque broke down and clogged his heart valves. He died suddenly in the morning circle as the group was planning their daily activities.

Clifford guided me back to our hotel room. My biggest concern was for John. I called him in California and told him we would fly there as soon as possible.

"In the meantime, think of everything about your dad that you loved," I said. "Tell your friends who are with you anything you can remember about being with him." I knew that John and Jim hadn't been getting along recently, and I was concerned that John would feel guilty.

Lufthansa upgraded us to business class when they learned we were changing our flights due to a death. Ironically, the movie being shown on our flight was *A Few Good Men*, in which Jim had played a small but interesting role. Clifford held my hand as I cried while watching Jim do the thing he'd seemed born to do, the thing he'd let no one get in the way of, being an actor till the end. I was so grateful to Clifford for his patience around my relationship with Jim. Clifford's constant love and support allowed me to heal from the wounds that Jim and I had inflicted on each other. Clifford really fulfilled all the qualities that I had written in my journal years before when I was longing for relationship; he wanted to be in a committed relationship, he supported my devotion to John, and he was a God-loving man filled with goodness on a spiritual path.

We arrived in L.A. in time to help John and Jim's brother and two sisters make funeral arrangements. I strongly discouraged the family from having an autopsy performed. One of the beliefs of Anthroposophy is that the body should be peaceful for three days after death to allow the etheric or life force to gently separate from the physical body.

A friend of Clifford and mine who was a Christian Community priest in L.A. had recently become good friends with Jim. He agreed to celebrate the Act of Consecration for Jim at Forest Lawn Cemetery. My friend Suzi Clark and I were the servers at the service. It was one of those moments when I felt karma very strongly playing out: Jim had introduced me to Anthroposophy years earlier, which had become my spiritual path that led to sending John to a Waldorf School, to my work with Dr. Hauschka, and to my meeting Clifford. It seemed fitting that I was standing at the threshold as Jim passed over to the spiritual world, surrounded by his Hollywood community who were witnessing a side of Jim that few knew—other than me.

A memorial service organized by Jim's close friends followed a few weeks after the funeral. I was the only woman asked to speak, which seemed ironic since we had been separated for fifteen years and Jim had a large circle of women in his life. It felt like another karmic sign that, although our relationship had been painful, it had been very necessary. I was recognized as having been a significant person to Jim because we'd had a child together. It was easy to speak about him because he was such a big character; one line that seemed to resonate with everyone was when I said: "He was a tenant in our hearts, behind in the rent, but impossible to evict."

One of the filmmakers in the audience borrowed the description and used it in the movie *Playing by Heart,* which I saw later that year. But the character it referred to paled in comparison to the challenges I'd had with Jim as a tenant in my heart.

At age twenty-four John inherited a large house and significant resources from his father. Clifford and I saw less and less of him after his father died. He remained in L.A., where he co-produced a film titled *Overnight,* a story about the rise and stumble of a filmmaker and musician. He also began to work on the James Bond films. When he did visit us, he usually arrived late, slept a lot, and departed early, leaving me feeling hurt. I was confused about our relationship; I felt as if I was deader to John than his father was. I couldn't see how much he was struggling. I rationalized his behavior, believing that he was suddenly wealthy and living a wild, Hollywood life, and that eventually he would find his way home.

Several years after Clifford and I married, I miscarried a second time. Clifford and I talked about adopting children, but our business was very demanding, and our plans to build a family together remained just talk until Clifford saw a play at the local Waldorf School. As he watched children of several of our friends perform, he became quite moved. Later he told me he was very sad that he'd never experience having young children. I spontaneously said, "Let's adopt."

After eighteen months of adoption applications, classes to prepare to adopt older children, and a failed adoption effort from an orphanage in Lithuania, on September 1, 1999, we brought our daughter Rossibel, a five-year old girl, home from a foster home in Guatemala. Her older brother, Emilio, followed a year later, when he was seven.

I made the mistake of thinking that, because I was successful in business, I would be successful in other areas of my life, too. But Jupiter must have been looking down, smiling from his grandeur, surrounded by glorious rings and moons, and thinking, "Oh, dear girl, the Jupiter years offer opportunities to grow in wisdom. It does not mean you already have the wisdom!" While I was enjoying great success and developing new capacities at Dr. Hauschka both domestically and internationally, I was approaching my own personal darkness.

It began to manifest in my impatience toward my mother, whose failing memory translated into subsequent neediness. I resented having felt like the parent for my whole life, and I was blind to my mother's need for quiet moments with me over a cup of tea and my undivided attention. I was in complete denial about how lost John was, and I still refused Jim's long-ago advice that I needed help in understanding addiction and the part I played in the illness. And regarding adopting older children and ignoring all advice from friends and family that it might not be a sensible task for us as we entered our fifties, I held on to the illusion that organic food, lighting a candle at each meal, prayers before bedtime, Waldorf education, 100 percent cotton clothes from Garnet Hill, and sailing and soccer lessons would heal all wounds. The slogan that adoption is a process not an event was a lesson I hadn't yet grasped. Prenatal trauma was a concept I had not yet heard.

The more challenging my personal life became, the higher my Dr. Hauschka star rose. Clifford was very happy to carry more of the parenting role as I travelled and started new projects. Our PR efforts continued to pay off. *House and Garden* magazine agreed to do a photo shoot and story about the WALA gardens. Beauty magazines called to ask what made our products so special and what biodynamic agriculture meant. As the spokesperson for the company, I was able to answer questions and throw interesting asides on topics such as WALA's rose projects in Bulgaria, where we converted a cooperative of rose farmers to biodynamic methods and prepurchased the rose oil so the farmers could buy adequate equipment, thus meeting our growing demand for rose oil and helping to improve their standard of life; and on how WALA converted a number of farmers in Iran who once had grown poppies to cultivate roses instead, and how we paid them a better price for the roses than they'd been receiving for the poppies that were headed to drug lords. As much as I loved those stories, the beauty editors were more interested in which stars used our products. (It would be decades before mission-driven companies became interesting to the press.)

The more I spoke about the products and the underlying philosophy, the more interested I became in the history of Elisabeth Sigmund, the medical-student-turned-esthetician who had been greatly responsible for developing the line together with Dr. Rudolph Hauschka in the 1960s. She had actually started to add his remedies to her handmade products as an esthetician in Vienna before she'd met him, and, when she began to see very dramatic healing results, Elisabeth contacted Dr. Hauschka about her success. He invited her to visit Eckwälden, and thus began their collaboration.

I often joked that, if I'd been the one to develop such brilliant skin care products, and if we were all living and working in today's world, I would be on the cover of *Vogue* magazine. Thankfully, times had changed since the 1960s, and women were finally being recognized not just for having "family names," such as Elizabeth Arden or Estee Lauder, but also as business leaders. In addition, the products were innovative, effective, and growing in popularity, and the story behind them was a marketing dream. However, during the time of Elisabeth's innovative work, WALA was pretty much a male-dominated business; when I first visited, only a few women in the esthetic department had acknowledged her. Now that I'd begun to thrive in spite of the male-dominated culture, I wanted to meet Elisabeth and hear her story. (I sometimes wondered if my success working with men had stemmed from having grown up playing touch football with a neighborhood full of boys.) My studies in Biography and Social Art convinced me that yes, that childhood experience had prepared me to catch anything thrown my way and to run for the goalpost.

Interestingly, several of my women friends at WALA repeatedly talked about how strong and forceful I acted with the directors in the company. One of my German friends even asked me if it wasn't painful for me to be so forceful. Though she'd said "forceful," I think she'd meant aggressive. And though I always felt well-respected, I was continuously bewildered that so many beautiful, creative, intelligent women didn't have more authority in the company. Was it a cultural difference between the United States and Europe? I finally realized that, while, in fact, I could be a bit aggressive as the American woman coming and going to and from the German headquarters, the women working within the company still had ceilings to shatter. But the U.S. sales were second only to Germany's, so my behavior, though thorny to the delicate, rose-like company culture, was tolerated.

I arranged to interview Elisabeth Sigmund in September 2002. Jupiter was in full orbit, and I liked what was happening.

— 22 —

Elisabeth and Me

WHEN I INTERVIEWED Elisabeth Sigmund, the thought of her as a spiritual mother crossed my mind, much the way the thought of adopting Rudolph Hauschka as a spiritual father had done twenty-two years earlier on my first trip to WALA. Elisabeth and my mother were born a year apart, both in the month of October. That was where the likeness ended.

Elisabeth was pleased that I was interested in her work and especially that I was bringing her life's work to the United States.

"It's wonderful for me to receive you in my home and answer your questions," she said. "I'll celebrate my eighty-eighth birthday soon and this is the best gift—to know that others find value in what is so important to me."

We sat together for three delightful golden autumn afternoons in her simple yet elegant living room. It was filled with bookcases and Russian Icons that her husband had painted while recuperating after the war. I had seen several pictures of Elisabeth as a young woman when she had dark hair and was quite thin; I thought she'd looked a little like Coco Chanel and Jackie O. Even that afternoon, her brown eyes and strong gaze spoke to me of a sharp mind and confidence born out of interest and success in the world.

A friendly colleague who had arranged the meetings acted as our translator. Elisabeth spoke no English; I spoke only a smattering of German and no Swedish. I asked questions and she replied; during the pauses between our exchanges, the translator built the bridge for us to meet. Through it all, Elisabeth looked at me with warmth.

Frau Sigmund told me to call her Elisabeth, and then she shared her memories, focusing on her lifelong study of esthetics and medicinal plants. Like most young girls, Elisabeth had played with her mother's and grandmother's beauty creams, but unlike most young girls, she visited the pharmacist who had made them and asked how he did it and what was in them. She even offered him suggestions of plants to add to his potions, plants she'd discovered in the garden at her grandmother's estate in the country where Elisabeth had spent her childhood summers.

Later, as a young medical student, one of only three women in a class of men, she discovered the absence of any mention of or treatment for skin problems. It surprised her that skin disharmonies were ignored by the medical community. She knew that the skin was an organ, a universal organ that reflected the health of the inner organs. She intuitively felt that cosmetics were the daughter of medicine and should be developed from a therapeutic perspective.

Sadly, however, Elisabeth had to leave medical school due to an illness. But while she was recuperating, she began to study old manuscripts about medicinal plants that were being grown at a local monastery. The more she read, the more the path to her future became clear: she decided to devote her life to esthetics. It was a bold choice for such a cultured young woman from a wealthy Austrian family; when she told her mother, the woman berated her, calling it common and reckless. I shared a bit of my own story with Elisabeth; I said that my parents had been very upset with me when, after I'd graduated from college, I'd taken a job working in an herb garden and learning how to grow medicinal plants biodynamically. She smiled her approval and reached over and patted my hand.

She then shared her journey of discovery that led from Austria to her skin care studio in Stockholm, and to her eventual collaboration with Rudolph Hauschka in Germany with a detour to India where she studied Ayurveda for a year.

In addition to following the process through which—rather than by simply studying symptoms of the skin—Elisabeth had developed products to support skin function, I also learned her intention behind the Classic Treatment. During World War II, she'd worked as a nurse for the Red Cross; in the early years after the war, and drawing from that experience, she began to develop concepts and practices for what she referred to as soul esthetics. I was most interested to hear Elizabeth say that her clients were still struggling years after the war ended. Everyone had suffered losses and had deep wounds, and, although they came to her for a beauty treatment, she intuited that they were coming to seek healing and wholeness in their lives. It reminded me of the many times when my clients and therapists who took our esthetic trainings said, "This isn't just a facial; it also feels nurturing and healing."

I was even more astonished to learn that Elizabeth thought of a treatment as being a yearlong process. By that, she meant that she would see her client once a month to consult about products and healthy nutrition. The Classic Treatment would help bring harmony and restore balance to the wellbeing of the client. Elizabeth understood that it took a year for someone to respond deeply to such a healing impulse. As an aside, she joked that she and her client took a yearlong journey around the sun together in her studio. It took me a few moments to realize that she meant it takes a year for the earth to circle the sun. After a year, she suggested that her clients come to her at least once each season to adjust products to help the skin adapt to seasonal changes.

What she was telling me made even more appreciative of the role that an esthetician could play in a client's life. I further learned that, in addition to creating a beautiful physical space in her salon, she also tried to create a beautiful soul space. Before every appointment she allowed for meditative quality time as well as space for each person; she sat, alone, in meditative silence and thought about the client who was expected. She felt that each face had its own beauty, an almost architectural structure, and that each client had her own unique story.

By meditating before the client arrived, Elisabeth felt she'd carved out "a beautiful quiet space for my client to unfold during our time together."

I first heard the term "objective love" from Elisabeth when she explained that a Dr. Hauschka therapist needed to develop a deep respect and love for the individual who had been placed in her hands. Because she felt it was important to touch each client with objective love—while carefully avoiding being invasive or sentimental—she spent the extra time and care to prepare to meet her clients so she'd be prepared to be totally present for each person she would touch.

Elisabeth had created a healing esthetic treatment in the early 1950s that continued to nurture the body, soul and spirit of twenty-first century women who were seeking their sense of self and their own unique beauty. The role of the Hauschka esthetician suddenly made sense to me. We focused on healthy functions in the skin but also on supporting the soul beauty of a client. Elizabeth had left medical school, which had addressed illness, and developed what I called "the newest profession"—one that addresses the body, soul, and spirit of an individual. What seemed like a disappointment in her biography when she had to leave medical school was actually a great gift.

I felt overwhelming gratitude for my time with Elisabeth. I told her that during my initial visit to WALA, when I'd received the Classic Treatment for the first time, I had felt a great sense of healing at a time when I was deeply wounded. As my colleague translated my remarks Elisabeth took my hand and smiled. I leaned over and lightly kissed her hand.

The greatest gift that Elisabeth offered me was her calm, humble demeanor, which was seemingly void of egoism. Although she'd worked closely with Dr. Hauschka to develop the entire product line of the brand as well as her signature treatment and training, she was happy to let the name Dr. Hauschka be the name that the world would see. Initially, one panel on the product boxes was labeled "Dr. Hauschka" with the name of the product below it, like "Rose Cream." Then, a side panel on each box had read "Healing Cosmetics from Elisabeth Sigmund" and was followed by a brief biography of her. When calling cosmetics "healing" became problematic for legal reasons, and when it was determined that having two names on each box created a marketing challenge, Elisabeth said that the name of the products should simply be Dr. Hauschka.

"People will take them more seriously if there is a doctor associated with the brand," she said.

Prior to our meeting, I'd come to realize that Elisabeth was a role model for many women, women who were on a path of inner development and were seeking to celebrate their unique, authentic beauty, women who were learning to mother themselves. But after getting to know Elisabeth, I also learned to appreciate my own mother in a new way. I understood that my mother hadn't caused my problems, but that we were working on similar challenges; I now had the luxury of going a step further, because she'd done the best she could as a parent. It came as a surprise when I realized that my mother and I were actually quite alike: hardworking and talented but lacking in self-worth and confidence. Unfortunately, for many years I had blamed her for my struggles; my journey with Dr. Hauschka had become a healing process along which I developed my sense of self-worth and confidence. The words of Rudolf Steiner that I'd read as a young woman—"We are born ill, and life is our healing"—finally made sense to me. I came to believe that those words mean that we're born neither finished nor whole, and that our lives are merely steps toward becoming more whole, more human. There is a similar thought in the words of a Leonard Cohen song: "There's a crack in everything. That's how the light gets in."

I recorded her story and offered a copy of the interview as a gift to WALA and to the U.S. Dr. Hauschka community. I had no idea that I would find a spiritual mother in Elisabeth—the same way I'd found a spiritual father in Rudolph Hauschka. One of the gems of meeting Elisabeth was when I learned she believed that *every* woman should be in *Vogue*, because every woman had a story to tell and a beauty to unfold.

After my interview with Elizabeth, but before I headed home, I attended an advanced training session for international esthetic trainers at WALA. When I related some highlights of my conversations with Elisabeth to the group, one of the trainers said it would be great to have a book about Dr. Hauschka and the treatment for their clients to read. I decided to consider the suggestion.

As it happened, one of my Amherst neighbors, Linda Roghaar, was a literary agent. Upon returning home, I asked her if she thought that writing a book would be a good idea. Linda spoke with an editor from Clarkson Potter Publishers, who was interested in seeing a proposal for the project. But, because I'd never written a book before, she suggested that I work with a professional writer. Enter Tom Monte, another Amherst neighbor as well as a well-published author. Tom agreed that we could work together, but it had to begin with me.

More changes were in store as my Jupiter years ended, including Clifford's and my decision to leave the area and move to Jamestown, Rhode Island. Our choice was based on several factors: the school department in Jamestown offered excellent remedial support for Rossibel and Emilio; my mother had begun to have memory issues, and she needed more care; and we were beginning to think about life after Hauschka. During the slow transition, Clifford and I took turns commuting to Hatfield to manage the company. The busier I was, the better. And, as I jumped headlong into writing the book, I realized that, though I believed that recycling, healthy food, and skin care are important lifestyle choices, I was at the beginning of another quest for health—this time, health for my soul. In short, I needed to find a way to bring harmony between how I looked to the outside world, and how I felt on the inside of *me*.

23

So What, Who Cares, What's in It for Me?

WHENEVER I WAS HOME, it was only long enough to get my next assignment from my Hauschka universe and to discover what personal challenges dotted the horizon. In January 2003, the company was invited to be a sponsor at "Media That Matters" held at Sundance in Utah. The conference was going to showcase short independent films about social justice that had been made by filmmakers who were referred to as "cultural creatives," people who have woken up to the social, economic, and environmental problems of the world. I believed that Rudolph Hauschka was a cultural creative long before the term was used. The conference was a great match, as our company was trying to change the world by the way we did business.

Because the event was to take place around the same time as the Sundance Film Festival, many actors, especially socially conscious ones, would be attending. I invited John and whomever he wanted to bring to be my guests at the event. I thought he would appreciate both the conference and my gesture, especially when I'd heard talk that the film *Overnight,* which he had coproduced, would be shown at an alternative event. It looked like a perfect way to spend time with my son.

When the day arrived, however, John was late. He missed the lunch that Dr. Hauschka had sponsored for Erin Brockovich, fell asleep during the film *People I Know,* and went to take naps in his rented vehicle during other activities. On the final day, he and I had breakfast before I needed to leave for the airport. Although he was sitting at the table, he wasn't really "there"; he looked exhausted and vacant. That's when it finally dawned on me that John might be ill; he looked traumatized, much like someone who had been to war.

As my blinders began to slide off, I felt like I was in an emotional undertow being swept into dangerous waters. I was scared, sad, and unable to completely grasp what was happening or what I could do. I begged him to come home with me, to rest and eat healthy food. He finally said he might see a therapist back in L.A.

Before I boarded the shuttle to go to the airport, I hugged as much love into John as possible. And as the bus drove away, I watched him slowly walk toward his room. I hoped he'd look back and wave, but he didn't. I remembered what Jim had said about the "Irish virus," and I finally realized that John might have an addiction.

I still didn't understand that I, too, needed help because of the effect that addiction had on my own life and my behavior. The pain that I'd felt while living with Jim resurfaced—compounded now by the strong sense that John might be struggling with alcohol and drugs, too. It was difficult for me to focus or to have any "normal" feelings when I thought of John. At unexpected and too-frequent times, deep grief suddenly seized me; I thought I would die if anything happened to my son. I worked hard to mask my feelings and walk through my life with Clifford and the children; I stumbled through the motions of being a wife and a mother. I took some comfort in a prayer that Rudolf Steiner suggested saying for one who isn't able to help themselves. It was a prayer to the other person's guardian angel about building a bridge of love to the person who is ill. Whenever the grief and worry about John paralyzed me, I said the prayer. I found myself praying more and more.

May 2004 was a month to remember and to celebrate. John did see a therapist when he returned to L.A. after the Media That Matters conference; he then checked himself into a trauma treatment center and began his road to recovery.

That same month, I received an advance from the publisher and began another journey deeper into the Dr. Hauschka story.

Tom Monte and I worked very hard to meet the publisher's deadlines, which were scheduled to accommodate a book launch date of May 2006. At the time, our company was working with the Susan Magrino Public Relations Agency, who recommended that I take what seemed like a very expensive one-day intensive marketing instruction session in New York City in order to prepare me to promote *Awakening Beauty the Dr. Hauschka Way*. When the day arrived, the elevator dropped me off in a corner office that was filled with floor-to-ceiling windows that overlooked Fifth Avenue as it snaked toward Central Park. As it was my habit to arrive early, I was invited to sit in their small reception area to wait. I glanced at the round glass table in front of me where glossy magazines were fanned out and a crystal vase with a single stem of pink flowering lilies greeted me. I closed my eyes. I'd recognized the blossoms as one of the many signs

I'd had over the years that my baby girl, Lily, was always with me in a spiritual way. I even thought of her as a spirit guide. The sorrow of having lost her had lifted, but the sight of a lily often brought me back to that long-ago wound that never quite healed. Her death had catapulted me out of growing a family with an unwilling partner and into a career with Hauschka that might not have been otherwise possible.

I took a slow, healing breath, opened my eyes, and looked beyond the lily and out the window. I had a quick flash of memories of driving with John into New York, of the first apartment Jim and I shared, and how, back then, I could never have dreamed I'd come as far as I'd come, or that I'd become a successful businesswoman, standing on the twentieth floor of a Fifth Avenue office building, in full view of the city where my future had started. It all seemed more than a little unreal, because, though the scars that I'd suffered had faded, they were still visible to me.

The woman we'd hired to train me stepped into the reception area. I squared my shoulders and stood to meet her. She looked very glamorous in stilettos, black slacks, and a cream-colored ruffled blouse with a plunging neckline. I had on my moss-green hand knit sweater, a pair of Jeans for Humanity, and my new Mephisto Allrounder suede walking shoes that were embroidered with red silk. Dressing that morning before sunrise, I had felt a certain casual elegance about my wardrobe choices. But now, compared to her, I had "living in granola valley" written all over me.

We moved into a tastefully decorated office; a film crew quietly encircled us; a young assistant in a pencil straight skirt, also wearing stilettos, clicked among us with steamy cups of coffee as I expressed to my coach the points that I thought were important to convey to consumers: how to treat yourself with a loving touch, the importance of biodynamic growing methods for medicinal plants, how to create a healthy rhythm in one's life, the importance of spending time in nature, and how essential healthy nutrition is.

At one point, she stopped me and said, "Look. The American consciousness is like a precocious teenager who is asking the questions, 'So what?' 'Who cares?' and 'What's in for me?' I need you to pick three points you want to make, and no matter what anyone asks, you need to link your reply to those three points."

My homework assignment was to go home, turn on the news, and pay close attention to how politicians answer questions from the media. "They know how to link the points they want to make to answer any question they're asked."

The film crew then videotaped me as if I were being interviewed about my book. I felt comfortable about the process until they played back the clip. I looked washed out and underdressed, and my answers seemed far too long. It was clear that I wasn't ready for "prime time." Prior to this training, my coach had not told me *how* to dress for it but had said I should wear whatever I typically would for a quick trip into New York. She also had not prepared me to keep my answers short. Pushed into cold water; I now felt the shock. I learned that it isn't necessary or advisable to tell someone everything you know about a topic.

"Sexy short bullets; that's what people remember," my coach said. Then she added that these were hard lessons, but ones that I needed to learn. At the end of our training, I told her I'd never paid anyone so much money to make me feel so bad. She laughed and assured me that I didn't need to wear a plunging neckline but to "always wear a V-neck blouse. It's more flattering." Lessons learned.

The big life questions that Rudolf Steiner and other philosophers like Plato and Aristotle had posed — "Who am I?" "What is life's meaning?" "What is my purpose in life?" — had guided the work of Hauschka and Sigmund, but they seemed light-years away from the New York culture of "So what?" "Who cares?" and "What's in it for me?" Writing the book *Awakening Beauty* seemed easier than bringing it to market was going to be. The challenge was to find a digestible message of a very big story about health and authentic beauty and to present it in a creative and interesting way to a culture that seemed conditioned to want only quick fixes.

We met the book deadline; the book was published in May 2006. Clarkson Potter arranged for me to do twenty-five radio interviews over a period of several months, during which time I honed my newly found skills of linking to my three points of discussion that encompassed how healthy skin and healthy aging went far beyond what products we used but were the result of a lifelong lifestyle choice.

The Magrino Agency landed me a television spot on *The Martha Stewart Show*. I did a twelve-minute segment on the positive effects of healing baths using our four bath concentrates—rosemary, lavender, lemon, and spruce—and explained how they related to the human temperaments. (For example, if one has a fiery, choleric temperament, lavender can be an effective, soothing way to calm inflamed skin and heated emotions.) John was in the audience with one of my assistants. During a commercial break when I looked their way, John smiled and gave me the thumbs up sign, but my staff member mouthed the words, "Don't move around so much." But I had to move because Martha stood very still next to me at the table where I was demonstrating how to create a vortex when stirring the bath concentrate into a bowl of water. I had to lean in front of her to reach the bowls that had been laid out for the demo, while simultaneously explaining the four temperaments and how they related to skin conditions and bath concentrates. It was a bit challenging and added to my anxiety about being on television.

A few days later, I went on NBC's *Weekend Today* with Campbell Brown to talk about nutrition, especially antioxidants, and how they support healthy skin. That time, the problem was time. We had requested a display of various foods such as leafy greens, berries, green teas, grains, and healthy oils, as well as foods to avoid such as sugary pastries. We were supposed to have an uninterrupted six minutes to discuss the various foods and which ones supported healthy skin. A minute before the segment began, we learned that they'd cut the segment to three minutes.

"Hold on!" I cried. "We have to plow through this in half the time?" I quickly edited the thoughts I'd extensively prepared and picked out the topics that were most important. Again, I heard echoes of my coach-in-stilettos and as she stressed my *three points*. But I figured I'd be lucky if I had time to deliver one.

The camera turned to us, and Campbell introduced me. I focused on the benefits of green teas and lots of green leafy vegetables, referring to them as the kamikaze pilots fighting antioxidants. As the segment was about to end, Campbell pointed to the plate of donuts and croissants and said that was what she still wanted to eat. I did not want to end on that note, so I stepped in front of her and pointed to all the healthy foods on display and I told her that, if she ate all these foods several times each week, she could have something from the pastry plate once a month. Campbell, a good host, smiled, and the director cut to a commercial. I was exhausted.

John was waiting for me in the Green Room. He gave me a big hug and told me that his sponsor had been watching and had called him to say I was a fox. Which was pretty funny because at that point I felt like a deflated birthday balloon.

That same month, in honor of Mother's Day, my daughter, Rossibel, and I were included in an article titled "Passing Down the Beauty" in *O, The Oprah Magazine*. Several mothers and daughters were photographed together; each mother was asked to share her biggest challenge as a beauty expert and a mother, the most opportune teaching moment for her daughter, and her best advice. My biggest challenge had been to help Rossibel see beauty not simply as a reflection of others' opinions of her but as a reflection of her unique spirit. In the article, my "opportune teaching moment" read:

Rossibel came home from school one day and told me she wanted red hair like a popular girl in class. She has this incredible black hair, so I said, "Let's talk about what looks good on you," assuring her that her black hair is beautiful and that she didn't need to change what she had. My advice was: "Don't try to be someone other than who you are; don't believe in quick fixes or a miracle in a jar. Remember that 'beauty is a gift in youth and an art as we age.'"

Rossibel lost interest in dying her hair red after she saw the photo of the two of us in *O*.

Several importers invited me to do book events in their countries, so I traveled to London, Dublin, Berlin, Amsterdam, Helsinki, and Tallinn to promote *Awakening Beauty the Dr. Hauschka Way*. The more I talked about the messages in the book, the more I appreciated how healing my career had been for me. It had been a thirty-year learning curve that had demanded that I, too, look in the mirror and ask myself the big questions:

Who Am I? I'm a spiritual girl, living in a material world, trying to transform my darkness and learn what it means to be a free and loving human being. Really I'm trying to understand what it means to have a soul and a spirit in a world that mostly acknowledges only the material aspect.

What is the Meaning of Life? I think life is an opportunity to unfold a little more of who I am becoming; I think the earth is my partner in my development and deserves my respect, love, and care because this is where I'm learning to be me.

What is my life's purpose? I think my life's purpose is to learn to listen with love, develop empathy, and to create opportunities for others to share their life stories through Biography and Social Art and remember their purpose. But mostly what I've learned is that I'm still emerging even with all the weedy patches in my life; maybe even *because* of the weeds in my life. Perhaps that happens to everyone.

24

The Perfect Swarm

"HEY, BEEKEEPER, let's go catch a swarm!" Clifford called out to me as I pulled into the driveway and unloaded groceries. He was standing by one of our empty hives with some bee wrangling equipment, our beekeeper's hats and jackets strewn at his feet.

I left my bags on the path and hurried over to where he was scraping resin from one of the frames of an empty hive. Two of our three hives hadn't made it through the winter in spite of my efforts to get more involved with them.

Recently, Clifford had said that he was too busy to be a bee-keeper any longer. Between the constant sailboat improvements he'd been making (hoping to get me more enthusiastic about sailing), mending the fence around the garden, building a screened frame to protect the blueberries, and splitting logs for the woodstove, he was giving up. Clifford enjoyed beekeeping when our younger children found it fun to help him, but as they got older they found less time for the bees.

"Well, I'll take over the bees. I can't just let them die," I said, surprising myself. Since it hadn't been my idea in the first place to get bees, it felt like a sign of opportunity for me—but it was also a little intimidating. Deep down, I was afraid I couldn't do it alone.

Clifford agreed to show me what to do so that gradually I could take over their care. I boosted my confidence by reminding myself that if I could run with the bulls at midnight I should be able to handle sweet little honeybees.

"Do we have to start now?" I asked.

"You're the one who still wants the bees," he replied and nodded at the hand clippers and a large cardboard box on the ground. Then he picked up an extension ladder and headed to the car. "Julie called this morning right after they swarmed, so now's the best time." Julie was another beekeeper in Jamestown.

I'd already learned that, just before honeybees swarm, they gorge themselves on enough honey to survive several days until they find another home. It makes them quite docile and easy to handle when their stomachs are full. Clifford was right. This was our moment. It was also good that they were from a local hive; they'd been naturalized, and the hive had produced the queen. Which is always a good sign.

We had been keeping bees for five years, with some early success and several recent failures. It had begun when, several years after retiring, I'd decided to write a graphic novel. The colorful 156-page result, *Beecoming Sophie*, is about a young teenage girl adopted from Guatemala who decides to adopt a queen bee that flies into her room one rainy night. The girl, Sophie, discovers that she can talk to the bee, a shaman bee who calls herself Queen Phoebee and who leads Sophie on a bee-conscious adventure. Sophie begins a crusade with her family, school, and community to save honeybees. The characters are loosely based on our family.

Clifford decided—really, he insisted—that, if I was writing a book about bees, WE HAD TO GET BEES! In the 1970s, he had worked as a bee inspector for Fresno County, California. At one time, he even had ten hives of bees, but had sold them before moving to England to go to college.

Julie was in her yard when we arrived. She pointed to a hive about thirty feet off the ground in a large tree. "My friend Jeff is coming to catch that one." She then led us to a privet hedge that bordered her neighbor's property. "There's one on the other side of the hedge that I thought you'd like to catch. It's not too high up."

We peeked through the hedge leaves and saw the cluster. I put on my bee hat, jacket, and gloves.

Clifford only put on his hat and jacket. "It's easier to grab them without the gloves," he said.

We climbed through an opening in the hedge. "I'm going to cut the branches where they're clustered," he said. "You hold the box steady, so they don't tip out."

Slowly, we moved into the open space among the bushes till we got a close-up look at the swarm. It was perfectly formed in the shape of a heart. The low, murmuring sound coming from the furry little beings sounded like a mantra being sung by meditants. As Clifford pruned the branches around the swarm, hundreds of bees buzzed around us in the small cave-like space where we were crouched. I took a deep breath, remained still, focused, and experienced firsthand how docile swarming bees can be. I held the box firmly and waited. Then Clifford cut a final branch where the swarm was attached, and all heaven broke loose. We were enveloped by thousands of bees moving at top speed in their own kind of sensitive chaos until the pulsating swarm landed in the box; Clifford scooped up handfuls of bees that had fallen to the ground and gently dropped them in. We walked gingerly back out of the maze and prayed that the queen was among those in the box.

We thanked Julie as we were walking across her lawn, and the three of us repeated our hopes that we had captured the queen. "You'll know by tomorrow," Julie said. "They'll come back and look for her here if she isn't with the swarm."

Back home at our hive, Clifford gently brushed the bees into the wooden structure that he had already prepared. I ran into the kitchen and brewed bee tea made from several herbs including chamomile, yarrow, and stinging nettle, and mixed it with honey and water then fed it to the bees close to the opening of the hive. I hoped it would welcome our guests to their new home.

The next day we watched the swarm settle in and circle closely around the hive. We knew by their behavior that their queen was safely inside. It had been a perfect swarm, and it resurrected Clifford's interest as a beekeeper—providing I'd assist him in the future.

In August 2006, when we placed the Dr. Hauschka Skin Care business into a foundation to eliminate individual ownership, we retired and moved to Jamestown, back to where my life had begun so many years ago. Clifford was delighted to let go of the business. He is, in the words of Bob Dylan, someone who "don't look back." I, however, felt completely lost. I wondered who I was after having been the queen bee in the Hauschka vortex for thirty years. My identity was so entwined with Dr. Hauschka, I remembered how when I opened my skin care center in New York several people had even thought that I was Dr. Hauschka. Now it was difficult to let go. I realized that the word "twin" is at the center of the word entwined.

We decided to renovate our house, which was too old to be functional and too new to be interesting. Clifford worked with the architect and builders to increase the footprint of the house in order to provide plenty of space for our family; two geriatric cats; our Chesapeake Bay Retriever, Lughnasa, who acted like a puppy her whole life; and friends, new and old.

I lost and found myself by working outside, first with a landscape designer to give the two acres some form and lots of beds to fill with roses for rosehip tea, as well as lilacs, peonies, lavender, anemone, and calendula for wayward bees. Then I corralled Clifford and our younger son, Emilio, into building a fence for a large vegetable and herb garden. Clifford, I've come to discover, does everything in a big way: he insisted that the fence be eight feet high and buried two feet below the surface to deter deer from jumping over it and rabbits and groundhogs from burrowing under it. It wasn't a beautiful garden; I jokingly called it Alcatraz because of the wire fence. The excavation for the new garage had unearthed three enormous smooth boulders that Clifford placed in the garden to gather warmth for early plantings of greens sown in front of them. I called them the RIP stones because they reminded me of headstones found in historic graveyards.

Although the garden wasn't as beautiful as others on the island, it was part church and part therapist for me. It's where I cried, talked to the bees about my mother's failing memory, and about the challenges our adopted children encountered in school with their unique ways of learning. It is where I watched nature die and become new through the seasons. My interest in bees had started in the garden, as I read articles about how honeybees are needed for pollinating the plants we eat but how they are, sadly, vanishing from the landscape. Gardens and bees are meant to be together. I included a garden for the bees within my garden and filled it with borage, holy basil, and native asters. I let the native milkweed go to seed, and it spread by itself. I gained respect for it when I discovered that it provides good nectar flow for bees.

My gardens had been the thread in my life that I picked up and followed after leaving my Dr. Hauschka career behind. They became the background for the home we created, the kind of home I'd always wanted as a child. There was room for everyone. I put vases of fresh flowers throughout the house from springtime through autumn; I made dried lavender sachets to slip into pillowcases for peaceful sleep and sweet dreams. Best of all, it was the first time our entire family had lived together in the same house. John had been living in L.A. when we adopted Rossibel and Emilio. Luckily, he moved in with us for several years to work on the sets of movies that were being filmed in Rhode Island. Emilio turned into a bee charmer and captured eight swarms of bees one year, several of which we donated to the Meadowbrook Waldorf School along with the hives and equipment to start a small apiary. He did his North Kingston High School senior project on sustainable beekeeping before heading off to volunteer at Ruskin Mill, an adult education center outside of Stroud, England. Rossibel created a monologue for her senior project at High Mowing High School titled "Do you know what war is?" inspired by my friend Zainab Salbi's book *If You Knew Me, You Would Care*. In college Rossibel studied American Sign Language, and then she went to California for a gap year.

My mother sat in my garden doing crossword puzzles as I weeded, harvested, and planted new seeds. On one of her last visits before she lost her memory, broke her hip, and moved to a retirement home where she soon died, she asked me, "What's a four-letter word for the place Dante made famous?"

"Must be hell," I replied. "You know, Dante's inferno."

She filled in the letters, put down the puzzle, looked over at me, and asked if I knew that her mother had been an alcoholic. I was stunned, not about her mother's illness but because my mother was admitting it to me and to herself. It was a final piece of my life's puzzle that helped me understand the generational effects of alcoholism. I finally knew why, years before, in my pumpkin-colored New York kitchen, Jim had told me that I needed help when he revealed that he was an alcoholic.

My sister, who lived in Florida, spent summers with us, and we celebrated her eightieth birthday in September 2017 two months before she died. My older brother, who had chosen me for his team to play touch football and often threw me the ball, did not like to travel, but he came whenever I invited him. He told my sister and me that he had cancer, perhaps exacerbated by the effects of Agent Orange from his time spent in Vietnam. My heart broke when he said his time was limited.

Most incredible of all was that, when John wasn't working on the films in Rhode Island, he traveled the country to be trained to do interventions for those suffering from addiction and for their families. It meant that he spent less and less time at home in Jamestown, but my heart was full and happy for him. I finally found a fellowship for the families of alcoholics and continued my own soul recovery.

Through all the riches and loss, I continued to garden. I made big batches of ratatouille; tomato sauce; arugula, parsley and basil pesto; strawberry and rhubarb chutney. I served fresh greens with dinner for eight months of the year and got very creative with kale. It always felt wonderful to run out to my garden and harvest fresh mint, thyme, and hyssop to mix with dried rose hips for tea for anyone who was suffering from anything.

In January 2012, I was invited to join the board of the Biodynamic Farming and Gardening Association, which I happily accepted. During my five years on the board my hive was gradually becoming empty, as my mother, then my brother, and finally my sister were gone. Our children had left to start their own lives and returned only occasionally for honey and a hug. I was freezing more of the bounty of the garden than serving it fresh to a full house.

Being a board member on the BDA was very rewarding. It reminded me a little of being connected to the Dr. Hauschka community. The WALA/Dr. Hauschka international community was trying to enliven medicine with a new paradigm based on supporting health rather than waging war on illness. They knew, of course, that both views were important and should be under one umbrella: the practice of conventional medicine together with all the modalities to support health. WALA also was trying to change the world by how they conducted business. Profit was used to accomplish its mission to heal the earth and the human being. The BDA was trying to birth a renewal of agriculture, heal the soil, and restore the connection between community, food, and economy.

There were biannual retreats with other board members, monthly video calls, and wonderful conferences that attracted over 700 farmers, gardeners, and consumers from around the country. I offered a workshop during the conferences titled *Bees, Borage, and Biodynamics* to encourage backyard gardeners to make compost and to use at least some of the BD preps on the soil and compost pile.

Then, because of my experience with writing and publishing two books, the Executive Director of the BDA turned to me when a publisher approached the association to write a book for backyard gardeners. But while I worked on the book proposal something didn't fit. I soon realized that, although I loved gardening, I wasn't really a master gardener. For me, it wasn't only about the gardening itself, but how gardens had been an essential thread of my life, how they always had offered me peace and harmony. And love.

When I reached that awareness, a different type of book called out to me to write: a memoir. I realized that my life was an interesting story with three large themes: addiction, adoption, and Anthroposophy. Gardens were the thread that had led me through my life as I followed my journey of self-discovery through sometimes difficult karma. But when friends asked me what I was doing these days, I second-guessed myself for a while as I switched from confidently saying, "I'm going to write a memoir" to "I'm thinking of writing a memoir." During the time of going from being confident to doubting my writing skills and goals, three things happened.

First, while sitting on the back stairs of the deck looking out at the many projects that needed to be done in the yard, I realized that I was also sitting on the metaphor for my life. I had spent a lot of years living on the back stairs of my life and entering through the front stairs of other people's lives. I was the grand mistress of serving others, taking care of and promoting their dreams and goals.

Next, a sailing friend gave me a rough-looking amaryllis bulb planted in a round metal container wrapped in green tissue paper as a New Year's gift. The bulb looked like it would never grow, would never realize its potential but remain dull and jagged in its mossy home. But slowly, as the light and air met its boundaries, first one, then four strong, green, sword-like leaves appeared. A straight stalk gradually emerged with a large bulb on top. I became fascinated by the plant as I watched it grow, and I secretly hoped it would flower by my birthday, February 19th. Over the weeks, it continued to grow in complexity and beauty, a hint of a vibrant coral-red flower emerging from its womb of green. It was still emerging on my birthday; its glorious flower appeared a few days later. It gave me the insight that I, too, was still emerging; I had been a wallflower who wanted to step off the wall.

Then, when I spoke to my former Dr. Hauschka colleague Mary Wynne and mentioned that I was writing a memoir she said, "Susan, if you're going to write a memoir, you need to take a Biography training." It didn't take long for me to research the Biography and Social Art training and sign up for the three-year program. After the first two weeks of the training, it was obvious that it would be a great help for the memoir process. I soon was connected to the new community of trainees as we explored our biographies and shared them with each other. When I told several of the students that I was writing a memoir, one of them said, "I didn't know you were famous."

I replied, "You don't realize how interesting your life is." But during the next three years, together we all discovered just how interesting, precious, and mysterious each human biography is. I realized that everyone in our group could write a memoir about a theme in their lives.

And I finally was ready to begin.

When Clifford and I admitted that, though we loved our beautiful home, where I still tried to maintain the gardens long after our perfect swarm of bees had left, it appeared to be time to downsize—or, as I called it, to right-size. It was as though the nature spirits heard our decision. Suddenly ground hogs and bunnies were boldly burrowing under the garden fence to feast on late autumn greens. Clifford had given up his attempt to find the exact place that the unwelcome visitors entered the garden. I sat alone in the garden on the warmer autumn days, enjoying quiet moments between the surges of decluttering that were necessary for a move. On one especially beautiful day, I was inspired to get down on the ground on the straw path between two beds, and I did the comforting yoga Child's Pose. While in the pose, I kissed the ground and thanked the earth. I couldn't help but recall my time as a child when I crawled around my aunt's garden looking for ladybugs.

It felt very much as if Clifford and I, too, were swarming once we became open to the idea of right sizing. We became filled with the richness of life that our beautiful home and garden had filled us with. Good friends of ours, who were looking for a house big enough for their grandchildren and extended family to gather in frequently, had sent an email to a few close friends; they had looked at dozens of houses for sale in Jamestown and wanted to know if any of us knew of a house for sale. I half-jokingly said, "How about ours?" They responded within minutes, "We'll take it."

The last celebration at our home was an engagement party the day after Christmas 2017 for our son John and his fiancée, Audra. They were living in Ocala, Florida, where John and his partner had just opened a Trauma Treatment Recovery Center called the Guest House, named after a Rumi poem. The human being is the guest house and each day a new visitor arrives: joy, depression, sadness, loss, or sometimes a fleeting awareness. Rumi welcomes them all because each is sent from a guide beyond. The party was a beautiful event for a joyous occasion, and the planning kept me moving along past any sadness of leaving the house and my much-loved gardens.

In January, I packed up boxes to ship to John in his new home, some to storage for Rossibel and Emilio, and others for the small condo in "downtown" Jamestown where we were going to land for a while. I remembered something Rossibel used to say when she was a little girl and was just learning to speak English. When she knew we were all going out to visit friends or to a school event she quickly put on her coat, so she was often ready to go much sooner than either Clifford or me. She would follow us around as we slowly prepared to leave and say, "I am sooo waiting, I am sooo waiting." I had felt the yearning in her words to go on the next adventure with us. And now I felt that yearning in my heart quietly whisper: "I am sooo waiting to see where the next garden leads me."

Susan West Kurz and her husband Clifford divide their time between Jamestown, Rhode Island, and Ocala, Florida. She is the author of *Awakening Beauty the Dr Hauschka Way* and *Beecoming Sophie*, a graphic novel about saving the honeybees. She is a certified facilitator for Biography and Social Art. You can learn more about Susan at biographyandsocialart.com.